Churchmen and the Western Indians

Churchmen and the Western Indians 1820-1920

EDITED AND WITH AN INTRODUCTION BY

Clyde A. Milner II and Floyd A. O'Neil

UNIVERSITY OF OKLAHOMA PRESS : NORMAN AND LONDON

By Clyde A. Milner II

With Good Intentions: Quaker Work Among the Pawnees, Otos, and Omahas in the 1870s (Lincoln, 1982)
(coeditor) *Churchmen and the Western Indians, 1820-1920* (Norman, 1985)

By Floyd A. O'Neil

(editor) *The Southern Utes: A Tribal History* (Salt Lake City, 1972)
(editor) *The Zunis: Self-Portrayals* (Albuquerque, 1972)
(coauthor) *A History of the Uintah-Ouray Ute Lands* (Salt Lake City, 1978)
(coeditor) *Churchmen and the Western Indians, 1820-1920* (Norman, 1985)

Library of Congress Cataloging-in-Publication Data

Main entry under title:
  Churchmen and the western Indians, 1820-1920.

    Papers from a conference held at Utah State University, Aug. 6-7, 1982, which was sponsored by the National Endowment for the Humanities.
    Includes index.
    1. Indians of North America—West (U.S.)—Missions—Congresses. 2. Missionaries—West (U.S.)—Biography—Congresses. I. Milner, Clyde A., 1948-   . II. O'Neil, Floyd A. III. National Endowment for the Humanities.
E78.W5C48   1985   266'.008997078   85-40477
ISBN 0-8061-1950-0 (alk. paper)

Contents

Illustrations

MAPS

vii

Acknowledgments

The six chapters contained in this book were first presented at Utah State University on August 6 and 7, 1982, at a research conference sponsored by the National Endowment for the Humanities. The editors wish to thank the Endowment for its generous support. For their participation in the conference we also thank a distinguished group of commentators whose ideas were of great help in the subsequent revisions of each essay. They are Robert F. Berkhofer, Jr.; Alison R. Bernstein; Henry Warner Bowden; Carter Blue Clark; Donald L. Fixico; and Arrell Morgan Gibson. In addition, R. David Edmunds, Margaret Connell Szasz, Doris Dwyer, Gregory C. Thompson, Paul A. Hutton, and Carol A. O'Connor attended sessions of the conference and made many useful suggestions.

During and after the conference colleagues and staff at both Utah State University and the University of Utah supported this project. We wish to acknowledge the aid of William F. Lye, F. Ross Peterson, Charles S. Peterson, Carolyn Buchanan, Sheridan B. Pew, Connie H. Baer, Jan Chambers, and Lee M. Austin at Utah State. At the American West Center of the University of Utah, we thank S. Lyman Tyler and John R. Alley.

John N. Drayton, Editor-in-Chief of the University of Oklahoma Press, encouraged our plans for publication and gave excellent advice on the production of the book. Finally, we thank our four contributors who joined in this collaboration from the earliest stage of original research to publication of their work.

Logan, Utah   CLYDE A. MILNER II
Salt Lake City, Utah   FLOYD A. O'NEIL

Editors' Introduction

Toward the very end of the fifteenth century two "old worlds" began an ongoing process of cultural conflict and interaction in which religion has played a major role. By the nineteenth century the Europeans in what they considered a "new world" had established many new nations. One of these nations, the United States, had begun to move aggressively westward across the Mississippi River onto the lands of older, native nations. Expanding American nationalism included a desire to increase the influence of European Christianity. Yet no one denomination had become a national church for the United States. The effort to persuade native peoples to give up their old ways of worship became the undertaking of distinct Protestant denominations and the Roman Catholic church. Within these differing Christian sects, many individuals felt called to convert America's Indians to what they considered a true faith. Some, but not all, of these men and women worked as missionaries among the native peoples. This book examines the careers of six men from six different denominations who attempted to Christianize the Indians of the American West.

Yet this volume is not exclusively a study of missionaries, nor is it an exercise in narrow biography. The interaction between the western Indians and these six churchmen is a major focus of each chapter. This focus highlights several comparative themes, such as the use of native language by some of the churchmen and the role of native converts as intermediaries. Most significantly each chapter allows the reader to consider both the churchmen's and the Indians' willingness to change and adapt, or their unwillingness to do so. In terms of the individual histories that unfold, several of the churchmen seem more rigid in their expectations than do the Indians.

Examination of such diverse peoples as the Choctaws, Chippewas, Kiowas, Utes, and Nez Percés reveals a complex layering of responses to attempted Christianization. Conversion to Christianity on Indian terms appeared viable for many individuals, who then, despite the desires of most of the churchmen, did not fully sacrifice their native identity. Apparently these Indians had their own uses for Christianity. In addition, the introduction of this new religion did not always produce simple acceptance or rejection by a tribe, nor did it always fragment and factionalize the native society. Thus for some individual Indians, as well as for larger segments of their tribes, partial acceptance of Christianity may reveal an adaptive form of cultural self-determination.

Nonetheless, most of the western Indians studied in this book did not become devout examples of Christian converts, nor did they fully accept the assimilationist ideals advocated by most of the six churchmen. These general results would seem to indicate failure of the churchmen's enterprise. Yet this measurement of results may be too simple. The nineteenth-century insistence on cultural homogeneity within the United States gave way, by the late twentieth century, to an emerging acceptance of cultural heterogeneity. In the case of America's Indians, adaptive self-determination combined with the historic failures of assimilation may explain their continued existence as part of this diverse national culture. In short, Indians have changed, but they have not vanished.

As the chapters in this book reveal, neither the western Indians nor the churchmen represented cultural monoliths. Each case study underscores the diverse factors that influenced the interaction between Christian white Americans and American Indians. It is not the purpose of this book to

create a strict comparative structure in all six chapters. Nonetheless, comparisons do emerge. The role of tribal and church
organization, for example, is an important part of several
chapters. In addition, the six chapters have been paired to
stimulate the reader's consideration of certain themes.

Part One: THE PROTESTANT PARADIGM

Protestantism dominated the nineteenth-century religious
identity of the United States. Mission efforts by Protestant
denominations reached out to the frontier regions of the
nation and also established work among many Indian tribes.
The first two chapters examine the careers of a Presbyterian,
Cyrus Byington, and a Methodist, John Jasper Methvin. Each
man worked as a missionary among Indians in what is now
Oklahoma. The chronology of their missionary careers stretches
from the early decades of the nineteenth century, for Byington, to the early decades of the twentieth century, for Methvin. In many ways the careers of Byington and Methvin can
serve as a reference for mainstream Protestant missions. What
each missionary attempted in terms of conversion and "civilization" indicates the basic aspirations behind the Protestant
enterprise.

Nonetheless, while they are of the mainstream, each man's
career is distinctive. W. David Baird emphasizes the importance of Byington's study and use of the Choctaw language.
Eventually Byington's linguistic efforts not only produced
numerous conversions but also helped establish, by the late
1860s, a "*bi*culture, evincing both EuroAmerican *and* Choctaw elements." Bruce David Forbes shows that Methvin insisted on cultural imperialism more than Byington. Methvin
did not learn to speak Kiowa and maintained that the Indians
must fully assimilate white ways if they were to survive extinction.

A comparison of Byington's and Methvin's attitudes raises
the possibility that expectations for the Indians may have become more culturally rigid after the Civil War. Perhaps the
fervid nationalism of the post-Civil War era that produced

significant examples of political imperialism explains, in part, this ardent cultural imperialism. Two other figures from the post–Civil War period, Albert Smiley and Henry Whipple, also held strong views on assimilation.

Part Two: FRONTIER VARIATIONS

For obvious theological reasons, neither Roman Catholics nor Mormons fit into the Protestant mainstream of nineteenth-century America. In addition, each had discrete, highly centralized forms of church organization. In Indian relations this church polity played a vital role. Joseph M. Cataldo, S.J., drew on the impressive resources of the Catholic church to recruit religious workers from outside the United States to serve in the mountain West. George Washington Bean, on the other hand, became one of the multifaceted pioneers who helped establish the Latter-Day Saints in their Great Basin kingdom. Both men moved from task to task as dictated by the authorities in their churches. Bean's assignments often coincided with frontier pacification and settlement, whereas Cataldo often aided school building and church building.

The Mormons created their Zion in the midst of the Utes and Paiutes, whereas Cataldo did not bring his entire church onto the frontier when he began his work with the Nez Percés. Floyd A. O'Neil points out that Mormon theological idealism could have permitted the integration of the Indians into the Church of Latter-Day Saints. This one-sided merger happened only rarely. Cataldo, as a Jesuit, could operate more broadly. He managed to merge partly into the Indians' culture through the use of language, dress, customs, and manners. Yet, as Robert C. Carriker explains, Cataldo also wanted the Indians to merge with white forms of education. Ultimately he established a college in Spokane to educate white and Indian boys.

Cataldo outlived the frontier era, whereas Bean did not. Similarly, the Catholic enterprise toward the Indians did not become mired in the dynamics of frontier conquest and settlement. Catholics like Cataldo seemed able to serve religiously on both the Indian and the white sides of the frontier. Bean, or his leader, Brigham Young, may have been viewed as a friend by some Indians, but in the nineteenth century the Mormons and their missions existed primarily on their own side of the frontier. Of course, the Catholics could call on centuries of missionary experience with non-Christian peoples. But the Mormons needed to firmly organize and establish a new church, and so they focused their missionary efforts on fellow Christians in Scandinavia and England who were ready for conversion.

Part Three: NATIONAL REFORM FIGURES

As advocates of reform in government policy, some churchmen had great influence over Indian affairs on the national level. Yet how directly did they interact with Indians themselves? The careers of the Quaker reformer Albert K. Smiley and of the Episcopal bishop Henry B. Whipple reveal contrasting experiences. Whipple visited extensively among the Santee Sioux and the Chippewas. He also carried on correspondence with Episcopal associates and native missionaries who lived and worked among these Indians. Albert Smiley began his limited visits among the western Indians only after the president of the United States appointed him to the Board of Indian Commissioners. Like the Mormons with their special theological views, Smiley inherited the near-legendary reputation of the Quakers as special friends of the Indians. And as with the Mormons, the realities of Smiley's efforts did not match the ideals that he inherited.

Both Smiley and Whipple agreed on the ultimate goal of assimilation, which they felt could be accomplished through Christianization, education, and "civilization." In this view they showed themselves to be mainstream humanitarian reformers. Indeed, nearly all the individuals, including Whipple, who attended Smiley's annual Lake Mohonk Conference of the Friends of the Indian, shared this commitment to assimilation. As Clyde Milner explains, antiassimilationist Indians were not invited to Lake Mohonk to argue against plans for detribalization. So the reformers at these conferences had little reason to question their desire to transform Indian culture.

Martin Zanger shows that cultural values cannot be easily eradicated. The Chippewas responded to Whipple and others' attempts at Christianization in a variety of ways that may have heightened the Indians' religiosity. Zanger indicates that attempted religious conversion, rather than producing a step toward assimilation, may have increased the Indians' sense of identity even if it included a Christian aspect. His chapter notes the cultural damage that can occur from missionary efforts, but it implies that religious conversion has limitations as a tool of cultural transformation. So even though men like Smiley and Whipple wanted Indian assimilation, Indians like the Chippewas demonstrated an adaptive form of cultural self-determination.

We hope that readers recognize the importance of these case studies not only as separate chapters but also as a collective whole. We also hope that this volume may serve as a source and as something of a model for additional studies that will increase the range of comparisons and distinctions presented here. We encourage other scholars to produce collections that compare different denominations, diverse native peoples, and distinctive individuals, especially churchwomen. We trust that such future studies will range beyond our focus on the nineteenth-century United States to consider developments in other centuries as well as other places. Whatever the case, we ultimately hope that this book contributes toward a broader understanding of the complexities of religion and culture as they affect societies and individuals.

Churchmen and the Western Indians

Part One   The Protestant Paradigm

1

Cyrus Byington and the Presbyterian Choctaw Mission

W. David Baird

Nineteenth-century Christian missionaries are frequently pictured as misguided persons who destroyed North American Indian cultures under the guise of religion and "civilization." The generalization is not wholly inaccurate, but exceptions are sufficiently notable that it cannot be accepted uncritically. A case in point is Cyrus Byington and his colleagues, who composed the Presbyterian Mission to the Choctaw Indians. Sponsored by the American Board of Commissioners for Foreign Missions and active after 1818, this contingent of missionaries proclaimed the Christian Gospel so effectively that by 1860, 10 percent of the tribe held membership in Presbyterian churches and the Choctaws as a whole were identified by interested observers as a Christian people. The two keys to this success were that some Choctaws, especially members of the mixed-blood power structure, responded to the Gospel message for purposes of national rather than spiritual salvation while others, primarily full-bloods, found it possible to convert to Christianity without losing their Indian identity. However and whenever the Choctaws responded to it, the message of the missionaries dramatically affected them, both individually and corporately. From the beginning Byington and his brethren anticipated no less a result.

At the onset of the Presbyterian Mission the Choctaws resided in what is now central and northern Mississippi. As a people they hardly resembled those of their ancestors who had encountered Europeans some three centuries earlier. Warfare and trade, intermarriage with whites, and myriad diplomatic negotiations had destroyed the tribe's economic independence, transformed its cultural fabric, and restricted its land base. Yet over the years the Choctaws had retained their distinctiveness as a people, in large part because they had learned to accommodate to new and unexpected circumstances. Indeed, by 1818 the willingness to entertain change had become a tribal trademark. Such a disposition obviously made the more than 20,000 tribespeople a ripe field of labor for dedicated Christian missionaries.[1]

The Presbyterian ministers and workers who made up the Choctaw Mission were sent under the auspices of the American Board of Commissioners for Foreign Missions. Founded in 1810, the American Board became the vehicle for the missionary activities of the Presbyterian and Congregational churches, initially of New England but later of the whole North. Administered by the Prudential Committee, the board was passionately committed to the propagation of the Good News of Christ among the heathen. The Gospel message energized by the Holy Spirit, it believed, had the power to convert men from paths of destruction and to assure spiritual salvation.[2] Equally important was that it could facilitate the civilization of the "savage." Indeed, the men of the American Board hardly distinguished between the Gospel and the New England virtues of literacy, frugality, and democracy. Critical to both salvation and civilization, however, was English-language literacy. Without it the Indians could not hope to understand the Bible or assimilate the habits and manners of their white neighbors. So civilization, salvation, and English-language literacy were inextricably intertwined for the leaders of the American Board. Together the three constituted a practical, though hardly scriptural definition of the Gospel message that, through formal education and sustained proclamation, they proposed to take to American Indians.[3]

The board established its first mission in North America among the Cherokee Indians in 1817. In the following year the New Hampshire–born and Andover-trained leader of that work, Cyrus Kingsbury, was commissioned to commence labors among the Choctaws as a consequence of an invitation received from the tribal leadership. The initial contingent of the Choctaw Mission arrived in the tribal domain in August, 1818, and established its first station, Elliot, on the Yalobusha River near present Grenada, Mississippi. Within a year it had become a model mission with a boarding school, a demonstration farm, a blacksmith shop, and a Presbyterian church. In August, 1819, Kingsbury attended a council of the entire Choctaw Nation, reported on the progress of the work, and presented the needs of the mission. The assembled tribespeople were so impressed that they committed from their treaty annuities $3,000 a year for the support of the station and donated on the spot $1,800 in cash and eighty cows and calves.[4]

Kingsbury and the American Board intended to evangelize the whole tribe. In 1820 an opportunity to establish another station presented itself when David Folsom, a mixed-blood, and John Pitchlynn, an intermarried white, invited Kingsbury to build a station near their residences in the northeastern district. Kingsbury promptly selected the site, just west of present Columbus, Mississippi, and christened it Mayhew, although it was not until the following year that the mission school and other facilities were fully operational. By that time much-needed additional workers had been sent out by the American Board.[5]

Among those who arrived in the second contingent of laborers was Cyrus Byington. Born on March 11, 1793, in Stockbridge, Massachusetts, Byington was one of nine children whose father was a tanner and small farmer. At the age of fourteen Cyrus entered the home of Joseph Woodbridge to study French, Latin, and Greek and prepare for a legal career. In 1814 he was admitted to the bar, though it was not until the following year that he opened his own law office. Under circumstances that are not clear, Byington professed religion early in 1816, closed his office, and that fall entered the seminary at Andover to study Hebrew and theology. He completed his studies in September, 1819, was licensed to preach by the local presbytery, and promptly volunteered to serve as a missionary of the American Board to the Armenians in Turkey. Instead the board commissioned him to raise money in its behalf in the Massachusetts region. One year later it asked him to accompany for "several hundred miles" a group of missionaries assigned to the expanding Choctaw work. Specifically, he was to act as an "advance man" for the party as it proceeded down the Ohio and Mississippi rivers to the mouth of the Yazoo. In addition to arranging receptions at principal river towns, he was to preach and to obtain donations for the mission.[6]

Leaving Pittsburgh on November 1, 1820, the group did not arrive at the Yazoo until January 27, 1821. The "Ark" that provided them transportation was a three-oared, fifty-six-foot-long flat-bottom boat. Always arduous and trying, the trip became incredibly more difficult upon reaching the mouth of the Yazoo. Three in the mission group died before a relief party could arrive. Byington was spared this particular trial, for he had earlier gone to Natchez to meet and assist the touring secretary of the American Board, Samuel Worcester. He finally reached Elliot on April 17, 1821, having apparently received permission from Worcester to join the Choctaw Mission permanently.[7] He relished the opportunity. "Here," he wrote three months later, "let me continue to live. Here let me labor till I die, and find rest in the tomb." His words may have resulted from youthful enthusiasm, but they were nonetheless prophetic.[8]

Initially Byington devoted his talents to the classroom, in keeping with both the needs and the philosophy of the mission. It was widely agreed that the saving and civilizing Gospel could best be propagated among the tribespeople by beginning with the young. From this conviction flowed an educational system based upon the boarding-school concept as first employed at Elliot and Mayhew. Choctaw parents were expected to leave their children at the schools, where, beyond the influence of the home environment, the students could be both "instructed and inured to labor."[9] As members of the mission family they would also be exposed to role models who personified both civilization and salvation. The envisioned relationship was not dissimilar to that Cyrus Byington himself had enjoyed in the household of Joseph Woodbridge. Once at the school the student's education began in earnest. Following a custom inaugurated by board missionaries in Bombay and Ceylon, the youngsters were given pronounceable American names and issued clothing appropriate for their new life-style.[10] To instruct the male students in the "useful arts of life," the mission farms were utilized as outdoor classrooms in agriculture, dairying, horticulture, and animal husbandry. They could also learn blacksmithing and carpentry. Girls obtained similar practical training in the household arts by caring for the school kitchen, dining room, and other areas, and by making, mending, and washing their own clothing and that of others. Initially few of the students objected to the practical training. "The children are docile, obedient, and ready to perform any kind of labor," Cyrus Byington wrote. "They are active and very useful."[11]

In the classrooms of the mission the Choctaw youngsters were taught to read and write English. As reading material the teachers initially used selected passages from the Bible and Christian catechisms. The method of instruction was the Lancastrian Plan, whereby brighter students under the direction of an adult instructor taught other students. The most advanced classes read in the New Testament, recited by memory important passages from Genesis and Exodus, and became knowledgeable about the life of Christ. All the students also received instruction in basic arithmetic and elementary geography.[12]

Given the nature of the curriculum, the success of the educational system depended upon a well-disciplined student body. Instances of open rebellion, if they occurred, went unreported; even references to youthful misconduct were rare. The most difficult discipline problems involved the reluctance of the students to engage in manual labor and the unwillingness of parents to leave their children in school until the end of the term. Aside from lecturing the tribal council on the necessity for students to submit to their authority, the missionaries sought to correct the problems by selecting as students even younger children, whose habits were still malleable, and by launching a long-range effort to educate parents to the importance of discipline within the family. In the meantime they suffered the loss of some of their more able scholars to the Choctaw Academy in Kentucky, an institution supervised by the Baptists that required no manual labor of its students. As the decade of the 1820s progressed, the ill will generated by the discipline caused the missionaries to place less emphasis upon boarding schools and more upon day and Sabbath schools. By the end of the decade they were prepared to abandon the whole boarding-school concept.[13]

In the reorientation of the philosophy and system of education Cyrus Byington provided important leadership. While laboring at Elliot as a classroom teacher, he devoted increasing amounts of time to mastering the Choctaw language. For periods as long as a week he resided in villages where only the vernacular was spoken. By early 1823 such experiences had enabled Byington and Alfred Wright, a native of Connecticut and another Andover graduate, to devise a system of orthography for the native language based upon the Roman alphabet, establish some rules of spelling, and conjugate at least one verb. Recognizing the value of this work, in the following year Byington's colleagues directed him to further his knowledge of Choctaw and to become fluent in speaking it. To this end he moved to Ak-ik-hun-nah, a settlement thirty miles west of Mayhew near the home of David Folsom, a politically prominent mixed-blood who understood and wrote English. By May, 1824, the missionary was able to preach in Choctaw, using written sermons prepared with Folsom's aid. Within six more months he was writing his own lessons, and at year's end he had delivered about thirty sermons in Choctaw on 176 different occasions, generally to good crowds.[14]

These initial linguistic efforts of Byington, along with those of Wright and Folsom, culminated in 1825 with the publication of the first edition of a Choctaw-language book. Entitled *A Spelling Book, written in the Chahta Language with an English translation* and printed in Cincinnati by the American

Board, the volume had only one objective. It was designed to facilitate comprehension of the Gospel by teaching Choctaw students how to read and write English. Put differently, it demonstrated that salvation, civilization, and English-language literacy remained merely different facets of the same Christian message.

But after 1825 that perspective changed. The missionaries began to emphasize both in and out of the classroom the teaching of Choctaw as opposed to English. Previous experiences had shown that while students, especially full-bloods, might read and memorize English, they did not understand it. Byington himself had also demonstrated that the tribespeople were most receptive to the Good News if and when they heard it presented in their own language. Since the implementation of this new approach required additional printed materials in the native language, Byington enlarged the much used *Spelling Book* to about 160 pages, and Alfred Wright and Loring S. Williams, the latter at the mission from the beginning and a student of the vernacular as well, prepared two other manuscripts of 15 and 144 pages. Byington spent most of the year 1827 in Cincinnati supervising the publication of the three books. He took the occasion of that pleasant sojourn to arrange his ordination as a minister and to court and marry twenty-seven-year-old Sophia Nye. By February, 1828, Byington was back in the Choctaw Nation with several thousand copies of three new books and a new wife.[15]

The Choctaw-language publications had an immediate impact on the work of the mission. By 1829 the more than 170 students in eight mission schools were taught to read Choctaw before and even if they did not learn English. Of the thirty-six students enrolled at Mayhew, for example, thirty read in Choctaw, while only six read in English. Additionally, several schools were established in which Choctaw alone was taught. One of the schools, Yok-nok-cha-ya, was at a new station seventeen miles south of Mayhew, to which Byington and his wife moved in early 1829.[16]

The new books also facilitated an energetic program of adult education. At each of the stations the missionaries and some of their advanced scholars conducted Sabbath schools for the adults and children in adjacent neighborhoods. On such occasions these special students, utilizing the publications prepared for the purpose, received instruction in the rudiments of the Choctaw language. The tribespeople responded enthusiastically to these opportunities: in one full-blood settlement where there was no mission school, about thirty-five individuals knew or were learning how to read their own language, and in another settlement about fifty-five students were pursuing the same objective. Reports from the missionaries in different sections of the Choctaw Nation made clear that the Sabbath schools with their vernacular training had greater potential for transforming the tribe than any other mission enterprise.[17]

For Byington the native-language publications and instructional programs provided an avenue by which the masses of the tribespeople could be reached with the saving message of the Gospel. Churches had been established shortly after the arrival of the Presbyterian missionaries, but the response of the Choctaws to evangelistic efforts had been noticeably unenthusiastic. Indeed, in the first decade of the mission the only converts were black slaves and a few white women. Of course, it was not particularly easy to become a convert. One had to become serious about his spiritual condition, give evidence of his piety by appropriate conduct, recognize his election, indicate knowledge of the Scriptures, accept Divine Grace, and repent of his sins—all of which took time. And it took longer if one had to know English and to adopt different cultural mores and customs. The missionaries were committed to these prerequisites for church membership, but they were nonetheless frustrated and disappointed by their inability to convert the "heathen." The new books and emphasis upon instruction in the vernacular, they hoped, would improve the record.[18]

And it did. Significantly the first Choctaw to respond to the spiritual message of the Gospel was a full-blood adult male about fifty years of age named Tunnapinchuffa. A resident of the community in which Cyrus Byington preached and referred to as "Abraham" within the mission family, Tunnapinchuffa heard the Good News in the vernacular and became serious about his spiritual condition in late 1827. He spent much time in fervent and expressive prayer, describing himself and his people in deprecating terms and asking God to take pity upon them. On frequent occasions he exhorted his family and friends to throw away their "black and dirty garments," and he worked diligently at transforming his own "bad thoughts" and overcoming the temptation of strong drink. His new life-style brought ridicule and even pity from some quarters, but he persevered in his conversion despite the costs. In March, 1829, the missionaries accepted him as a member of the Presbyterian church. Tunnapinchuffa "adorns his profession," wrote one, being a "man of prayer; very industrious, meek and humble; a good but not a great man."[19] The old gentleman retained his Christian commitment until his death in June, 1834, becoming an elder in the church and composing original hymns that were later published.

At the same time Tunnapinchuffa never lost his unique Choctaw identity. The fact that a deer remained in one place until he could go leisurely to his camp and get his gun and return to kill it he interpreted as a sign and present from his "heavenly Father." He also utilized the services of native doctors until late in life, despite the disapproval of the missionaries. And like all other full-blood Choctaws, Tunnapinchuffa was vigorously opposed to removal of the tribe from its homeland. Moreover, he accepted Divine Grace without abandoning his native tongue; indeed, he never learned English. That Tunnapinchuffa was both Choctaw and Christian vindicated the new evangelistic philosophy and methodology employed by Byington and his colleagues.[20]

By the time Tunnapinchuffa finally united with the church, a full-scale revival was under way in the Choctaw Nation. It apparently had its genesis in the northwestern district, where Methodist missionaries had been at work since at least 1827. Alexander Talley, a physician turned preacher, had succeeded in converting the district chief, Greenwood Le Flore. At a large camp meeting in the summer of 1828, one of the participants was affected with bodily exercises, and at a similar meeting in October there was even more widespread excitement. Within a year about 1,000 Choctaws had been converted, and within another year 3,000 more. Rather than denigrate this phenomenon by critical references to the Methodist philosophy of conversion, the Presbyterian missionaries rejoiced at this "work of grace."[21] Indeed, they moved to take advantage of it, if not imitate it, by launching a series of three- and four-day protracted meetings of their own.[22]

As in vernacular preaching and instruction, Byington seemed to take the lead in using the protracted meetings. At one attended by about 500 natives, 270 Choctaws took places on the anxious seats.[23] At another meeting, where more than 400 were present, "Many wept, and many looked as though they were too full and solemn to weep." On this occasion thirty-three persons, seven of whom were captains (clan leaders) and twenty-four of Choctaw descent, were examined and admitted to the church. "Surely," said Byington, "it is a time of the Lord's power."[24] And so it must have appeared. Continuing through 1830, the revival in the woods brought a harvest of some 360 church members, including 2 district chiefs, thousands more who sought relief on the anxious seat and began to pray, and more than 240 baptized children.[25]

Although none questioned the power of the Word, Cyrus Byington and his colleagues realized that factors secular in nature accounted for the revival. In 1820 at Doak's Stand the Choctaw leadership had reluctantly consented to cede a third of the tribe's remaining Mississippi domain in return for a tract of land that encompassed all of what is now southern Oklahoma. Federal officials hoped that the Treaty of 1820 would encourage the Choctaws to begin a gradual but sustained removal to the new domain. The mixed-blood and intermarried power structure of the tribe, however, opted for another course, one based upon the historic willingness of the tribespeople to accommodate change. Assuming that their white neighbors demanded removal primarily because Choctaw society was "uncivilized," they determined to encourage the transformation of the cultural habits of their people to the extent that they would conform to so-called "civilized" standards. With the Choctaws similar to their neighbors in all but color, perhaps then the government would forget about tribal removal.[26]

The Presbyterian missionaries arrived almost simultaneously with the decision to foster a cultural transformation of the tribe. Happily, their Gospel had both secular and spiritual elements. The mixed-blood leadership, therefore, enthusiastically supported the mission schools, especially their emphasis upon English literacy and mathematical competency, and commended the station farms as examples of activities to be imitated. It also endorsed the Gospel's demand for abandonment of "heathenish" customs that lowered the white man's estimation of the Choctaws. Particularly objectionable was pole pulling, a rite that involved placing poles around the grave of a deceased person, daily mourning, and the subsequent removal of the poles. Equally questionable were the practices of infanticide, the use of conjurors, the killing of suspected witches, polygamy, and adultery.[27] Because of vested property interests, the mixed-bloods also welcomed missionary sermons on the family structure as revealed in Scripture, sermons that implied criticism of the sex roles and matrilineal descent system traditional in Choctaw society.[28]

Although such cultural customs were deeply ingrained in tribal lifeways, immediate transformation was imperative given the impending danger of removal. To this end and with the blessings of Byington and his colleagues, the mixed bloods sought to hasten the working of the Gospel by employing the force of law. As early as 1822 the chief and council of the southern district of the tribe enacted ordinances suppressing intemperance, infanticide, and adultery, laws which were then enforced by the lighthorse, a company of armed and mounted police. The action was taken, said the chief, because "we wish to follow the ways of the white people."[29]

Yet a more permanent and extensive cultural reformation seemed to require extensive alteration of the overall political structure of the tribe. Such a change occurred in 1826, when the rising mixed-blood leadership, specifically David Folsom,

Greenwood Le Flore, and John Garland, deposed the full-blood chiefs, adopted a constitution, and enshrined a government they themselves controlled. The latter then quickly identified as crimes against the Choctaw Nation theft, murder, polygamy, infanticide, perjury, the killing of witches, and the liquor traffic. It also guaranteed the principle of the father as head of the household and provided for inheritance through the male line. This action at the national level encouraged similar responses locally. In July, 1828, the northeastern district chief and council made the custom of pole pulling illegal.[30]

The new moral code and the endorsement of educational activities would have heartened the Presbyterian missionaries had they been accompanied by some evidence of religious piety. For a decade they were not. Instead, the mixed-blood leaders of the tribe embraced selected elements of the Christian message with the objective of saving their nation rather than their souls. But in 1829 that self-serving response changed. In March the Mississippi State Legislature extended legal jurisdiction over the Choctaws and acted to abolish tribal government. With ten years of effort designed to prevent removal seemingly for naught, the mixed-blood leaders turned to prayer and sought actively the protection of Divine Grace. Men like David Folsom even exhorted their full-blood followers to abandon their sinful ways and accept the saving message of the Gospel. Such timely conversions further fueled the revival fire then ready to sweep the Choctaw Nation. To his credit Byington was fully aware that the threat of removal had finally impressed upon the Choctaw leaders the need to make an effort to save themselves and their people. Still, he believed that the source of this "good effect" was not so much removal as it was the fact that "the father of mercies smiles upon them and blesses them."[31]

The certainty that the civilizing and saving power of the Gospel was at work among the Choctaws caused the Presbyterian missionaries to support the tribal leadership's effort to resist expulsion. In communications to the American Board they documented the religious and social transformation of the Choctaws and lamented that the tribespeople could not be left in their homeland to continue their progress. In private correspondence Cyrus Byington labeled the demands for removal as "cruel and unjust," while his wife condemned the source of those demands, President Andrew Jackson, as a *"wicked man."*[32] Ironically, the Gospel message itself apparently worked to moderate the resistance of the mixed-blood chiefs to the prospect of tribal emigration. Having embraced the doctrine of God's omnipotence, David Folsom by early 1830 was prepared to leave the matter of removal to Providence. "For myself, I do not feel distressed now as I have been," he observed. "If it is the will of our Heavenly Father that we should go, we shall go. But if it is not, we shall stay."[33] Greenwood Le Flore, a Methodist convert more given to free will than predestination, merely concluded that the cause of religion among the Choctaws could best be advanced in the West.

For whatever reason the mixed-blood leaders settled upon a course that resulted initially in political chaos and ultimately in removal. In March, 1830, a general council of the tribe acted to make Le Flore chief of the entire nation. He then produced a manuscript copy of a treaty in the handwriting of Alexander Talley which consented to tribal removal upon certain conditions. Endorsed by the council but not accepted by the federal government, the proposed treaty occasioned among the Choctaws a violent political reaction and strong antimissionary sentiment. More tragically, many of those who had recently accepted the Gospel message were ridiculed, tempted, and tried. And laws passed designed to demonstrate the moral advancement of the people were soon repealed.[34]

This climate of political and religious anarchy prevailed in September, 1830, when the Choctaws assembled at Dancing Rabbit Creek to negotiate with federal officials concerning removal. Given their commitment to the welfare of the tribe, Cyrus Kingsbury and others of the Presbyterian Mission made it a point to be present. The federal negotiators, however, feared their influence and ordered them to leave the council ground. After registering strong complaints, they accepted the inevitable and returned to their stations. The Choctaws adopted the same fatalistic posture. To pacify their different constituencies, both full-blood and mixed-blood leaders initially remonstrated against removal, but ultimately they consented to a treaty that provided for the removal of the tribe within three years to those lands west of the Mississippi previously assigned to them. For the Presbyterian missionaries, the members of their congregations, indeed, the entire tribe, the removal treaty signaled the end of a historic era.[35]

Organized by the federal government, Choctaw removal to what is now southeastern Oklahoma extended through 1833. During this period virtually all pursuits identified as civilized ceased to function, including education, government, and religion. Yet despite the confusion and the distress of the removal process, the Choctaws had sufficient resources— especially their characteristic willingness to accommodate change—to enable them to restructure and rebuild another community in the West. The reservoir upon which they drew, significantly, consisted of those secular elements of the Gospel message that the mixed-blood leadership had selectively accepted during the previous decade. But what role the proclaimers of that message would play in the new community was not immediately apparent.

From the point of view of the American Board in Boston there was good reason not to continue the Choctaw Mission. After twelve years of labor, the establishment of eight to ten stations, the service of sixty-six men and women (though no more than forty-four at any one time), and a total investment of $140,000 ($60,000 from the board, $60,000 from the Choctaws, and $20,000 from the federal government), the spiritual harvest of 360 souls and four churches had not been particularly gratifying. Moreover, the Prudential Committee was not all that certain that the Choctaws would survive the trauma of removal and offer fertile soil for the Gospel. Also the antimissionary sentiment rampant in the tribe might effectively neutralize any evangelistic efforts.[36]

But there was also good reason to continue the work. When compared to other board outreaches, the Choctaw Mission had been relatively cost-effective. The Hawaiian Islands effort had garnered only 185 souls despite even larger investments of time and money. Moreover, the Choctaw ministry had reached an average of 208 students annually in nine to eleven schools at a total cost of only $56 per scholar. Additionally the vernacular had been reduced to writing, souls had been awakened, churches had been organized, and "uncivilized" habits had been reformed. Most important was that an impressive number of Choctaws wanted a Presbyterian missionary delegation to accompany them to the West.[37]

Ultimately the Prudential Committee determined to continue the mission but with a new look and different emphasis. For one thing, it stipulated that there would be no more boarding schools or demonstration farms, restricting the educational function of the mission to day schools and whatever Sabbath schools might be established. Such changes suggested a subtle redefinition by the American Board of what constituted "civilization" in the context of salvation. As the life of Tunnapinchuffa had demonstrated, individual acceptance of Divine Grace did not depend upon English literacy, agricultural proficiency, skills in commerce and industry, or abandonment of all traditional recreational habits. Temperance, appropriate dress, monogamy, a male descent system, and restrictions on pole pulling were probably demanded, but within the tribe such behavioral patterns already were either widely practiced or had been significantly modified. Thus the board's concept of "civilization" had come to encompass much that was Choctaw either by tradition or by recent adoption. For the Indians the redefinition meant that salvation was available without the necessity of dramatic cultural change; for the missionaries it meant freedom to focus their energies upon proclaiming the saving message of the Gospel and upon preserving those who had already accepted Divine Grace.[38]

Whether Cyrus Byington would be part of a new mission was not immediately clear. In October, 1832, he accompanied some full-blood members of his church to their new homeland, but once they were safely situated, he returned to his old station where his wife and by this time two children, Edward and Lucy, awaited him. At the direction of the Prudential

Cyrus and Sophia Byington during their eastern tour, ca. 1857. Courtesy Smithsonian Institution.

Committee his principal task was to complete a grammar and dictionary of the Choctaw language, a work that was more difficult than anticipated and remained unfinished in late 1833. In the meantime the government had completed the removal of the Choctaws, and Cyrus Kingsbury had disposed of the remaining assets of the board in Mississippi. The committee, therefore, encouraged Byington to continue his language and ministerial work in the West. He accepted the assignment eagerly. "The missionary cause is a good one— a great one," he wrote, "& one that will triumph yet in every land." Moreover, for him the time spent in his previous labors had constituted "the happiest days of my life." Thus in the spring of 1834 he took his wife and two children to Marietta, Ohio, where they could stay with his inlaws until he had found a new mission site.[39]

Because of an extended visit to other Indian missions, Byington did not reach the Choctaws until December, 1834. Warmly welcomed by those people among whom he had previously labored, he found that his colleagues Alfred Wright, Loring Williams, Ebenezer Hotchkins, and others had already reestablished stations at four sites, opened or planned eight day schools, were operating four Sabbath schools, and had organized three churches. Over the next several months he settled upon Eagletown, just west of the Arkansas line in what is now southeastern Oklahoma, as the location of his own station. In March, 1835, he traveled back to Ohio to make the arrangements for his family to accompany him back to the Choctaw country. During his absence a third child had been born, Cyrus Nye.[40]

Delaying the trip until Sophia and the baby had gained strength, Byington returned to the Choctaws in November, 1835. With him he brought teachers for the day school that would be established at the mission and a married couple who could look after the secular concerns of the station. The Choctaws in the neighborhood voluntarily erected for him a dwelling and a schoolhouse, the former with two doors and a floor made of planks, not planed and not joined. Two glass windows were soon added. Although rather primitive, the physical facilities were better than those of his neighbors. He named the station Stockbridge in honor of his Massachusetts hometown.[41]

In concert with the goals of the mission, Byington immediately undertook his evangelical and ministerial duties. Beginning with the remnants of the flock initially collected in Mississippi, he organized a church at Eagletown, where, along with five or six other sites, he preached regularly. Occasionally, when there was sufficient interest, he also conducted or participated in protracted meetings near his station as well as at distant locations. His primary area of service encompassed 1,800 square miles and more than 3,000 Choctaws. Although a number of prominent mixed-blood families lived nearby, Byington generally focused his attention upon the full-blood majority to whom he always preached in the vernacular. Like Tunnapinchuffa, these "genuine" Choctaws received the Good News as a system of thought and style of life not incompatible with being Indian. The mixed-bloods, on the other hand, generally accepted the Gospel for secular reasons, seeing Christianity as a means of achieving social and political acceptance by the whites. However the Choctaws responded to his message of Divine Grace and circumspect behavior, Byington encouraged them all by baptizing their children, comforting them upon the losses of loved ones, and nursing them at times of ill health. Within a short time he was prescribing and providing medicine for about 500 Choctaws a year.[42]

Although he was frequently distracted by the spiritual and secular concerns of the mission, the ministerial work that Byington most enjoyed was the study and translation of the Choctaw language, work which, he said, was "reviving to the mind." To complete the grammar and dictionary were his passions, but he recognized that printed materials in the vernacular had more immediate value because they facilitated evangelistic endeavors. Thus following the formal reorganization of the mission, he, Alfred Wright, and Loring Williams prepared additional Choctaw books for publication. Byington generally concentrated his efforts on revision of materials that dealt with language instruction and on translation of Scripture from Hebrew into Choctaw. Between 1836 and 1844 he prepared an annual edition of a *Choctaw Almanac,* which contained statistical information about the tribe and used a measure of time more effective than the familiar bundle of sticks.[43] Byington had responsibility for the total linguistic effort after Wright's death in 1853. Williams had left the mission sixteen years earlier.

In terms of volume the cumulative results of this work by Byington and his colleagues were impressive. By 1848 about 95,000 copies of fifty-seven different publications containing a total of about 3,000 pages had been printed on the presses of the American Board. The following year the American Bible Society published the New Testament in Choctaw, a good portion of which Byington himself had translated with the assistance of such native preachers as Jonathan Dwight and Pliny Fisk. In the old nation both of the latter had been students and converts whose bilingual talents proved most helpful after removal both in the pulpit and in the translation into Choctaw of English-language materials.[44]

The American Board considered religiously oriented publications of highest priority and eschewed printing vernacular materials that had only literary merit. Byington himself was directly affected by this policy. In 1851 he traveled to New York and Boston to oversee the publication of a "definer" for the schools and to translate and see into print portions of a new hymnbook, biographies of biblical heroes, and five of the Old Testament books. During his extended stay he urged the board to publish the grammar upon which he had labored for twenty-five years. To his great disappointment the board declined to sponsor publication on the grounds that the grammar had little religious content. For a time Byington hoped that the Smithsonian Institution would publish it, but officials there finally asked for further revisions and expansion. This reception of a labor of scholarship and love left him "not a little vexed." It had caused him a great deal of extra work, he wrote to Sophia, for which he got nothing, not even wages. Still, he believed, "The Lord will take care of this book and me too. I needed something to bring me down."[45] Even with additional revisions the grammar was not published until two years after Byington's death. The other scholarly passion of his life, a Choctaw-English dictionary containing more than 12,000 words, was not published until 1915.

Despite the reaction of others, Byington always intended his linguistic work to be merely a means of enhancing the Gospel message. Achieving as a consequence of it literacy in the vernacular, the tribal majority could then read printed materials that spoke of little but the way of salvation. Nourished upon such food, which was further interpreted and explained by both white and native preachers speaking their own language, the Choctaws could be prepared to accept Divine Grace. And it worked largely as it was planned, producing a spiritual harvest of significant proportions. To the 180 church members brought together in 1833 by the mission, only 45 had been added by 1840. The next year the number increased by one-third. There were 450 members in 1843, 769 in 1846, 959 in 1849, 1,158 in 1856, and 1,768 in 1861. During the same period the number of congregations increased from three to seventeen. By the time of the Civil War, therefore, 10 percent of the entire tribe were members of Presbyterian churches; an equal number belonged to other Christian fellowships. That the growth in membership coincided with the proliferation of vernacular literacy and literature vindicated the value of Byington's work and demonstrated the success of the general mission effort.[46]

The growth further reflected the wisdom of having emphasized evangelism and ministry in reconstituting the Choctaw Mission and the value of redefining Christianity in non–New England terms. But some Choctaws, especially the mixed-bloods, remembered vividly the earlier missionary concept of "civilization" and its emphasis upon formal education as the door of opportunity and the guarantor of nationhood. That the civilizing elements of the Gospel separate and apart from salvation had not served them well before removal was forgotten. Thus they had no more than reached Oklahoma when they made plans to establish an extensive system of neighborhood schools. In addition to the day schools at the different mission stations, they encouraged the government agent to establish and finance similar ones from treaty funds. By 1837 at least eleven such schools were in operation.[47]

But for the mixed-blood leaders this represented only a beginning. Under their influence in 1842 the tribal government created a system of two male and five female boarding schools that would provide an advanced educational curriculum. Later another male school was established. For assistance in operating these institutions, they looked to Presbyterian and Methodist missionaries. Four of the girls' schools were offered to the American Board on a contract whereby the Choctaws would supply operational funds in the amount of $7,800 annually to be matched by only $1,800 from the board. For the entire eight-school system the Choctaws planned to spend almost $20,000 annually, utilizing federal government annuities that had previously been allocated per capita.[48]

With the frustrations of administering boarding schools at Elliot and Mayhew a vague memory, the Presbyterian missionaries urged their sponsoring board to accept the challenge of directing the fortunes of the new schools. The Prudential Committee weighed the matter and ultimately consented to the relationship proposed by the tribal government. The resultant contract committed the American Board to double both its level of funding and the staff assigned to the mission. In anticipation of this decision the missionaries themselves had already assigned the four female schools to different superintendents. One of the institutions, Ianubbee, was placed under the direction of Cyrus Byington at Eagletown.[49]

Byington's surviving correspondence suggests that he was not particularly excited about supervising a large boarding school. Nonetheless, before 1844 he selected a site for the facility about one and one-half miles north of his ten-year-old station, began negotiations that would result in construction of a school building, laid out another farm and pasture, and moved his family to a new house near the school. Much of the burden of Ianubbee fell upon the shoulders of two additional female teachers as well as a steward and his family recruited by the board, all of whom arrived just before the scheduled opening of the school in late 1844. Byington retained general oversight of the institution and had special responsibilities for the spiritual instruction and welfare of the students.[50]

He also wrestled with the nature of the curriculum pursued by the twenty-four boarding-school and forty day-school scholars, some of the latter being boys. The problem was not the usual fare of reading, spelling, writing, arithmetic, geography, botany, music, and domestic arts. The difficulty was English versus Choctaw as the language of instruction. Under pressure from both tribal and federal government officials, Byington and his counterparts at the other schools eventually settled upon English, even demanding that the girls speak to each other in that language. For *genuine* Choctaws, he rationalized, the mother tongue was better, but for patrons of the schools, presumably the mixed-bloods, English was altogether best. Byington superintended Ianubbee through 1852, when, because of ill health, lack of help, and growing frustration with the American Board, he asked to be and was relieved of his responsibilities.[51]

In the meantime the Choctaws continued their remarkable commitment to public education. In addition to eight boarding schools which had enrolled 445 students by 1860, they supported as many as twenty-two neighborhood schools that reached about 500 scholars. The Choctaws even appropriated sums of money to underwrite dozens of missionary-inspired and conducted Sabbath schools that reached hundreds, perhaps even thousands, of adult learners. Like the neighborhood schools, these too were conducted by native teachers and preachers. The result of this enthusiasm for formal and informal education was impressive. According to historian Angie Debo, tribal literacy in the Choctaw language had been achieved by 1860.[52] Moreover, after no more than a generation following removal, many participated competently in an increasingly sophisticated economic system, all recognized the authority of constitutional government and a written code of laws, and the leadership sustained the rights of the Choctaws in frequent diplomatic negotiations with the federal government. Institutionalized first by the Presbyterian missionaries and endorsed by mixed-blood leaders concerned about national survival, formal and adult education had produced a "civilized" nation.

Although the Choctaws, and particularly the rising mixed-blood class, concluded differently, Cyrus Byington and his associates had reason to believe that the Gospel had been misserved by the boarding schools. For one thing, parents enrolled their children with the object of social and material elevation rather than spiritual good. Also, instruction in English raised the students so far above their parents that, according to Cyrus Kingsbury, "they became vain in their imaginations, and their foolish heart was darkened." The moral and religious interests of the tribe, he believed, would have been better served had the students been taught the vernacular rather than English. As it was, few of those educated in the boarding schools west of the Mississippi ever gave evidence of piety.[53] Put differently, education had contributed to the civilization but not the salvation of many Choctaws, just the reverse of what the missionaries had once anticipated. Yet in secular terms that result was precisely what the mixed-blood leaders *had* planned.

If boarding schools seemingly inhibited the acceptance of Divine Grace by some Choctaws, they also involved the missionaries in the politics of slavery. Introduced into the tribe by intermarried whites well before the Presbyterians had initiated their mission, the institution had been carried west at the time of removal and had prospered in the new nation. Its importance, especially to mixed-blood planters, caused the leaders to be ever watchful that criticism within and without their domain did not curtail its use. For that reason as early as 1836 the tribal council made it illegal to teach slaves how to read, write, or sing and directed the banishment from the country of any missionary or preacher who promoted abolition. Later laws forbade free blacks to live in the nation, restricted slaves from holding property, and prevented emancipation of slaves except upon petition of the owner. And in 1852 the council restated its opposition to children of slaves being taught to read and write.[54]

For their part the missionaries unanimously opposed slavery. Byington, for example, frequently spoke of the "evils and horrors" of the institution. Yet before and especially after the removal of the tribe to Oklahoma he and his associates had to confront and deal with the reality of the slave system virtually on a daily basis. For one thing, the missionaries needed physical assistance in carrying out the work of the mission, help that was almost impossible to find among the Choctaws or to recruit from the states. They soon began the practice of employing slaves of Choctaw owners to provide the necessary manual labor, and for this purpose on twelve occasions they even purchased slaves, who after five or six years of work were given their freedom. Also the missionaries encountered the slaveowners who themselves became "hopefully pious" and sought admission to the church. At such times these candidates were admitted to membership without reference to slavery. By 1848 there were 38 slaveholders in fellowship with the churches as well as 104 slaves.[55]

However the missionaries dealt with the "peculiar" institution they encountered severe criticism. Some of their number, including Cyrus Kingsbury, were accused by the Choctaws of being abolitionists. These charges accounted for the departure of four members of the mission from the nation, the transfer of one school to the care of another sponsor, and the apostasy of one native preacher. At the same time Byington and his brethren were labeled soft on slavery by some influential supporters of the American Board as well as some of their own, younger colaborers. Initially the Prudential Committee itself sustained its Choctaw Mission in the use of slave labor and in the view that ownership of slaves had no bearing upon acceptance of Divine Grace and church membership. In so doing, the committee endorsed its historic position that evangelism took precedence over societal reformation.[56]

By 1848 the growing strength of the antislavery movement worked to make this mainstream Presbyterian approach to missions unpopular within the circles of the Prudential Committee. More acceptable was the view that social reform, that is, abolition of slavery, had equal standing with evangelism in the mission field. The pervasiveness of this more liberal perspective became apparent in February, 1848, when S. B. Treat visited the Choctaw Nation. A corresponding secretary for the American Board, Treat embodied the new disposition. As such he was a firm opponent of slavery and was deeply troubled that the missionaries did not publicly condemn the institution, even if that condemnation impeded the proclamation of the Gospel. Before returning to Boston, he requested that the brethren prepare at an early date a detailed statement which would rationalize their traditional position on the issue of slavery.[57]

The following month Cyrus Byington and his colleagues responded to this directive. With reference to the debate over slavery, they wrote, in their *"sphere of labor"* they had determined upon a course of neutrality. Only as a matter of necessity did they employ slave laborers, and the admission of slaveholders to church membership was in accordance with Presbyterian doctrine on church polity. Nowhere in "the plain language of the Bible," they argued, was the morality of slavery addressed, nor did it record any efforts to reform systematic civil wrongs. Thus, as they saw it, the duty of the missionary was to preach the Gospel and let the Lord, in due season, perfect human society. This view was consistent with their willingness, manifested since the great revival of 1829, to accept other than New England standards of social behavior from potential converts and to permit church members to be both Christian and Choctaw—even slaveholding Choctaws.[58]

With this argument Treat and the Prudential Committee were not impressed. If in the interest of evangelistic expediency they had once been willing to broaden their definition of Christianity for the benefit of Choctaw converts, they no longer were. In June, 1848, in a long response to the mission's policy statement, Treat agreed that congregations theoretically could determine their own membership. At the same time he insisted that board missionaries must preach against the sin of slavery, that slaveholders were not eligible for church membership, and that those who were members should be instructed on the evils of the practice. Moreover, the hiring of slaves was "altogether inexpedient." Put differently, the practices of the Choctaw missionaries relative to slavery constituted thirty years of error.[59]

This was a bitter pill for Byington and the others to swallow. Although in April, 1849, they consented not to employ slave labor except in cases of extreme need, they nonetheless chafed under Treat's censorious condemnation and what they identified as untraditional and unscriptural proscriptions of their conduct. Following an unsatisfactory interview with the secretary two years later when he was visiting the East Coast, Byington wrote to his wife that, since "Mr. Treat has undertaken to manage the mission on antislavery principles, let others have an opportunity to go on the Indian mission and work under a burning sun—and be complained of for hiring slaves." Indeed, he almost came to the point of defending slavery. Compared with Irish emigrants in Boston, he exclaimed, "Why the negroes on Mountain Fork are princes." He added that there was "no laboring population on the globe" as well provided for or with so much religion as "our blacks."[60] But these comments were exceptional, flowing from painful frustration. The real Byington was the man of compassion who raised sufficient funds to purchase the freedom of "Uncle" Simon Harrison, a Choctaw slave convert who later served as a board missionary in Liberia.[61]

Byington's extended stay in the East demonstrated, in part, why the Choctaw missionaries were at odds with their sponsoring agency. He was shocked that the people of New York wore only "new clothes" and was horrified that a church had spent $1,000 for a single window. Moreover, he learned that the interest and focus of mission activity had shifted from American Indian to East Asian peoples, which made it difficult to find laborers for the Choctaw work. Sixty-two ministers had sought a single appointment at a church in Connecticut. "But," he asked, "who among them thinks of the Indians or of Africa?" Obviously Byington had become a victim of time and geography. His views and practices had been acceptable in New England thirty years earlier but now they no longer were. Unlike the people to whom he had dedicated his life, ironically, he found it difficult to accommodate such dramatic change.[62]

During the decade of the 1850s the relationship between the Choctaw Mission and the American Board became increasingly tense. Byington and his senior colleagues continued reluctant to speak out against slavery and to discipline slaveholding church members, a posture that the Prudential Committee viewed at best as "an embarrassment." On two different occasions Treat urged Choctaw missionaries to seek a relationship with the Foreign Mission Board of the General Assembly of the Presbyterian Church, a board that had a more traditional view of missions and had been active in the Choctaw Nation since 1845 without inciting abolitionist fears of the tribal leadership. On both occasions Byington and his brethren declined to initiate a transfer. Accordingly, on July 27, 1859, the Prudential Committee with some reluctance informed the missionaries that it would forthwith discontinue its support of the Choctaw Mission. At the same time it authorized payment of a lifetime pension for Byington and Kingsbury in consideration of their long service and advanced ages.[63]

It was hardly a fitting culmination to four decades of toil and sacrifice. The two did not accept the offer. Instead they and their colleagues on January 7, 1860, entered into an arrangement with their own Presbyterian church denomination whereby its Foreign Mission Board would assume responsibility for and fund their ministerial and educational activities. The Prudential Committee accommodated the move by transferring title to any equipment and property belonging to the American Board to the new sponsor. Although not everywhere applauded by the leaders of the denomination, the Presbyterian Board welcomed the Choctaw Mission to its ranks if for no other reason than that it included seven ordained missionaries, six native preachers and helpers, ten stations, and twelve churches with an aggregate membership of 1,467.

In addition, there were three day schools and three boarding schools with a total enrollment of 455 scholars.

If the Choctaw Mission brought numbers, it also brought problems. The most immediate of these was an incident involving Cyrus Byington and members of his church.[64] In late December, 1858, Richard Harkins, a prominent mixed-blood, had been murdered by his black slave Prince. Upon being apprehended, Prince had implicated a female slave in the crime, confessed to the killing, and then escaped only to drown himself. The enraged relatives of Harkins in the presence of his wife then burned to death the accomplice, Lucy, who maintained her innocence to the end. Both Lucy and Mrs. Harkins were members of Byington's church. In the wake of the tragedy Byington visited the widow regularly and urged her to appear before the ruling elders of the church and submit herself to their discipline for her part in the affair. Involving the mixed-blood elite of the tribe and occurring at the height of abolitionist criticism of the Choctaw Mission, Byington felt constrained not to broadcast the news of the event, which was well known and perhaps even condoned in the Choctaw Nation.[65]

Two years passed before the circumstances of the slave burning were published in the United States. Within abolitionist circles Byington was severely criticized and condemned for his failure to report the incident and because he had not insisted that Harkin's wife be denied the communion and fellowship of the church. These critics interpreted the event as evidence of the tacit support that the Choctaw Mission gave to the sin of slavery. More recent interpreters have followed the same interpretation. Yet for Byington the unfortunate affair reflected more his strict evangelicalism and biblical literalism than his attitude toward slavery. Among a people who were more and more defensive of the institution, he knew that proclamation of the Gospel depended upon a narrow and neutral course.[66]

That there was no alternative to such a role was soon confirmed. Under the general supervision of the Presbyterian Board, the Choctaw missionaries continued their ministries and made plans to enroll classes in the boarding schools during the fall term of 1860. The ensuing academic year was more notable for the series of events that signaled the permanent close of the schools than for educational achievement. The election of Abraham Lincoln, the secession of southern states, and the bombardment of Fort Sumter combined to cause the Choctaw leadership to embrace the cause of the Confederacy. Southern patriotism was so strong that those missionaries suspected of abolitionist sentiments were forced to flee the Choctaw Nation in fear of their lives. Among those who fled was the superintendent of the school at Byington's station. Other mission workers sympathetic with the North also abandoned the field. In July, 1861, the Choctaws formally allied with the Confederacy, thereafter focusing their attention and money upon the furtherance of that cause. The three female boarding schools then under the supervision of the Presbyterian missionaries were forced to close. As Cyrus Byington had feared, the inability to separate the Gospel from secular reform had damaged the effectiveness of the mission, and only a handful of workers now remained to preach the Good News.[67]

In September, 1861, without Byington's presence and acting in behalf of the Indian Presbytery, the residue of the mission disassociated itself from the General Assembly of the Presbyterian church. That organization, it stated, had supported a government that had refused to fulfill its treaty obligations with the Choctaws, had withdrawn its troops and exposed the Indians to the wild tribes of the West, and was engaged in a war against the Confederate States with whom the Choctaws were "politically, socially, and ecclesiastically connected."[68] In December, 1861, when the Southern Assembly of Presbyterian Churches was organized, the Indian Presbytery immediately associated with it. Although the new denomination then assumed responsibility for the Choctaw Mission, it was never able to fulfill its financial commitment after military conflict began in earnest. During the course of the war, therefore, Byington and his brethren were virtually without support. The ensuing years were difficult indeed.

Fortunately, the previous four decades had prepared Byington to cope with what appeared to be the disintegration of his lifework. He had always been hard pressed financially. The American Board had never provided him with funds beyond those necessary for his immediate needs. It even claimed ownership of the house he occupied. Because his father had virtually disinherited him, Byington had had to look to the gifts of friends and family, especially his in-laws, to finance the education of his children.

In addition to economic hardship, personal affliction and grief had inured Byington to the trials of the war years. Slight in body, he frequently suffered ill health. By 1851 a persistent throat problem so drained him physically that Sophia felt compelled to warn members of her family whom he would visit not to be startled. "You will find him *greatly changed,*" she wrote. "*Fifteen years* in the *down hill of life, must make changes.*"[69] More important, Byington had also buried two sons near "his home in the wilderness," his oldest in 1840 and his youngest in 1846. On both occasions he was almost overwhelmed with grief. When his last-born, only thirty months old, died in his arms, he could only write, "It was best for me that I should be humbled by his death and be more weaned from this world and be better prepared for death."[70] A sister who had come for a visit and was the first member of his family he had seen in twenty years he had buried earlier.

If trials prepared Byington for the war years, then love sustained him. The relationship he had with Sophia approached the marvelous. It was founded upon mutual respect as much as affection. He knew of no one who worked as hard as she did, and he understood her need to visit family and friends in Ohio despite the cost. She in turn accepted the necessity of his long absences to preach in distant places and to oversee the publication of his books. During Byington's long stay in the East during 1851-52, Sophia joined him earlier than expected. "I took him by surprise," she wrote, "but he seemed *right glad* to see me." After a pleasant summer together, during which they visited Massachusetts, Sophia returned to Ohio. He adjusted to her absence very slowly and at one point wrote that "what I miss most I begin to suspect was carried away in your old shoes." Their love was quiet and subdued, and it lasted for forty-one years.[71]

The same kind of relationship existed between Byington and the two children that survived childhood. His only daughter, Lucy, was ten years old when he sent her to Ohio to live with her uncle and go to school. She did not return to the Choctaw Nation for eight years, but during the interval her father wrote long letters of counsel, encouraging her to pursue her religious life, to write home more regularly, and, when she did write, to be careful about her spelling. Lucy married George Dana, of Belpre, Ohio, in February, 1852, when Byington was on the East Coast. On the way back to the Choctaw Mission a year later he stopped to visit her and left her a note that suggested his measure as a father. "You have," he wrote, "done much to comfort me and very little at any time of your life, even while a child, to grieve me. I regret I have not been more faithful to all my children, the living or the departed." He commended her and her husband to the Blessed Savior and enclosed a fifty-dollar bill.[72]

Lucy's brother, Cyrus Nye, did cause his parents some grief. At the age of sixteen he left home to attend school and over the next several years struggled with his studies, his religious commitment, and his use of tobacco. He returned to his father's house after a seven-year absence, found employment as a store clerk, married, and moved to Arkansas. After the war he helped dispose of the family property at Eagletown. He died in September, 1867.

Finally Byington's religious faith enabled him to continue his labors in an inhospitable environment. He had long since committed himself to the Lord, and in that commitment he was not about to waiver. He believed fervently in the Gospel message and that God's will would be done. Man's duty was to serve and to wait, not to ask why or when. So Byington after 1861 could look at what appeared to be the destruction of a life's work and not be dismayed. A biblical text used as the basis of a sermon in 1864 clearly reflected his state

Allen Wright, full-blood principal chief of the Choctaw tribe between 1866 and 1870. He attended American Board schools in the Choctaw Nation West, was graduated from Union Theological Seminary in 1855, and was ordained a Presbyterian minister. To Byington and Kingsbury he was proof of the saving and civilizing power of the Gospel. Courtesy Oklahoma Historical Society.

of mind: "But God has brought you into union with Christ Jesus, and God has made Christ to be our wisdom; by him we are put right with God, we become God's own people, and are set free."[73]

Although his health was beginning to fail, Byington spent the war years preaching, prescribing medicine, working on his Choctaw grammar, and translating the Pentateuch. When peace came to the Choctaw Nation in June, 1865, he determined to go north to visit Lucy and to see through the press the work he had completed. Sickness kept him at his station until July, 1866, and it delayed him in Ohio until September of the following year, when he finally arrived in New York. In the meantime Sophia left the Choctaw Nation in May, 1867, saw her husband in Ohio for a few weeks, and then joined him again in New York in November. Together they received the news of Cyrus Nye's death, read proof, and again visited Massachusetts, where Byington continued to revise his grammar. With his health deteriorating, they both returned to Lucy's Ohio residence in May, 1868. On December 31, 1868, at the age of seventy-five, Byington died. Sophia survived him for twelve years.

When Byington died, the Presbyterian Mission of the Choctaws had been active for fifty years. He had been a major force in the mission almost from the beginning. Although his contributions were many, his work in reducing the Choctaw language to written form was undoubtedly the most important and that which most distinguished him from his colleagues. This labor of love and scholarship had more than merely linguistic implications. With reference to the Choctaws, at least, it forced a reevaluation of the whole philosophy and methodology of the work and goals of Christian missions. The New England concept of civilization which was to accompany salvation had to be redefined, and the techniques leading to salvation were modified. Rather than concentrate its efforts on an English-speaking, mixed-blood elite, the Choctaw Mission turned its attention to the full-blood masses who spoke only the vernacular. Evangelism rather than civilization, therefore, became its principal goal. The vehicle of

civilization, formalized education, was simultaneously rede-
signed to focus upon day and adult students and to emphasize
Choctaw-language literacy. In the boarding schools, which
were once abandoned but were reestablished to accommodate
the wishes of the mixed-blood leadership of the tribe, English
remained the language of instruction, but by 1860 this decision was judged to have been a mistake. In the view of the
mission those fluent and literate in English had evidenced
little interest in religion.

Yet during Byington's lifetime more than a few Choctaws
were awakened to the saving message of the Gospel. A total
of at least 2,700 accepted Divine Grace, and by 1860 more
than 10 percent of the tribal population had united with a
Presbyterian congregation. An additional 10 percent held
membership in churches of other denominations. To Cyrus
Kingsbury, Byington's long-term colleague, such statistics
indicated that the Choctaws had become a "Christian Nation,"
in the popular acceptance of the term. As further evidence
he noted that there was no other religion among the tribespeople but Christianity, that those who were not church
members were believers in Scripture, that the Sabbath was
observed, that the sessions of the General Council were opened
and closed with prayer, that the name of God was used to
affirm oaths, and that no person who denied the being of
God or future state of rewards and punishments, could hold
civil office.[74] If these practices did not denote the work of
the Spirit and the success of the Choctaw Mission, Kingsbury
would have asked, to what else could they be attributed and
by what other criteria measured?

If the Choctaws had become a Christian people, it was
because Cyrus Byington and his brethren had enabled them
to be Christians without abandoning their Choctaw identity.
Specifically, they had revealed the Gospel to the Choctaws
in their own language both in speech and in writing. Since
language is the medium and hallmark of culture, those Choctaws who retained exclusively their native tongue, despite
other changes, also retained their cultural identity. For converts who continued to speak and cherish the language of

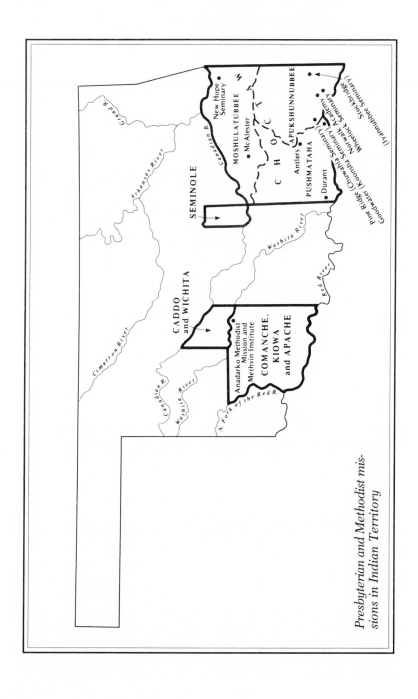

Presbyterian and Methodist missions in Indian Territory

their forefathers, then, to be Christian was not anti-Choctaw. A result of Byington's work, this perspective explained the ability of the Presbyterian Mission to win converts and give birth to a "Christian Nation." It also explained why the Choctaw work, in terms of church membership, was more successful than that of any other mission sponsored by the American Board, except perhaps the one in Hawaii.[75]

If the presentation of the Gospel in the vernacular awakened some Choctaws to an acceptance of Divine Grace, the Gospel message as an agency of civilization also provided them opportunities to demonstrate their worthiness as a people in a world that was increasingly non-Indian. Usually concerned only with the secular elements of the Good News, the mixed-blood power structure of the tribe enthusiastically embraced institutionalized education, a male descent system, a settled agriculture economy, a written code of law, and restrictions on objectionable customs and rites. And for the full-blood masses they even welcomed Choctaw-language literacy. The conscious objective and desired result of this selective process was the creation and emergence of a bicultural society wholly different from that encountered by the Presbyterian missionaries in 1818. Yet the end product in 1868 was *bi*culture, evincing both Euro-American *and* Choctaw elements. The essential native component was a vital mother tongue used in both oral and written communication, the legacy of Cyrus Byington.

Most Choctaws understood Byington's importance. "His translation," wrote Sampson Folsom upon learning of the missionary's death, "will ever be read and had in commemoration of his exemplary and laborious Christian character, so long as the Choctaw language exists." "His life," Folsom concluded, "shows conclusively to me, and ought to those who were the objects of his Christian love and training, that to live and die for the cause of Christ is great gain." Byington would have appreciated this evaluation of his work, but as a summary of his life he could have identified better with the words of Cyrus Kingsbury, who said of him, "He endured unto the end."[76]

2

John Jasper Methvin
Methodist "Missionary to the Western Tribes" (Oklahoma)

Bruce David Forbes

In the summer of 1885, John Jasper Methvin, the president of a Georgia college, received an invitation to become the superintendent of a Methodist Choctaw school in Indian Territory. He accepted, inaugurating twenty-three years as a missionary to American Indians, serving as a preacher, a missionary visitor to native camps, and a principal of three boarding schools. The following chapter examines his life and ministry, attempting not only to construct a biographical narrative but also to raise several themes of importance to the general history of missions among American Indians. Six issues receive particular attention along the way: Methvin's justification of the conjunction of evangelizing and "civilizing" tasks, revivalism as a mode of evangelism, the questionable effectiveness of Methodist itinerancy as a missionary strategy among American Indians, the role of native leadership, Methvin's theological evaluation of native religion and culture, and Indian responses to this mission's activity. Such themes, illustrated in the case of Methvin, may serve as a basis for comparison with other mission figures and other denominations.

John Jasper Methvin was born December 17, 1846, near Jeffersonville, Georgia, to John and Mourning Glover Methvin. His education in Georgia schools (first rural schools, later Auburn and Talmadge institutes) was interrupted in 1862 when, at age sixteen, he joined the Confederate army and served for two years in what he called "that senseless war."[1]

He studied law and was admitted to the bar in Georgia, but he functioned as an active attorney for only a short time before feeling called to preach and teach.

In 1870, Methvin was licensed to preach in the Methodist Episcopal Church, South, and in 1874 he was ordained a local deacon. Through the 1870s his professional employment was in education, as the principal of Nachochee and Cleveland, Georgia high schools, serving concurrently for some years as Superintendent of Public Instruction of White County, Georgia. In 1873 he married Emma Louise Beall, and eventually they had five children.

In 1880, Methvin became president of Gainesville College; from 1883 to 1885 he acted as president of another Georgia institution, Butler Female College. He was reelected to that position in 1885, but Methvin wrote that "the situation was not satisfactory to me for the reason that the college was a city school and under the domination of petty politics and denominational prejudices." His "wish and prayer was for some school under the auspices of the church, where I could without embarrassment cultivate the religious and spiritual interests of the pupils as well as the mental and cultural."[2]

Thus, Methvin resigned the presidency of Butler College and accepted an offer from Bishop Robert K. Hargrove to become superintendent of New Hope Seminary, "a Choctaw female school under the auspices of the church" in Indian Territory. In September of 1885 Methvin was ordained an elder and admitted on trial to the Indian Mission Conference of the Methodist Episcopal Church, South. In that same month the fall term opened at New Hope Seminary, and John Jasper Methvin entered upon the focus of the remainder of his active ministry, which consisted of missionary efforts among Oklahoma Indians.

Methodist Indian work in what is now Oklahoma preceded Methvin's arrival by more than sixty years, when missionaries began following Methodist converts among the "civilized tribes" as they were removed into Indian Territory. Beginning in 1821, ministers such as William Capers and Alexander Talley were appointed as missionaries by various annual conferences in the southeast, to work with tribes located in their midst: Choctaws, Chickasaws, Creeks, Cherokees, and only minimally, Seminoles. From the 1820s through the 1840s the federal government forced these tribes to relocate to the newly designated Indian Territory, a widely known tragic story of brutal transition. Two historians of Oklahoma Methodism estimate that more than four thousand members of the five tribes had accepted Methodism prior to removal.[3] Thus, as tribes moved into the new territory, the Mississippi, Missouri, and Tennessee conferences continued to send missionaries among them.

In the familiar Methodist pattern of conferences taking responsibility for initiating ministry in neighboring, unorganized lands, eventually producing new conferences as offspring, Missouri gave birth to the Arkansas Conference in 1836, which in turn took over supervision of Indian work from other southern conferences.[4] By 1844, Methodist Indian work was substantial enough that the Indian district of the Arkansas Conference was organized as its own Indian Mission Conference, with the great bulk of its work within present-day Oklahoma. The same (national) General Conference which organized the Indian Mission Conference also authorized a north-south division of the church over the issue of slavery. As a result, from its beginning the Indian Mission Conference was part of the Methodist Episcopal Church, South. The Methodist Episcopal Church (North) and the Methodist Protestant church both attempted some limited missions among Oklahoma Indians, but the southern church was the dominant Methodist missionary body among Indians in the area. The three national Methodist groups did not reunite until 1939.

Consistent with its beginnings, the bulk of Methodist activity was among the five "civilized tribes"; efforts also developed among plains groups that preceded the five tribes in eastern Oklahoma. Yet all of the significant effort remained in the eastern part of the territory. In 1887, Methvin would be credited with finally extending Methodist missions to the western portion of Indian Territory.

Narratives of Oklahoma Indian work before Methvin tend to emphasize two themes. One is the conversion and church leadership of notable native leaders, such as Samuel Checote and James McHenry (Creek), Greenwood Le Flore (Choctaw), and John Ross (Cherokee). A second theme is the priority given to schools. Leland Clegg and William Oden, historians of Oklahoma Methodism, claimed that "from 1848 until the Civil War, the primary work of the Indian Mission Conference was educational."[5] The federal government financially encouraged the emphasis by permitting churches and missionaries to administer schools funded by the federal government through Indian agencies and Indian national councils. Methodists established thirteen Indian schools in Oklahoma during this period, including New Hope Female Academy, founded in 1847.[6]

Methvin arrived in time to preside over the demise of the Methodist relationship with New Hope. The school was administered by the Methodist Episcopal Church, South, under a contract with the Choctaw Nation, with funds provided by both the church and the nation. Methvin reported that "we endeavored to give prominence to religious instructions and keep prevalent a strong religious sentiment, and God blessed us most wonderfully." In November, 1885, twenty-five pupils joined the church, and in the following January, "at our usual chapel service on Sabbaths the Holy Spirit came in great power, and fifty-seven more were converted to God."[7] In the fall of 1885 the Choctaw Council, seeking more tribal oversight, annulled all contracts with mission boards relative to tribal schools, including New Hope.[8] Methvin claimed that "this was done in opposition to the wishes of all good people in the Choctaw Nation."[9] With a new building and about one hundred pupils, most of whom were said to have converted to Christianity during Methvin's brief tenure, Methvin believed that the school's last year as a Methodist institution was its best. He mourned July 1, 1886, as a "sad day," when the school passed out of mission hands.

In 1886, Bishop Charles B. Galloway appointed Methvin to the Sasakwa Circuit, which was reported in 1886 to have twenty-four Indian, eighteen white, and three "colored" members, and concurrently as superintendent of another Methodist contract school, Seminole Academy. In the spring of 1886 Methodists had completed their sixth annual term in contract with the Seminole Nation. The Academy, with about forty students, taught a wide range of subjects: orthography, reading, penmanship, geography, arithmetic, grammar, anatomy and physiology, calisthenics, vocal and instrumental music, and housework. In addition to such subjects, Christian religious interests were given prominence. W. S. Derrick, the superintendent who preceded Methvin, reported that "we open and close the day by reading the Bible, singing and prayer; Sunday-school and preaching on Sunday; a weekly prayer-meeting by the pupils." Thirty of the forty students had professed faith in Christ.[10]

Within a year under Methvin's superintendency Seminole Academy also passed out of Methodist hands. Sidney Babcock's brief biography of Methvin offered this explanation:

There were forty students in the school. All of them came from Baptist families. When Methvin discovered that the gospel was being supplied to the Seminole Indians by the Baptists, he recommended that the contract which the Seminole nation had with the Methodist church be terminated. The Seminole Council readily agreed and the school passed from under the care of the Methodist Church.[11]

However a report presented to the 1887 Indian Mission Annual Conference (not written by Methvin) hints at quite a different story:

It was seen during the past year by the superintendent that the contract under which we were operating was not such as to subserve the best interests of the cause of Christ, and by the direction of the Board of Missions, he submitted certain important changes in the contract, which the Seminole authorities refused to grant. So, in consequence, this school passes out of our hands.[12]

What were the proposed changes? Evidence uncovered thus far by this writer provides no answer but only a tantalizing mystery and temptations for speculation.

With Methodist responsibilities for the Seminole Academy terminated, Methvin made a "reconnoitering trip" among the "western tribes" of Oklahoma, especially Kiowas, Comanches, and Apaches. Contrasted with the settled, agricultural life-styles and cultural adaptations of the "civilized" tribes, Methvin and others referred to these as the "wild tribes." Methvin found little missionary effort among them and in later reminiscences painted their situation as almost hopeless. "A people wholly given over to superstition and idolatry, nomadic in their habits, with no settled homes, a babel of unwritten dialects, habits and customs degrading, corrupted to even a lower degradation by the vices learned from contact with white men and Mexicans, did not present a very inviting field."[13]

Methvin wrote letters to the Board of Missions and to Bishop Charles B. Galloway, encouraging the Methodist church to initiate missionary efforts in the West. At the 1887 Indian Mission annual conference session, in an era when appointments were kept secret until the closing of conferences, Methvin was surprised to hear his own name read as the initiator. In later personal correspondence he recalled:

I did not anticipate that I was one of the missionaries to be sent. Inasmuch as I had a wife and five young children I did not judge myself eligible for so difficult but glorious task. So I was startled into quickened heart beats when I heard Bishop Galloway in his clear, musical voice read, "Missionary to the Western Tribes, J. J. Methvin."[14]

Methvin's appointment was "to all the western tribes to be found west of the Indian Meridian and from Kansas on the north to Texas on the south and west."[15] After "taking a survey of the whole field," he chose Anadarko as a base, the location of a federal Indian agency. Although the agency dealt with ten or twelve tribes, Methvin's efforts quickly focused upon the Comanches, Apaches, and especially the Kiowas.

The Kiowas were a people of transition in the last decades

of the nineteenth century. Tribal legends included memories of western Montana mountains, Devil's Tower, and the Black Hills, but by the 1700s they apparently moved out of the mountains to the northern plains, obtained horses, and shifted southward. Abut 1790 a Kiowa and Comanche peace alliance (also involving the small tribe of Kiowa-Apaches) formed a confederation which virtually controlled the southern plains. Both groups were "typical" plains tribes. Mildred Mayhall notes that "there was no such thing as a Plains culture of Plains Indians, aboriginally." The introduction of the horse and borrowing of culture traits here and there, however, gave rise to a culture pattern which quickly diffused, prompting Mayhall to classify eleven of the thirty-one tribes on the plains as typical, one of which was the Kiowa.[16] The "hub of the wheel" of this plains culture was the horse, introduced on the plains in the early 1600s, enabling mobility which made the plains habitable. Dwellings, clothing, weapons, and other material goods were accommodated to the mobile lifestyle. The horse also facilitated the pursuit of buffalo, on which plains Indians were very reliant, with little domestic agriculture, fishing, or food gathering to augment their subsistence patterns.

The rise of this plains culture was meteoric, but it lasted only about a century, from 1775 to 1875. As an increasing white presence progressively circumscribed the plains, and as the federal government moved "foreign" tribes into their midst, cultural disruption reigned. The changes were not easily or quickly accepted, however. The Kiowas and Comanches became noted as plains warriors, raiding Texas and Mexican settlements, attacking caravans of intruders passing through their lands, and resisting government efforts to restrict them on reservations. From the first Kiowa treaty with the United States government in 1837 to the final major military campaign waged by the government in 1874, treaties and hostilities swung on a fierce pendulum. By 1875 the major Kiowa battles were over, leaders such as Kicking Bird and Stumbling Bear encouraged peaceful accommodation, and leaders of resistance were imprisoned in Texas and Florida. The buffalo had disappeared, the horses were taken away, and the restricted Kiowas, on foot, faced the task of creating or adapting a culture for new circumstances.

Spiritual traditions of the Kiowas of the plains included the sun dance, the sweat lodge, vision quests, and legends of a supernatural boy Hero, child of the Sun and an earthly mother, who gave himself to the Kiowas as medicine. Keepers of medicine bundles or Ten Grandmother bundles were highly respected for cures and for spiritual guidance. Yet some of the traditions seemed tied to the old, fading lifestyle, and as the end of the nineteenth century approached many Kiowas turned to religious alternatives in attempts to revive the past or to adapt to a new age. In 1881 a medicine man-prophet, Datekan, began preaching the return of the buffalo and advocated rituals to bring it about, but his efforts yielded no substantial results and were discredited. In 1887, Pa-ingya revived similar teachings, and the ghost-dance religion of the northern plains sparked interest in 1890, but excitement about both was short-lived. More significant was the appeal of peyote religion, called "mescal worship" and worse by some missionaries. Earlier use of peyote as medicine by the Kiowas was followed by increasing use of the cactus button in a cultic religious context, eventually leading to the later establishment of the Native American church among Kiowas and neighboring tribes. In the very period of these various religious innovations, federal authorities actively interfered with some traditional ceremonies, especially the sun dance. The last publicly acknowledged Kiowa sun dance of the era occurred in 1887; in 1889 a planned dance was prevented by federal troops.[17] It was into this transitional situation that Methvin stepped, offering the Christian Gospel and the cultural patterns of Euro-America.

Methvin was not the first missionary in the region. Thomas C. Battey had arrived in 1871 at the Wichita agency (later known as Anadarko), teaching Caddo children there, and in 1873 establishing himself in Kicking Bird's Kiowa camp. A Quaker, Battey functioned primarily as a teacher and as a trusted broker in peace negotiations; he portrayed himself as "an instructor and civilizer."[18] He gave little effort to evangelization but felt, when he left in 1875, that he had contributed toward preparing the soil so that "the seed of the word of life" might eventually be planted.[19] J. B. Wicks, an Episcopalian, built a church at the Anadarko agency in 1883, but the Methodists claimed that his ministry was mostly with whites. The Baptists, whom Methvin acknowledged as "always forward in missionary enterprise," entered the field in the same year as Methvin, but their efforts focused north of the Washita River; Methvin considered the peoples south of the river to be almost untouched by missionary influences and chose to work with them.[20] A Presbyterian missionary arrived at Anadarko in 1888, intending to establish a church at the agency and eventually a school. Catholics also became involved in administering a government-supported school at the agency. Yet even in this context Methvin was frequently acknowledged as the first Indian missionary at Anadarko; he at least became one of the major mission figures of the area, laboring there from 1887 until his retirement in 1908.[21]

Methvin's ministry basically involved three forms of effort. First, he established in Anadarko a local church and parish ministry, serving whites, Indians, and blacks associated with the agency and its environs. Second, he visited native camps and later supervised others in camp work, attempting to evangelize Native Americans on their home ground. Third, he established another school, which became a major focus of his attention. Each effort merits extended discussion.

Within Methvin's first three years at Anadarko he built a parsonage with a small annex for church services. Whites attended the Sunday worship, but Methvin also attempted to appeal to Indians who would gather at the agency every two weeks for supplies. "They began coming to church," he reminisced, "at first three or four, then more, then less, then an increase, till the congregations filled the church annex so that the partition had to be removed to make room for the increasing numbers."[22] Methvin's appointment to the "Anadarko circuit," involving the development of a congregation, continued until 1894, when he was relieved of the local

John Jasper Methvin, Methodist missionary among the Kiowas and Comanches. Here he is with a group of Kiowa girls, ca. 1894. Methvin rode the bicycle. Courtesy Western History Collections, University of Oklahoma Library.

church responsibilities to concentrate more fully on the school
and camp work. Methvin and his family moved out of the
parsonage into another dwelling, and another minister was
assigned to the parish work.

Within months of his arrival, Methvin reported after one
Sunday that "in the morning I made a short sermon to Bro.
Hicks' [Baptist] congregation of Wichitas, in the afternoon I
preached to a negro congregation, and in the evening to the
white[s] here at the agency. The red, black, and white all
in the same day."[23] Such a description raises an issue common to many missionaries: competing demands for Indian
and white ministries. It is illustrated by the report of Sallie
Davis, who came to Anadarko in 1892 to teach Indian children but was unable to do so for months because of the need
to instruct white children, whose language and background
were different from those of the Indian children. "I am still
teaching the white children," she wrote in 1893. "It has been
nearly four months since I began, and it seems almost impossible to get anyone to come and take charge of them. . . .
Miss Gregory [teacher at the Indian school] needs me very
much; she is doing the work of two teachers; but it would
not do for me to leave the white school without a teacher,
as there is possibility of *some* of the pupils going to the
Catholic school. You see that the work here is assuming a
twofold nature, and there is much to be considered in making
changes."[24]

Methvin saw this as a major hindrance to Indian work,
"the absorption of the men and means by the white work
in their midst to the neglect of the Indian."[25] Oklahoma's
mushrooming white population at the time certainly posed
such a dilemma. From an estimated 7,000 white settlers in
the territory in 1880, the number climbed to more than a
million in 1906, the year before statehood.[26] The shifting
population was reflected in Methodist membership figures.
By 1889 white members in the Indian Mission Conference
outnumbered Indians 4,173 to 3,909; 1893 church records
counted 12,503 whites and 4,714 Indians.[27] The non-Indian
population at first was concentrated in the eastern region

among the Five Civilized Tribes. Yet even in the west Methvin encountered an increasing trickle of non-Indians (soldiers, government agents, traders, cattlemen, and others), and when western lands were opened for homesteading between 1889 and 1906, the trickle became a flood. In Methvin's case the solution was assigning another minister to the developing white congregation, allowing Methvin to continue his efforts among Indians. But he knew that his case was exceptional. He complained that "the whites have poured into the Indian country in such numbers that our ministry has been absorbed by them, to the neglect of the Indian. This will be our chief danger for the future."[28]

The second form of missionary activity engaged in and supervised by Methvin was camp work. It began with Methvin's reconnaissance travels and initial visitations in western Oklahoma, a practice which continued as teachers at the Methvin school visited native camps when school was not in session and eventually led to full-time assignments of women as camp visitors (most notably, Helen Brewster). Essentially, camp work visited natives on their home ground instead of expecting them to come to a missionary-constructed school or church, and it apparently focused upon women and children.

As described by Methvin, "the principal work of these women has been to visit the families in their homes, teach the women how to do things in domestic civilized home life, read the Bible, hold prayer meetings, etc., and thus, while improving their home life, reach them with the message of the Gospel."[29] Other descriptions referred to instruction in cooking and sewing, ministering to the sick, and "the myriad other lessons that can be taught only by association."[30] Both Methvin and the women emphasized that camp work involved evangelism through kindness. Mrs. M. B. Avant wrote that the camp visits intended to show "that we are really interested in them, and want to do them good."[31]

Methvin believed camp work was effective not only because it expressed personal interest but also because it was direct. "This feature of our work is very important," Methvin wrote, "since it brings the missionaries in more direct contact with the Indians in their home life."[32] Sallie Davis, a teacher and camp visitor, made a similar remark about the organization of prayer meetings among Kiowa women: "thinking that more good could be accomplished by taking the Bread of Life *to them*, we have the meetings at the camps."[33] Such camp visiting was a regular part of missionary reports, and it provided the base for the eventual establishment of Indian churches outside of Anadarko, such as Mount Scott, Ware's Chapel, and Little Washita.

Associated with such domestic camp work were camp meetings, firmly rooted in the American revivalist tradition of Kentucky and later frontiers. References by Methvin and others to camp meetings can be confusing, for they may refer to prayer meetings or gatherings of women to undertake domestic skills, or they may refer to long sessions of evangelistic preaching and singing, usually held outdoors. As an example of the latter, Methvin reported at one point that "we have held a camp meeting down on Little Washita, and I left Brothers Butterfield and Perez and native helpers still going on with it last night."[34] The style of Methvin's evangelism was clearly revivalistic, revealed in descriptions of conversion, such as the following: "I have seen rugged old Indians who, many a time have been on the warpath and jerked the scalp from many heads, under the preaching of this gospel come forward and with quivering forms and streaming eyes confess their sins and ask for help, and I have seen them transformed by this power alone and lead new lives."[35]

The phenomenal growth of Methodism among white and black Americans in the nineteenth century is partially attributed to its revivalistic style, and it is not surprising that Methodists applied the same form of evangelism to their Indian missions. Yet historians have seldom discussed how revivalist Christianity compared with Calvinist or Catholic alternatives in appealing to American Indians of various cultures. A full discussion of that issue cannot be attempted here, but perhaps two preliminary suggestions might be offered about how camp meeting, revivalist Christianity could relate to Kiowa traditions in this case study.

On one hand, the extended revivalist gatherings seem consistent with traditional Kiowa religious ceremonies in that both had overtones of a social gathering and could last long hours or days. The sun dance involved six days of preparation, four nights and four days of dancing, and was a major tribal gathering with much peripheral activity. A sweat lodge would take hours; a scalp dance or various forms of vision-seeking required days.[36] A contemporary religious alternative, peyote ceremonies, would last through the night. Extended, somewhat free-form camp meetings seemed a more natural successor to Kiowa religious traditions than a brief one- or two-hour liturgical service.

On the other hand, revivalism accents a disjunctive tendency in Christianity in calling for wrenching repentance, rejection of past life as sinful, and emphasis on a radical rebirth into new life. This dualistic inclination, revealed in contrasts between heaven and hell, Christians and non-Christians, wholly sinful past life and new life in Christ, contrasts with the unitary tendencies of many tribal cultures which give more emphasis to continuities.[37] A rejection of a notion of hell and an assumption that all tribal members would be together in an afterlife, a willingness to accept various religious paths as equally valid, and a pervasive emphasis on relatedness, all common to many tribal cultures, would not prepare one to accept Christianity's exclusive claims, accented by revivalism's call for radical conversion.

In addition to the Anadarko church and the camp work and camp meetings at native locations, Methvin's mission efforts included another school, the basis for much of his reputation because it carried his name. At the time of Methvin's arrival at Anadarko the government had a few schools operating in the region. Federal funds also supported a Catholic school near Anadarko, but Protestants like Methvin had difficulty recognizing that as a proper religious option. Surveying the situation, Methvin wrote that "there was need for

strictly religious schools with no political affiliation, where
unhindered the Bible could be taught and its truths emphasized. The Government schools did much good, but in the very
nature of things, could not emphasize the religious training."[38]
    Once again J. J. Methvin sought the kind of school he had
envisioned when he left Georgia. He applied to the government, on "behalf of the church, for land upon which to build
a church school."[39] It was granted. Methodist mission funds
supported construction of a building, and the school opened
in 1890. Methvin applied to the government for some kind
of contract arrangement in running the school but was informed "that the Government had changed its policy, and
would make no more contracts with church schools, and
would get rid of those already made as fast as the service
would permit."[40] Methvin then requested that supplies provided to all reservation Indians, such as allocations of cloth for
clothing, be supplied to the school in proportion to the number of students enrolled, which was granted.[41]
    The church thus needed to supply virtually all of the
school's financial support. In 1890 the Women's Board of
Missions took responsibility for the school, or, in the words
of one teacher, "the Women's Board . . . bought the Anadarko
School."[42] They recruited and supplied many female personnel, received regular reports from Methvin and various
women teachers and published them in the *Woman's Missionary Advocate,* and even sent board officials to visit the
school. In 1894 the Women's Board named the school Methvin Institute in honor of its founder and continuing super-
visor. Methvin expressed thanks but insisted that "I am sensi-
bly conscious of the fact that I do not deserve the honor.
God's blessings be upon the school in spite of its name."[43]
    Methvin Institute was a boarding school for Indians, al-
though some whites attended as day students, especially in
the early years. Attendance ranged from fifteen to one hundred, with an average of about thirty-five in the early 1890s.
The school had both "literary" and "domestic" departments,
involved in both intellectual and manual pursuits, usually
with separate teachers for each. Domestic activities included

sewing, cooking, washing, and other housework for girls, and farming tasks with cultivated land and limited stock for boys. Prayer services, religious instruction, and encouragement to attend Sunday services at the Anadarko church also were part of the school program. In 1892, Elizabeth Gregory, one of the teachers, described a typical daily routine at the school.

We rise at 6 o'clock, have prayer at 6:30, breakfast following. At 8 we go into the schoolroom, and remain until 12. The afternoon is devoted to industrial training. On Monday afternoon the girls assist with the washing. On Tuesday they do the ironing and mending. Wednesday, Thursday, and Friday they sew, and Saturday is cleaning day. We have an evening session of school from half-past six to half-past seven, and then prayers before retiring. The first half-hour in the morning and a part of the evening session are devoted to religious training.[44]

Eugenia Mausape, a Kiowa girl who entered Methvin Institute when she was about thirteen years old and stayed four years, was interviewed shortly before her death in 1967. When asked what they taught at the school she replied, "Well, they teach us in every way—readers and arithmetic and spelling and geography. Just like what they learning."[45]

Indeed, the claim that Indian students were learning just what whites learned had far-reaching implications. More than simply offering an education in certain subjects, the boarding school lifted young people out of native contexts and immersed them in white American culture. The intention was to raise godly, civilized, educated children, with all the implications that those words carried. The goals were difficult to achieve if the child remained in touch with old ways and life-styles; the separation of the boarding school made children more educable in new patterns.

A symbol of the break with traditional life was the Methvin school missionaries' inclination to give children new names. In oral reminiscences, Eugenia Mausape remembered being given her name by Mrs. Methvin, whose sister was named

Eugenia. Guy Queotone was named for the principal's brother. Ethel Howry remembers confusion when she was first called Ethel, for reasons she did not understand.[46] It is true that traditionally Kiowa names "could be changed and often were," making this practice less radical than would be the case in most Euro-American cultures, but the intention and symbolism of creating a new life remained clear.[47]

The school also taught in a new language, with virtually no attempt to bridge communication by mixing the use of native languages and English in the classroom. For Methvin the English approach was both necessary and desirable. It was necessary because the students usually represented at least four different tribes (Comanche, Chickasaw, and Caddo, with a Kiowa majority), and it seemed impossible to learn and manage the various languages. It was also desirable because of the need for Indian students to adapt to an advancing, dominant civilization. In Methvin's own words:

There are not less than ten different unwritten dialects here. Beyond a mere vocabulary of words and phrases with which to make known simple wants, it would be the work of a lifetime to acquire a thorough knowledge of these different tongues so as to be able to teach them. . . . This would be an endless task — a useless waste of time and means. The effort, therefore, is to get them to learn English. The white man is in their midst, and the necessity is upon them, and in another decade the lame method of working through interpreters will no longer be necessary.[48]

The general pattern of boarding school education has been much discussed, for instance in Robert Berkhofer's now classic *Salvation and the Savage*.[49] Although the Methvin school was half a century later than those summarized in Berkhofer's second chapter, "Nurseries of Morality," the pattern remained fairly typical. Male students had their hair cut and were issued clothing; names changed; the curriculum was generally similar to that for whites; inculcation of values such as industry and cleanliness was prominent; religion (Christian) pervaded the school day; conversion and Sabbath observance were encouraged.

It is one thing for an outsider or a later historian to describe cutting hair, introducing new names, and the like, but native descriptions of the experience bring to life feelings of fear, resistance, and confusion that were often provoked in new students. One of the most striking is an oral reminiscence by Guy Queotone, a Kiowa student at Methvin Institute who eventually became a Methodist minister. He recalled that his father "dedicated" him and sent him to mission school; his description deserves extended quotation:

At that time my braids was about that long, wrapped with otter skin fur. And I had a breastplate [of hair pipes]. . . . And they took me up there. . . . Told that boy that's there as an advisor to take care of me. He said, "Well, you folks go home. Don't you never come back for a month or two." I overheard them. He was talking Indian. He's a Mexican Kiowa captive, Andele, with the Mission. I begin to get excited when he said that because I know that they're going to hold me there. "We'll take care of him. You don't have to worry. Just don't come back for about a month or two before you come back. He'll be all right." But I was still in my costume. They took me in the other room and Andele Martinez and then a white man and then the barber and one woman—a white woman. And they shut the door. Mother was gone. She said, "I want that hair. Save that hair for me." They say, "All right. Go on, now. We'll take care of him. We'll change his clothes." They shut the door and about that time I get excited and they got a chair. This man set me there and they commence to hold me. He set me down in that chair and that lady talked to me and tried to get my attention. While I was talking to her—looking at her— this barber—while I was talking he come from behind and cut one side of my braid off. I knew what happened. About that time I jumped up and they grabbed me and hold me down. And I turned tiger! I commenced to fight and scratch and bite and jump up in the air! They had a time, all of them, holding me down. Cut the other side. Two men had me down there and that white lady tried to hold my head and then that barber cutting all the time. It was almost an hour before he finished cutting my hair. And you ought to see how I look. I sure hate a haircut! Then after I got a haircut I changed my clothes. They gave me a pair of old ration-government issued shoes. The government [had] issued the Indians clothing. And they issued Methvin [Institute] all kinds of clothes for the Indian children that go to school there. And they issue shoes. And I got a suit—jeans—kind of gray. And one of them shoes— they were about that long—big heavy shoes with a big brass buckle on them with holes and I'd stick that thing in there and bring the buckle back. That's how come my feet's so large—wearing over-sized shoes![50]

Girls felt some of the same dismay. Ethel Howry remem-bered going to the Methvin Institute and feeling that she knew nothing. She could speak no English, was given a dif-ferent kind of clothing, and was shown how to put on shoes and stockings. She was also given a new name, as mentioned earlier. Teachers would simply call a name repeatedly until the child, still not quite understanding what was happening, responded.

. . . so she says, "Come here Ethel." Here I went. Oh, she was so glad and she says "Good, good," she says. I didn't even know what she wanted. So she picked us all up and took us back to the school. To our building. Just then I don't know what she done but that was where she cleaned us up and we had the clothes on and she named us. And we went and oh we just cried and our brothers would come over and put us to bed, and we'd go to sleep, and they'd have to go back to their quarters. First thing in the morning they'd come. We didn't know nothing.[51]

Because of the students' separation from family and home culture, the Methvin school had problems with attendance. In 1890 one teacher reported, "We had great trouble to keep them at school, very few of them ever having slept in a house before. It is a difficult matter to get them accustomed to the ways of white people, both in regard to the manner of living and of dressing. But we could expect nothing else, as everything is so different to what they have in camp."[52] Methvin learned how important the support of parents was in keeping students in school. He acknowledged that he at first had tried to recruit students "promiscuously," to get the school started. Later he sought only those students whose parents sincerely wanted them in school; "then we can hold them with little trouble."[53]

Methvin (in front of door) and Methodist Church (South) Mission School employees at Anadarko, Oklahoma, before 1901. Courtesy Western History Collections, University of Oklahoma Library.

A short-lived day school initiated by Helen Brewster, one of the camp workers, provided an interesting contrast with the experience of the Methvin Institute. Miss Brewster's efforts seemed to be uncommonly successful and were repeatedly praised by Methvin.[54] Although she spent some time teaching at the Methvin Institute, most years of her missionary service consisted of full-time camp work in several locations. Significantly, she was the only non-Indian figure, other than Andres Martinez, associated with the Anadarko area Methodist mission who seriously attempted to learn the language of the people with whom she worked. In 1891 she began an experimental day school on the Little Washita and met a very positive response. Parents wanted to remove their children from government schools so that they might attend Brewster's, causing the government to forbid enrollment in the day school until the government schools were filled. She claimed to have nearly all the remaining children in the neighborhood in attendance and was excited that "their progress has been very encouraging indeed." In only seven weeks, she wrote, "my pupils have learned to read well on their chart, write quite legibly, know their figures and are beginning in addition."[55] In spite of this success, Methvin shifted Helen Brewster to other camps in later years to initiate ministries in other areas, with no attempt to continue the operation of the day school.

Why this commitment to the boarding school approach, with its cultural implications? The answer is found in the double intention of Methvin's missionary efforts in general. Like many other Euro-American missionaries to Native Americans, Methvin believed that Christian missions to Indians served two purposes. He wrote, "All along a double task has been set the Church, both of Christianizing and civilizing the Indian, both of changing him and his condition."[56] Later critics, with the benefit of hindsight and operating out of pluralistic assumptions, ask about the relationship of the evangelical and cultural tasks. Even assuming the missionaries' Christian commitment, were they so ethnocentric that they could not conceive of "authentic" Christianity being expressed in other cultural forms?

Methvin's discussions offer implicit answers, justifying the link between "Christianization and civilization" in two related ways. First, he did believe that thoroughgoing Christian conversion would lead to "civilization." Spiritual conversion of Native Americans was the primary mission concern, but cultural changes would follow naturally. "Change him," Methvin wrote, "and he will change his own condition." The Gospel,

faithfully preached, not only saves his soul, but qualifies him for taking on the habits of civilization. That adjusts him in relation to God and to man. Everywhere our missions have been planned and faithfully pushed this has proved true. Under the impulses of the Christian life the Indian has become industrious, built homes, planted fields, settled in contentment, till the white man's greed for more land demanded that he move on.[57]

As further evidence Methvin cited the testimony of Aoute, a Kiowa Christian, in conversation with Methvin: "When you came here and began to preach, I was a lazy, gambling, drunken Indian; but since this gospel took hold upon me I have a home, fifty acres of land in cultivation, a good crop, some cattle, and all this I have done myself. I find the Christian road is the working road, and I like it."[58]

Yet Methvin did not simply wait for cultural changes to grow from conversion; he promoted them. On a second level he would justify his advocacy of cultural changes as an enactment of Christian humanitarian concern. In Methvin's view introduction of the elements of "civilization" was a means of improving the Indians' condition, making possible happier, more stable, and secure lives. Even more it was a matter of saving Indians from a present threat of physical destruction. White American civilization seemed to be rolling across the continent, crushing all before it. Removal of southeastern tribes to Indian Territory was only a stage in an ongoing process. Methvin believed it was the Christian's responsibility, on humanitarian grounds, to aid Indians' adjustment to the "higher" civilization in order to assure their physical survival. He wrote,

There can be no preservation of the Indian as an Indian. He must be absorbed into the great body of American citizenship, and take his stand side by side with other men. If he is not prepared for it, he must begin unprepared, for it is at hand. There is no more territory to which he can emigrate.[59]

This was a major theme with Methvin. In another article he repeated,

As a race they are doomed. . . . The strain is upon them; the white man, designing, aggressive, persistent, is on every hand and right in their midst, and they must take on the spirit of his progress or go down before it. With their present life the latter is inevitable.[60]

Thus, Methvin advocated "civilization" because whatever its connection with Christianity, he believed that it was the only way to save American Indians from physical extinction. Yet he also claimed that "civilization" was best introduced through the Gospel. "Civilization alone does not civilize," he claimed, because "a veneering of civilization may be given or forced upon a people and yet leave them void of the real purposes and high aspirations of life and it soon wears off."[61] For Methvin, Christianity provided civilization its heart, its ideals, its staying power. A mere shell or veneer of civilization could be turned to evil as well as good.

Yet, because of their major concern about the physical destruction of Indians by the dominant culture, missionaries like Methvin did not feel impelled to examine the precise connection between Christianity and every feature of Euro-American civilization. One gains the impression that even if a convert could convince Methvin that some features of native culture were closer to Christianity than were the Euro-American cultural replacements, cultural change still would be advocated for the sake of survival. Indians had to be absorbed "into the great body of American citizenship" or perish. The much-discussed "blind" association of Christianity and Euro-

American culture by many missionaries may have been able to remain unquestioned, even when challenged by native converts, because many missionaries had an additional, over-riding concern about the physical extinction of Indians who did not adapt to the Euro-American mainstream. Later commentators may evaluate the fear of extinction as a premature obituary and offer other culturally pluralistic visions of the future, but for Methvin it seemed a real threat with only one conceivable solution.

Interestingly enough, though, on the verge of his retirement from active ministry in 1907, Methvin claimed victory. Against those who, "from the discovery of America to this day," speak of Indians "as a fading race, doomed to extinction, soon to pass away," Methvin claimed that "there is less prospect now than ever that he will soon fade away and become extinct. The causes which have militated against the Indian's rapid increase in the past have about all disappeared, and henceforth he will have about an equal chance with the white man for increasing and multiplying and replenishing the earth." Although Methvin promised to explain the causes of the reversal in a future article not located by this writer, he made it clear that a major factor was "what the Gospel has done for these Indians."[62]

To return to the boarding school which prompted this discussion of "Christianization and civilization," it must be acknowledged that some parents as well as missionaries believed an immersion in Christianity and white culture to be important for their children's futures. For instance, Eugenia Mausape's mother and stepfather enrolled her in Methvin Institute because, in her words, they "think it's good way."[63] Hunting Horse enrolled his son Cecil after Methvin taught the father "the right way of living."[64] Such decisions need not be seen merely as capitulations to a foreign culture but might be described more positively as attempts to find a new organizing center for lives which had suffered disruption. As Angie Debo wrote about the "civilized tribes," some persons "found in Christianity a steadying influence to compensate them for the disruption of their ancient ways."[65] Howard

Harrod has made a similar point, noting that "participation in missionary institutions may provide a needed center of social order and identity for Indians undergoing rapid social change—a conservative, stabilizing function."[66] Such perspectives, however, do not deny that mission activities also played roles in cultural destruction or at least insensitivity.

Yet issues of cultural transformation or dislocation were not the only memories of students. Eugenia Mausape, when asked how she liked her teachers, replied,

Oh, she's good. They don't whip us. They don't punish us. That's a good school. J. J. Methvin told the teachers and the employees, "Don't be mean to the Kiowas. We're staying on their land and we treat them nice. Treat them nice. If they don't know the lesson, they'll learn it some day. Don't switch them and don't slap them, no. No. It's not right to treat a children—"Oh, it was so nice. Great man, J. J. Methvin.[67]

That is precisely how Methvin wanted to be remembered. Although he did not believe that native cultures could continue, he sought in his own way to respect individuals and repeatedly criticized the actions of other border whites. He sought to distance himself from their greed and mistreatment, and he told stories illuminating the insulting attitudes and vulgar curiosity of tourists.[68] Although the Methvin Institute might be charged with cultural insensitivity common to the age, there is little evidence of other forms of disrespect or mistreatment. On those grounds Methvin saw himself as a defender and supporter of Indian people.

After seventeen years of service the Methvin Institute closed in 1907. Oklahoma Methodist historians Clegg and Oden indicate that the Women's Board "could no longer finance it," but Methvin bitterly charged that the closing also involved "vile misrepresentation" to the board by a greedy syndicate in Anadarko which wanted to obtain the Institute's property.[69] Methvin retired from the conference one year later at the age of 62.

Yet he remained active. Methvin's first wife died in 1904, and he subsequently married Ida Swanson, a teacher at the

Institute, who had assumed the superintendency from Methvin in 1904. He continued to attend conference events regularly, wrote a book-length history of Anadarko, and produced reminiscences for publication in *The Chronicles of Oklahoma.* Methvin died on January 17, 1941, in Anadarko.

How does one assess the legacy of Methvin's ministry and, on a broader scale, of the Methodism he represented? On a superficial level, one could simply point to continuing institutions. Six United Methodist churches still serve Kiowas in Oklahoma, with 804 members reported in 1973.[70] The Kiowa church in Anadarko carries Methvin's name. Mount Scott, Little Washita, Ware's Chapel, and Albert Horse Memorial all are continuing Kiowa or Comanche congregations whose founding involved Methvin. Several native ministers and their descendants have been former students of the Methvin Institute. Beyond such obvious citations, though, to what extent did the Methodist missionary system prove to be an effective instrument in accomplishing its aims? Obviously, Methvin's example is only a piece of a much larger story, but his experience in his denominational context prompts some concluding comments about both missionary strategy and theology.

First, regarding church polity Methvin had to contend with several hindrances of Methodist missionary history and strategy.[71] Although Methodists saw their whole system as missionary in character and prided themselves on the circuit riders' effective work in following the westward flow of white populations, Methodist missionary efforts were preoccupied with the white frontier. Aside from experience with American blacks, the church was relatively late in gaining experience in cross-cultural situations, both foreign and American Indian. American Methodism's first, limited foreign experiences did not come until the late 1830s, beginning in the independent nation of Texas, among black American colonists in Liberia (neither of which were radically cross-cultural situations) and in South America.[72] Among Native Americans the first official appointment of a Methodist missionary did not come until 1819; this was James Montgomery of Ohio.[73] Compared to some other denominations, Methodists were late in obtaining cross-cultural experience upon which to base missionary strategies.

The Methodist system also made it difficult to share the experiences once obtained, because of a decentralized mission system. Annual conferences rather than central mission boards took most responsibility for Indian missions within their borders or in neighboring lands, as is illustrated in the beginning of Oklahoma Indian missions. Thus, personnel were generally recruited from white contexts and given local responsibilities, with little or no special training and with little contact with former missionaries to Indians. Nineteenth-century Methodist mission boards were primarily funding organizations, not given to considerable development of mission theologies, strategies, or training; the American Board of Commissioners for Foreign Missions and the theological leadership of Rufus Anderson provide a provocative contrast. Early Methodist missionaries each had to "reinvent the wheel" until more centralized and powerful mission organizations developed, primarily in the twentieth century, or until missions clustered sufficiently in one region, as they did in the Indian Mission Conference.

In addition the circuit-riding system, built on the principle of itinerancy, was less appropriate for Indian missions than for the white frontier. The high mobility of the appointment system viewed circuit riders almost as interchangeable chessmen, who were moved from one appointment to another at least every three or four years. It was not unusual to take a minister from a white circuit, appoint him to an Indian circuit, and then a few years later appoint him once again among whites. Such mobility obviously made it difficult to adequately understand a culture or learn a language. M. A. Clark, a minister at Fort Sill who had visited and preached in Methvin's region in 1887 and 1888, complained in 1907 about this very hindrance. "Previous to this time," he noted, "our church authorities would not allow a missionary to stay on a charge longer than four years. Imagine a missionary being changed from China to Japan and from Japan to Africa every four years. What could the church expect of him?"[74]

Methvin was both an illustration of and an exception to this Methodist missionary pattern. His move from a white school in Georgia to an Indian school in Oklahoma seems to have been accomplished without a thought about cultural complications, and his early shifts from Choctaw to Seminole schools and then to western tribes seem unconcerned about the significant tribal diversity of languages and cultures. Once in Anadarko Methvin's continuing appointment there was exceptional, but he did not then show a strong inclination to learn languages or build upon knowledge of native cultures. Helen Brewster, who showed great interest in learning native languages, was shifted between Kiowa and Comanche camps, consistent with the Methodist itinerant pattern.

One factor which helped compensate for the cited hindrances of Methodist polity was the development of native leadership. Indeed, the early Methodist system in England and America was intended to rely heavily on local leadership while the circuit rider traveled a large circuit, sometimes returning to a specific point only every few weeks. Methvin declared an interest in utilizing native leadership and could point to several examples.

A letter Methvin wrote to the *Woman's Missionary Advocate,* published in January, 1895, provided his clearest statement of intentions in this regard. He noted that two employees at the school, John and Maggie Dunlop, were Kiowas and "faithful employees." He added, "I try to give encouragement to all Indians who want employment, and while for lack of training they cannot compete with the whites, yet some of them are very earnest in their efforts to learn."[75] He added:

It is my purpose as soon as I am settled for the year to organize a Bible and training class with such Indians, both male and female, as I can get interested in the matter and give them such training as will make them efficient in telling the story of Jesus as they go out among their own people. I hope to accomplish much in this way in permanent good.[76]

Non-Indians held virtually all teaching posts and leadership roles at the Methvin Institute, but, as Methvin noted, he employed some natives in positions such as cook and farmer. As young persons gained a formal "civilized" education, some would return as student advisers or interpreters.[77] Andres Martinez, the most noted native leader at the school, really defied such a classification. His family was of Spanish descent, but in 1866 at age seven Andres was captured by Apaches and then sold to the Kiowas, where he was known as Andele and became the adopted son of "Chief Heap O'Bears." After almost twenty years he was reunited with his Martinez family (mother and brother) and regained his facility in Spanish, but four years later he returned to the Kiowas. There he met Methvin, joined the Methodist church, and worked at the Methvin Institute as an interpreter and industrial teacher. He proved indispensable to Methvin because of his knowledge of Kiowa language and culture; in general, he played the crucial role of intermediary often filled by mixed-bloods in other settings. Methvin recounted an incident when he tried to speak to an angry crowd, with Andres interpreting. "But soon . . . . he took the leadership in his own hands, and poured out upon them an exhortation of such pathos and power that the whole wild element came pressing to the front . . . . and cried to God for mercy . . . . Many turned from the old way and started on the new."[78] Martinez later entered the ministry; Methvin was convinced that "there is no one so well qualified under sanctifying grace to lead the Indians to Christ."[79] Methvin also wrote a book-length narrative of Andres Martinez's captivity, which has taken its place among the classics of the genre.

Besides Martinez, Methvin influenced a number of Kiowa leaders, and several students at the Methvin Institute became ordained Methodist ministers. Stumbling Bear, a leading force for accommodation in the last Kiowa struggles with federal troops, attended Methvin's services. The younger Kicking Bird, who at first opposed Methvin's preaching "the white man's religion," converted, became an interpreter and local preacher, and in 1905 was the first Kiowa ordained deacon in the Methodist Episcopal Church, South. Hunting Horse became a friend of Methvin, accepted Christianity, and enrolled two

sons in the Methvin Institute. Both Albert and Cecil Horse
became ministers, as did Albert's son James. Guy Quoetone,
quoted at length above, became a noted minister, established
several churches, and was a leader in Kiowa tribal affairs.
The Ware family (Harry, Guy, Louis, Ted) was instrumental
in starting a church named Ware's Chapel near Hog Creek.
Others could be added to the list.[80] In the Methodist system
such native leadership was crucial.

In this attempt to communicate and persuade across cultures, the role of theology was also significant. Missionaries'
theological evaluations of native religion would strongly influence their strategies, determining whether they would seek
to build upon or completely overturn native ways. Traditional
Christianity claims to be the exclusive path to truth and salvation; more liberal Christian theological acknowledgment of
the mutuality of religions had few if any representatives among
nineteenth-century American evangelical missionary figures.
Yet even if virtually all missionaries assumed Christianity's
exclusive claim, they still had some choices in their views of
native spirituality. They might simply view native religions
as demonic, or as valid but incomplete religions that needed
fulfillment. In one view anything not clearly the work of the
Christian God must be a product of opposing satanic power.
According to the other view native religions could be acknowledged as a sort of Old Testament faith, worthy but needing
the completion of the Christian Gospel. One might expect
many Methodists to tend toward the first option, because of
the revivalist emphasis on the converts' rejection of past life
("put off the old nature," Ephesians 4:22, Colossians 3:9) and
because of previously discussed hindrances in learning about
native cultures.

Methvin's view did incline toward the first option, portray-
ing the Kiowas as "wholly given over to superstition and
idolatry."[81] "It is a long way," he wrote, "from the teepee
and tom-tom steeped in superstitious worship to the temple
of God with its songs of prayer and praise."[82] However,
Methvin's rejection of native religion was not couched in
language of the demonic; he almost always referred to it as

idolatry, a false human creation. Methvin explained that "in the absence of the true God, he [the Indian] seeks to choose or invent one for himself, and in doing so he selects or invents one in harmony with his own nature that can be made to pander to his own depraved passions and appetites, for in his ignorance the only conception he has of God is what he sees in himself."[83]

According to Methvin, "every religious system, other than the Christian, is built upon three perversions of the religious instinct"; the particular perversion most notable in Indian religion, he believed, was nature worship of the lowest order. Such worship led to many excesses, including "prostitution of the emotional nature, in beastly sensual indulgence, in cruel and blood-thirsty practices."[84] The most positive thing Methvin could say about such nature worship was that "they worship the *good* instead of the *Author* of the *good.*" Still, it amounted to idolatry, "a wall of darkness God alone can penetrate."[85]

Methvin's criticisms of the ghost dance and peyote religion were even stronger. About the "Messianic craze" he wrote, "A dozen maniac asylums turned loose together would hardly be equal to the scenes enacted by these tribes . . . . in their crazy, superstitious worship of the supposed Messiah as they dance day and night through heat or cold."[86] He called peyote ceremonies "a drug habit under the guise of religion."[87] From such a perspective Methvin was incensed by the activities of James Mooney, whom he almost never identified by name but referred to as "a representative of the Ethnological Department of the Smithsonian Institution." Mooney was "a crank upon Indian affairs" who "believes that any religion or superstition peculiar to a people is good for them, and so he teaches the Indian that the 'mescal worship' is good for them, that it is their religion, and it is well for them to go on it." Methvin could not understand Mooney's suggestions as a Catholic that "by being favorable to their 'mescal worship' he could more effectively carry out his purposes."[88] He noted with disapproval an Indian report that Mooney and "a Catholic priest, or bishop, were eating the mescal with the Indians not long since, and declaring that all that I had said or written against it was a lie, and that worshiping Jesus through the mescal was all right and good for the Indian."[89]

Methvin's writings give only occasional indication that he was prepared to use native beliefs or practices as bridges to understanding Christianity, on the model of Paul's appeal to the Unknown God in Athens (Acts 17:22-23). However, Helen Brewster tells about a time when she and Methvin visited an Indian neighbor, Kata Prooney, who mentioned that his name meant "the Unseen One" or "Holy Spirit." "Brother Methvin began to talk with him about his name, branching naturally from it to the Blessed Spirit, explaining his office and character. I never heard anything so natural, and at the same time so effective."[90] Also, Methvin commended the good traits, fervor, and liberality of the Kiowas.[91] In general, however, his assumptions tended to reject rather than build upon native heritage. For example, Methvin's description of Choctaw minister Willis Folson noted that "he had some of the Indian traits and peculiar idiosyncracies of his tribe lingering with him but none to mar his usefulness."[92] For Methvin almost all of native religion and culture was contradicted by Christianity and its accompanying civilization.

Significantly, though, it was otherwise for some of his converts. The most interesting example is Cecil Horse's account of how his father, Hunting Horse, "became religious . . . . in the white man's way." Hunting Horse had gone blind, and at his request he was taken up on Mt. Sheridan, after the "old Indian way" of becoming a medicine man. He prayed and sacrificed to the "Great Spirit" for four days. Cecil explained that "they had to go the hard way because they believe that some way God would bless them, even although it might be an idol-worshipper." After four days his sight was restored. Hunting Horse then went to Methvin, "one of his great friends," and told him he wanted to be baptized because the Great Spirit had returned his sight.[93] The story is a remarkable fusion of native tradition and Christian claims, for Hunting Horse came to believe in the Christian God through a quest obviously linked to traditional Kiowa spiritual practices.

In spite of the missionary inclination to deliver Christianity and Euro-American civilization as a package intended to fully replace native religion and culture, the Kiowas were capable of managing their own links with their past and were inclined toward selective adoption. Methvin himself quoted Stumbling Bear as saying, "White man's road heap good, better than Indian road. But not *all* of the ways of the white man better than *all* the Indian ways. Some Indian ways best."[94]

Part Two   Frontier Variations

3

The Mormons, the Indians, and George Washington Bean

Floyd A. O'Neil

By the late 1840s, under the leadership of Brigham Young, the Mormon church had established itself on the frontier in Utah. This location placed the Mormons in the midst of various groups of American Indians. Other major religious denominations in the nineteenth century sent missionaries to the Indians, but none placed their church so dramatically among them. Mormon-Indian relations, therefore, represented the dynamics of frontier settlement as well as the aspirations of religious conversion. George Washington Bean participated in settlements and missions, war-making and treaty-making. His life captures many of the basic elements that characterized the interactions between the Mormons and the Indians in the West's Great Basin.

From April, 1830, when the Church of Jesus Christ of Latter-day Saints was founded, to the present, the American Indian has had a special place in Mormon theology and missionary efforts. By late fall of 1830, Mormons had begun preaching to Indians on the Kansas River, where they left the *Book of Mormon* with a Delaware sachem.[1] Great conversions did not reward this initial venture, and federal officials shortly expelled the Mormons from Indian country for "disturbing the peace."[2] The church made some further missionary efforts in the eastern states; elders met with Cattaraugus people in New York, Wyandots in western Ohio, and Wyandots, Delawares, and Shawnees in eastern Kansas.[3] By

77

and large, however, the young church essentially abandoned missionary work among the Indians shortly after its first endeavor on the Kansas River. For this fledgling church with many pressing needs Indian missions were expensive to develop and slow to grow. Work among non-Indians, on the other hand, soon yielded converts who would begin almost immediately to contribute to the building of the new church. Yet even when circumstances mitigated against active Indian mission efforts, church theology maintained a special concern for American Indians, or Lamanites, as they were called in the *Book of Mormon.*

The theology of the Mormons presents a peculiar variant of the nineteenth-century American religious experience. The religion was born in that hotbed of American evangelical Christian strife called the "burned-over" district of upstate New York. Joseph Smith, the founder of the Mormon church, claimed to have found records of ancient inhabitants of the area which would explain the presence of the Indians. From these gold plates which were ostensibly found in a hill near the Smith home, the young receiver of miracles published the *Book of Mormon.*

The book is principally a history of two groups of people who came from ancient Israel to the New World. The first group under a leader named Jared came to bitterness and internecine war, which caused their extinction. Their historian, Ether, witnessed their end and deposited a record which was found by a second group of colonists who came to America six hundred years before Christ. This second group was divided into warring factions, and the forces of good (Nephites) were overwhelmed by the evil group (Lamanites). The Indians according to this version are descendants of Laman, hence Lamanites. The dark skin is a curse by God upon them. In the time of Joseph Smith the gospel was to be brought to these unfortunates. One of the reasons the Mormon church was "restored" was to convert the Lamanites before the Last Day.[4]

During the rule of the Nephites, according to the *Book of Mormon,* Christ had appeared in the New World and the

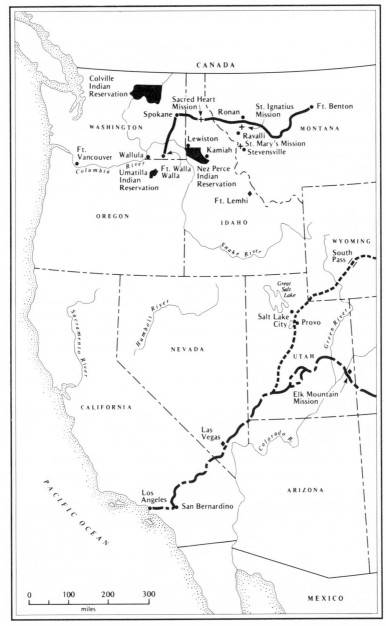

Roman Catholic and Mormon missions in the West. Dashed-dotted line is the Old Spanish Trail; the trail through Salt Lake City is the Mormon Trail; solid line is Mullan Road; crosses indicate Catholic missions; diamonds indicate Mormon missions

Indians had been for a time stalwart Christians, but then, through their "loss of belief they became 'wild,' 'full of mischief,' 'loathsome,' 'and full of idleness.' "[5] Further, they were cursed with a dark skin, a truly heavy burden in nineteenth-century America.

According to the Mormon doctrine these Lamanites were capable of redemption. They might be rescued from their despised state by becoming members of the Latter-day Saints religion and by living clean and upright lives. Through their virtue they could become "white and delightsome."[6] Thus the Mormons saw it as their destiny to uplift the fallen children of Israel. As two contemporary Mormon scholars, Leonard J. Arrington and Davis Bitton, have observed, the early Mormons' perception of American Indians combined the idea of the "noble savage" with the idea of the "white man's burden." On the one hand, Indians were viewed as noble and therefore somewhat superior because of their special history and prophesied future as presented in the *Book of Mormon*. On the other hand, Indians needed elevation to "civilization" within the present day. These concepts of the Latter-day Saints "combined under a religious canopy the duty to convert and civilize with a respect for the past accomplishments and the religious records of the Indians and with an attitude of awe toward a chosen people of destiny whose prophesied role in the divine economy was equal if not superior in some ways to that of white Mormons."[7]

Although theological concepts could produce a sense of awe or even superiority, the historical record of nineteenth-century Mormon-Indian relations reveals little of either. Instead, both the rhetoric of leaders like Brigham Young and the actions of Mormon settlers reveal an assumption of white superiority. As on other frontiers, there were acts of friendship between the two peoples, but ultimately the Mormons like other white settlers in the West readily occupied Indian lands and eventually displaced the native people. As with other religious denominations, missions, when they were finally established, did nothing to prevent this ultimate result.

The Mormon church was founded on the frontier and continued to exist on subsequent frontiers of settlement as it was forced ever westward to its Zion. The patterns which the new group assumed did not reflect so much its new theology as the realities of the frontier areas in which the Mormons settled. As we shall see after their arrival in Utah, daily necessities for these religious argonauts were more important than most obligations of their new faith toward the Indians.

When the Mormons moved west through Ohio, Illinois, and Missouri, their teachings about the Lamanites did not create a mission policy. Relations with Indians during this time seem to have been governed by necessity. On their hegira from Nauvoo, Illinois, to their new Zion in the mountains, most of the Mormons came into contact with Indians. Many of the beleaguered refugees spent the winter of 1846–47 on Indian lands along the Missouri River in western Iowa and eastern Nebraska. There the Indians of the region and the Mormons seemed to accommodate to each other. Not until the establishment of their new home in the Great Basin did missions begin to play a major role in Mormon-Indian relations.

A comparison can be made between the Mormons of the nineteenth century and their Puritan forebears of the seventeenth. Both groups had a passionate desire for insularity. Both felt that by taking up their work in the wilderness they could accomplish by ecclesiastical rigor and hard work the utopia which was the guiding star of their "errand into the wilderness."[8] Both had difficulties in accommodating to their neighbors. Both were firmly convinced that the truth resided only with them. Both knew that they were instruments in the hands of God to perform a special work for their era. And both did surprisingly little missionary work among the Indians. For example, the Mormons made no organized effort to convert the Utes in the years before 1855. The relations were actually adversarial. Brigham Young had come to the valleys of Utah with the idea that the Utes could be treacherous, an idea enunciated by Jim Bridger. In fact, by 1850 Brigham Young had started pressures on Congress to remove the Utes.[9]

In many ways the career of George Washington Bean typifies the problematic development of Mormon-Indian policy, relations, and missions in the church's first five decades. He was born in Adams County, Illinois, April 1, 1831, just a year after the founding of the church. His parents were among the many generous souls at Quincy, Illinois, who gave succor and refuge to the Mormons who had been expelled from Missouri. A persuasive Mormon elder whom they had sheltered converted the Beans to the new faith. In 1841 ten-year-old George W. Bean was baptized.

From the time of his entrance into the Mormon faith George Washington Bean became immersed in that swirl of activity that did and does characterize Mormon families. In 1845 his parents moved to Nauvoo, which was then the center of Mormon life. Young Bean, like most American boys of his time, took on the duties of adulthood at an early age. At fourteen years of age he worked as a laborer in construction of the new temple at Nauvoo, served as a member of a posse that aided the sheriff in arresting house burners then plaguing Nauvoo, was initiated into the higher orders of the Mormon priesthood by being named a "Seventy," and was ushered through his "endowments" in the temple, a rite now reserved to those of more mature years. At fifteen this intrepid young man traveled across Iowa to the Mormon camp at Council Bluffs. He and his father were then sent eastward to Missouri to work for provisions and seed grain. According to Bean's autobiography, the family spent the winter on Potawatomi lands.

Next, the seventeen-year-old crossed the plains to Utah, reaching the valley of the Great Salt Lake in October, 1847. His autobiography, like the standard histories of the Mormon community, records the difficulty of the Latter-day Saints' first months in their new home:

During the winter and spring lived on very short rations and had to resort to thistle roots and segoes to help out on the provisions.

In the spring of 1848 we put in one bushel of wheat and two acres of corn, but the crickets took the latter.[10]

George W. Bean. Courtesy University of Utah.

In May, 1848, Bean's parents arrived in Great Salt Lake City, but young Bean was not to remain with them. He soon received his first assignment in the colonizing of the Mormon kingdom. On his eighteenth birthday he arrived at the site where a new settlement, called Fort Utah (later Provo, Utah) was to be built. Bean helped to "locate" or lay out the fort, and soon this settlement began to rise at the center of a region traditionally used by the Utes. The valley surrounding Utah Lake contained the largest Ute band, who found nearby almost all that they needed to maintain themselves. The lake teemed with trout, such an important resource that the Ute band's own name for itself, Tumpanawach, meant "Fish-eaters." Canyons led from the valley, offering easy access to hunting areas in the mountains to the east. The materials the band needed could be gathered near the camps: lodges could be built without transporting anything from distant places; basketmakers could find the willow they needed; and wood for fuel was plentiful. Small wonder that the Utes were reluctant to give up such an area.

The Indians who dwelt in this valley were historically not a belligerent people. In their life-style the Utes were uncomplicated. The only known annual ceremony was the Bear Dance that celebrated the coming of spring. The Utes adapted to their environment in a highly efficient way as demonstrated by their use of medicinal plants, tanning techniques, food sources, fish traps, and a variety of tools. Each summer and fall of the year the people left their lakeside location and traveled to the mountain areas to gather and to hunt. These upland areas were easily reached through low valleys leading out of the valley of the Utah Lake. During this summer season the Utes met other divisions of their people. The various bands knew of each other and the areas in which each dwelt. Spanish explorers led by Fathers Dominguez and Escalante made the first white observations in late summer of 1776. They described a very peaceful and loving people. Yet as commerce and contact with the intruders increased over time, the Utes appear to have become more aggressive.

By the time the Mormons arrived, they had involved themselves with the fur trade and the horse trade and were demanding tribute of Mexican caravans that traveled through their country. These Mexican caravans also carried on a slave trade with the Utes, who captured people of neighboring tribes and sold them to the Mexicans. As a result of these activities by the 1820s and 1830s the Utes had grown very prosperous as compared to their earlier life-style.[11]

Yet, commerce with the fur traders and the Mexicans caused the Indian people to be increasingly dependent upon trade goods. The Utes especially prized horses and metal items. They also sought bridle bits, knives, metal arrow tips, and guns.

After the Mormons settled at Fort Utah, a pattern familiar throughout United States history repeated itself. Non-Indian attempts to take resources that Indians felt they could not give up led first to disputes then to armed conflict. Bean observed that "the Timpanodes, a large band of Utes lived on this stream [Provo River] and were often saucy and troublesome."[12] Soon Bean became a member of the militia formed to protect the settlement. Although the Indian-white conflict near Utah Lake in 1849 and 1850 was limited and relatively few people were killed, the new soldier sustained an injury. As he recounted:

An iron 6 pounder, [cannon] was mounted to overlook the houses. Sept 1, I was called on by Lt Wm Dayton to assist in artillery practice on the bastion, it was nearly sunset, and we hurried up and after firing once while ramming the next cartridge a premature explosion took place killing Lt Dayton and instantly and seriously maiming me. Our bodies were thrown about 30 feet and fell at the foot of the mound. My left hand was gone entirely and my body filled with splinters from the rammer, face burned and black with powder burns and was unable to see for 20 days.[13]

Fortunately for the desperately wounded man the U.S. Army Corps of Topographical Engineers under Captain Howard Stansbury had just arrived in Utah. A fellow militiaman

rode to Great Salt Lake City and returned with an army
surgeon who amputated Bean's arm to three inches below
the elbow and removed more than 200 splinters.

During his recuperation George W. Bean busied himself
learning the Ute language. He also worked as a school teacher's
assistant, became the first city recorder from Provo, Utah,
and assisted in the trade with the Indians. When Utah County
was established in 1852, he was made the first assessor and
and collector of taxes and served as deputy U.S. marshal.
The civil appointments to high local offices continued, and
Bean married and became a father. By 1854 he had recovered
enough to join Orrin Porter Rockwell in pursuit of the Ute
leader, Wakara, whom the Mormons called Walker.[14]

Through 1853 and 1854 the Ute-Mormon conflict erupted
in what became known as the Walker War. Suffering and
deaths on both sides increased, and the attitude of local whites
toward the Indians began to change: they wanted the burden
imposed by the Indians' presence removed from their lives.

It is clear from the record quoted below that the Indians
distinguished between Mormons and the rest of the Americans. They divided them into two differentiated groups. One
was called Mormonee the other Mericats. Yet the Utes did
not distinguish as carefully between each group in terms of
what each desired from the Indians.

The Ute people lost the Walker War. The Mormon pioneers,
well armed and well trained in the military science of the
day, held the upper hand. An extensive part of the male
population had served in the Nauvoo Legion since the early
1840s. In addition, members of the Mormon Battalion who
had served in the Mexican War returned to Utah with their
guns and their training.

The peace negotiations between Brigham Young and the
Indians held at Chicken Creek in Juab County illustrated
what had transpired in the six short years since the Mormons'
arrival. S. N. Caravalho, a Portuguese artist in Utah as a
part of the Frémont expedition, attended the peace negotiations. In a conversation with Brigham Young, Caravalho
learned that "Utah Indians possess rifles of the first quality."

These weapons had been acquired by trade with "American travelers," but others had been furnished by the Mormons so that the Indians could hunt for themselves instead of begging or stealing food at the Mormon settlements.[15]

At the first peace council Caravalho heard several Ute leaders explain that factors other than food created their antagonism. Two elderly speakers made especially touching yet forceful statements.

For five minutes intense silence prevailed, when an old grey-headed Utah chief got up, and in the effort, his blanket slipped from his body, displaying innumerable marks of wounds and scars. Stretching aloft his almost fleshless arms, he spoke as follows:

"I am for war, I never will lay down my rifle, and tomahawk, Americats have no truth—Americats kill Indian plenty—Americats see Indian woman, he shoot her like deer—Americats no meet Indian to fight, he have no mercy—one year gone, Mormon say, they no kill more Indian—Mormon no tell truth, plenty Utahs gone to Great Spirit, Mormon kill them,—no friend to Americats more."

The chief of the San Pete Indians arose, and the tears rolled down his furrowed cheeks as he gave utterance to his grievances:

"My son," he said, "was a brave chief, he was so good to his old father and mother—one day Wa-yo-sha was hunting rabbits as food for his old parents—the rifle of the white man killed him. When the night came, and he was still absent, his old mother went to look for her son; she walked a long way through the thick bushes; at the dawn of day, the mother and the son were both away, and the infirm and aged warrior was lonely; he followed the trail of his wife in the bush, and there he found the mother of his child, lying over the body of Wa-yo-sha, both dead from the same bullet. The old woman met her son, and while they were returning home, a bullet from the rifle of Americats shot them both down." He added, "Old San Pete no can fight more, his hand trembles, his eyes are dim, the murderer of his wife, and brave Wa-yo-sha, is still living. San Pete no make peace with Americats."[16]

Some leaders spoke for peace, but Wakara refused to make a speech even after a direct invitation from Brigham Young. Instead, he insisted, "I got no heart to speak—no can talk to-day—to-night Wakara talk with Great Spirit, tomorrow

Wakara talk with Governor [Brigham Young]."[17] On this somewhat religious note, the first parley ended.

That same evening Brigham Young served as host to the Indians at a feast and slaughtered an ox for the occasion. The next morning the governor pledged his love for the Indians and presented them with gifts of clothing, ammunition, and sixteen head of oxen. Wakara then spoke. His statement of peace showed that Mormon gifts and friendship as well as a message from the Great Spirit had swayed his decision:

Wakara has heard all the talk of the good Mormon chief. Wakara no like to go to war with him. Sometimes Wakara take his young men and go far away to sell horses. When he is absent, then Americats come and kill his wife and children. Why not come and fight when Wakara is at home? Wakara is accused of killing Capt. Gunnison. Wakara did not; Wakara was three hundred miles away when the Merecat chief was slain. Merecats soldier hunt Wakara, to kill him, but no find him. Wakara hear it; Wakara come home. Why not Merecats take Wakara? He is not armed. Wakara heart very sore. Merecats kill Parvain Indian chief, and Parvain woman. Parvain young men watch for Merecats and kill them, because Great Spirit say—"Merecats kill Indian"; "Indian kill Merecats." Wakara no want to fight more. Wakara talk with Great Spirit; Great Spirit say—"Make peace." Wakara love Mormon chief; he is good man. When Mormon first come to live on Wakara's land, Wakara give him welcome. He give Wakara plenty bread, and clothes to cover his wife and children. Wakara no want to fight Mormon; Mormon chief very good man; he bring plenty oxen to Wakara. Wakara talk last night to Payede, to Kahutah, San Pete, Parvain—all Indian say, "No fight Mormon or Merecats more." If Indian kill white man again, Wakara make Indian howl.[18]

The council dissolved after the ritual of smoking the calumet. Wakara further demonstrated his own peaceful, friendly intentions by accompanying Brigham Young on his visits to the Mormons' southern settlements. His party of more than thirty Utes provided safe passage for the Mormon leader through previously hostile areas.

The events of the Walker War and its aftermath demonstrated that Mormon-Indian relations still existed in the fron-

tier context of incursion, settlement, and attempted pacification by whites. The Utes and other Indians of the area
retained enough autonomy to make peace negotiations and
gift-giving a wise form of diplomacy by both Mormons and
"Merecats." Earlier encounters between Europeans and native
peoples had produced similar forms of interaction. But at
this stage of frontier development, with no one group fully
dominating a region, religious missions held little prospect of
success. Indeed, Brigham Young wished to establish his entire church, not just a few missions in the midst of these
Indians. Peaceful relations with the eventual domination of
the area by the Mormons remained Young's primary policy.
He clearly wished, therefore, that the Indians would view the
Mormons as better friends than other whites.

In a famous speech during the course of the Walker War,
Young told his followers not to do as "inhabitants of the
United States" have done and retaliate against an entire tribe
for depredations or killings carried out by a few individuals.
"We must shun this practice, and teach them [the Indians]
that the man who has committed the depredation is the man
that must pay the penalty, and not the whole tribe. It is our
duty to teach them good morals, and the principles of the
Gospel of Christ. We are their Saviours." Young also warned
that the Mormons not pursue the Indians up into the mountains ". . . for there are not soldiers enough here to contend
with them there. . . ." Instead, he counseled a harsh but
pragmatic policy.

> They [the Indians] came pretty nigh starving to death last winter;
> and they now see, if they are driven from these valleys in winter,
> they must perish; therefore they not want to make good peace.
> Treat them kindly and treat them as Indians, and not as your
> equals.[19]

Young's testimony showed that the wintering grounds of
the Utes had been taken. Fish-trap locations and camping
grounds had given way to plowed fields. The pattern of survival had been so drastically altered that submission or raiding were the clear alternatives for this displaced people.

Whether George Washington Bean held the same views as Brigham Young on Indian affairs is unclear. But after the peace council with Wakara, Bean continued his active life as a loyal member of his expanding church. In 1855 he joined an unsuccessful exploring party that searched for a more direct route from Salt Lake City to Sacramento, California. That same year Bean began his greatest work among the Indians. He spent part of the years 1855 and 1856 in the Mormons' Las Vegas, Nevada, Indian mission. Strangely, Bean largely omitted this activity from his autobiography. We know not why; it is usually impossible to find a Mormon diary or autobiography that does not dwell in detail on missionary experiences.

The "mission" system of the Mormons differs from systems of other religious groups in America. Catholic or Protestant missions in the United States of the nineteenth century normally contained at least one trained ecclesiastic who was to serve as the representative of a parish, area, or bishop. These established "missions" usually had a set location, buildings, and eventually a staff. The Mormons called men to serve for a limited time. Often they were mendicant, or as they put it, "traveled without purse or script." This was a necessary method, inasmuch as they were usually poor young men representing poor families and poor communities. The normal sojourn of a Mormon "elder" in the field was two or three years. Most Protestant and Catholic missionaries dealt with their "mission" as practically a lifetime endeavor. Some nineteenth-century Mormons spent time on two, three, or for some zealots, four missions. These individuals were rare; the usual pattern was for an adult to spent two or three years as a missionary. The pattern persists to the present, but the term of service is shorter.

In the "setting apart" ceremony of April 22, 1855, apostle Wilford Woodruff blessed Bean before he undertook his mission. Woodruff's prayer spoken as his hands rested upon the head of the neophyte missionary reveals what tasks a member of the Latter-day Saints hierarchy believed a missionary to the Indians should undertake:

We say unto you let thy heart be comforted and thy soul rejoice before the Lord for thou shalt receive thy reward for all thy labors and the trial through which thou shalt be called to pass. Thou shalt be mighty and have influence among the seed of Joseph, and thou shalt teach them to leave off all their foolishness, their shedding of blood and all their filthy and evil practices and abominations of every description. Therefore go forth with thy brethren and be full of faith before the Lord and He shall raise thee up and make thee useful in imparting the knowledge of the English language to thy brethren the Lamanites, and of impressing upon their minds the truths contained in the Book of Mormon and of the prophecies of the ancient prophets who lived upon this continent and who bore record of the great blessings that should rest upon their descendants. After that their curse and afflictions shall be removed and they become a delightsome people.[20]

Fortunately for Bean a detachment from Edward Jenner Steptoe's U.S. Army Company led by Lieutenant Sylvester Mowry had been detailed to go to California by way of Las Vegas. Bean was hired to accompany them. Thus he earned three dollars per day by acting as interpreter and by guiding the troops to "Las Vegas Springs, New Mexico [modern Las Vegas, Nevada]."[21]

The new mission faced many challenges. The struggle to raise food and maintain life in the desert posed a major problem for missionaries who lacked the survival skills of their Indian neighbors. Another missionary sent to Las Vegas, Aroet Lucious Hale, wrote that they spent the first three months in "Grubing Muskeat and Willows for Our Gardens, making Watter Ditches putting in our garding, makin Adobes for our Foart and Exploring for Timber."[22] That the missionaries built a fort suggests that the Mormons anticipated more than the peaceful communication of their religion.

As interpreter, George W. Bean had a central role in the missionary band of thirty-three men who took up their labors in the desert. Because his knowledge of the Ute language would not serve perfectly among the Paiutes, he had to learn a second difficult Shoshonean language. Bean diligently set out to accomplish this task. A. L. Hale commented in his autobiography: "George Bun [Bean] of Provo, Our Indian interpreter used to talk hours and hours to them, wheir Ever we could find them."[23]

The Paiutes in the area of the new Mormon mission lived on desert vegetation and hunted small game, such as rabbits. Extended family groups lived separately but came in contact at various times of the year. Communal activities were common, such as rabbit drives, deer hunts, and celebrations. The desert vegetation provided a remarkably varied food supply. Mesquite beans, grass seed, and dozens of small desert plants all had their uses among the Paiutes.

In summer the Paiutes went to the mountains where they picked berries, hunted, and fished. They skillfully wove baskets and used them for cooking, storing, and carrying. Many baskets were used in gathering and storing pine nuts, one of their principal sources of food. Some forms of pottery also were produced.

By the early 1850s at the time of the arrival of the Mormon colonists in the Paiute areas, agriculture had developed among these Indians. The complexity of this agriculture is revealed in the following passage from a contemporary history authored by members of the tribe:

Later in the spring or early summer was the time to till and sow the farmlands. The fields were carefully prepared: brush was burned, roots were dug out; and the ground was tilled and watered before planting. Corn, squash, beans, pumpkins, and sunflowers were grown. There were four different colors of corn — white, blue, yellow, and red. Some of each color were saved from the last year's crop. The crops usually were planted in rows, and holes were made for the seeds with a specially shaped stick whose end was flattened like a shovel. It is likely that the Nuwuvi [Paiutes] used a method of irrigation like that of the Pueblo Indians. Corn was planted in small mounds, and diverted water was let to flow into the fields. One known irrigation ditch was a half-mile long, four feet wide and four feet deep and had been dug through a gravel bed by using only wooden spades. A nearby dam was constructed of logs and brushwood and conveyed the water toward the farm.

Some of the Nuwuvi, especially those living in drier regions away from rivers, used another method of watering crops. Rather than planting in rows, pits about three feet across and six inches deep were dug. The plants were watered by allowing rain water to collect or by bringing water from springs.

Nuwuvi farmed along streams such as the Virgin, the Santa Clara, Ash Creek, Beaver Dam Wash, and the Muddy River, as well as at numerous springs.[24]

Overcoming the difficulties of the desert, the Mormon missionaries gradually became established, and their influence grew in the area. Hale reported that more than fifty Indians had been baptized. The fort provided a military presence in the area, enhancing the Mormon claim to the region at a time when the Latter-day Saints envisioned a domain much larger than the area of modern Utah. In addition to mission work the little band explored the region and carried on some commerce with California. The men traveled down part of the lower Colorado River and helped the church decide to try to establish a seaport on that river east of the Las Vegas mission (at Saint Thomas). A trail from Great Salt Lake City to the Los Angeles area afforded the mission communication with the outside world. Mail arrived once a month. The mission also became a way station in the desert, for it lay on the shortest Mormon route to a seaport (Los Angeles). While Bean served as a missionary in Las Vegas, LDS missionaries on their way to the Sandwich Islands passed through.

As Bean's sojourn in the desert aptly illustrates, there was more to the "mission" than the converting of Indians—in this case the placing of the mission along the route from Salt Lake City to Los Angeles might easily serve the aims of empire building more than that of gathering souls. Indeed, the "building of the Kingdom of God" as the Mormons put it, was a difficult concept to separate into neatly defined parts. While "mission" in Mormon lexicon meant carrying the gospel to unbelievers, it also meant missionizing among other faiths, and it could mean any special service one was called upon to perform in the name of the church. The "mission" was also used to "call" people to begin new settlements and establish a new "stake" comparable to a very small diocese. These settlements often occurred in areas that Brigham Young or later leaders felt best fit the growth and support of the kingdom.[25]

As for the actual conversion of Indians, this concept must be questioned, as it can be with other denominations. The giving of food and clothing at the time of baptism indicated an economic as well as religious relationship. And what did baptism mean? In all areas of Indian America, baptism did not necessarily mean conversion. Most Paiute converts in the Las Vegas mission did not show up in Mormon records after the notation of their baptism. The close relationship with church officials and congregations (wards) that characterized the Mormon experience for most other converts did not exist for the Paiutes who accepted baptism. Only a few Paiutes dwelling on the edges of the southern Mormon settlements were regular members of a congregation. Yet, these converts did not take up the same relationship to the church that, for example, European converts so quickly assumed. The Indian portion rarely included tithes paid, orders of priesthood conferred or full participation in the "gathering of Israel." In fact, these Indians rarely communicated with their new coreligionists at all.[26]

George Washington Bean eventually left his missionary labors, returning to his wife and young daughter in Provo. He found the valleys of Utah in a state of intense religious excitement. The "Mormon Reformation" had broken out. Its possible causes are numerous, but in part this reformation may be traced to the brute force and dedicated labor required to build an agricultural society in the deserts of the intermountain West. The raising of churches, civic establishments, and a military force; building of canals, roads, and bridges; funding and manning a large missionary system and a lay ministry demanded great personal effort. Small wonder that backsliding occurred.

Jedediah Morgan Grant, a counselor to President Brigham Young, led this movement to purify the Mormons. It powerfully resembled Protestant revivals that had broken out on earlier frontiers. Grant appointed missionaries, not to foreign parts or to the Indians, but to wards within the Mormon kingdom. The hellfire-and-brimstone sermons that issued forth must have reminded many of the Mormons of the churches they had left. The thrust of the movement attempted to make each member acutely aware of his or her own sins and shortcomings. Many of the guilt-stricken accepted rebaptism, an early Mormon practice that has since become rare. Many saw visions, and others spoke in tongues. Grant emphasized personal cleanliness and insisted that the local bishops wash themselves at least once a week. Homes were to be clean and tidy as a reflection of spiritual orderliness.[27] Yet the enthusiasms of the revival did not spread beyond the Mormon realm. It remained an insular reformation. Missionaries did not descend on the Indians of the region, despite the fact that earlier leaders like Wilford Woodruff had perceived "filthy and evil practices" among this "seed of Joseph."

George Washington Bean did not record whether he became part of this reformation. But he clearly demonstrated his devotion to the faith by entering the institution of polygamy. He married two additional women in December, 1856. His three marriages produced thirty children, twenty-six of whom lived to adulthood.

In 1857 a crisis occurred in the Mormon communities. President Buchanan sent an army to install a new governor of Utah to replace Brigham Young. The Mormons prepared for war, thinking that the army was being sent to impose military rule over them or to annihilate them. Brigham Young ordered his followers to be ready to abandon Utah and flee before the army.

In choosing a place of refuge, Governor Young used information about a "White Mountain," westward from central Utah, supposedly in south-central Nevada. Young sent George W. Bean as the leader of one of two exploring parties that set out in 1858. During the spring of that year, Bean and his men searched a large portion of eastern Nevada. They did not find the sanctuary.[28] In the interim a rapprochement between the Mormons and the federal government had been forged, and a sanctuary was no longer needed.[29]

In November of that year Bean was hired by Captain James H. Simpson, of the Corps of Topographical Engineers, to explore and locate a mail route from Camp Floyd to California. Bean worked on only the first part of the route. It appears that he did not tell Simpson that he had been in the area before. Simpson later criticized the Mormons for their lack of honesty, but his opinion did not affect Bean's reputation.[30]

By 1860 Bean had been appointed prosecuting attorney for Utah County, which indicates something of the stature he had attained. In 1862 he received an appointment as assistant collector of internal revenue. Of this position Bean wrote: "... had 11 distilleries in my District high tax reduced them to 3 in 1864."[31]

During the 1860s some of Bean's other activities entered the public record. Since the founding of Fort Utah in 1849 the Utes had posed a vexing problem to the Mormons. Conflict over resources escalated from minor hostility in 1849 to the armed encounters of the Walker War in 1853-54. As deaths increased, so did the settlers' desire to have the Indians removed to remote locations, as Indians had been elsewhere in the United States. During the Civil War years President Abraham Lincoln, hoping that the Mormons would not pose a threat to the Union, carried out a federal policy that called for giving the Mormons what they wanted as long as it did not cost too much. Since the removal of the Indians was among the Mormons' first desires, Lincoln attempted, soon after his administration was in place, to implement that policy in Utah.

The federal official in charge of Indian affairs in Utah, Henry Martin, recommended the Uinta Valley in northeastern Utah as a reservation. When Brigham Young learned about his choice, he asked for a delay and sent an exploring party to the Uinta Valley in August and September, 1861. The party reached the valley at a time when the vegetation had turned brown from the summer sun. Unimpressed, they reported that they "did not know why God had created it [the Uinta Valley], unless it was to hold two other parts of the world together."[32] Lincoln quickly set the valley aside as an Indian reservation, issuing an executive order on October 3, 1861. When the Utes were asked to remove to the Uinta Valley, however, they refused, saying it did not have enough food and the winters were too cold there. A standoff existed during the Civil War years: the Mormons urged the Utes to go and the Utes continued to refuse.

In the times preceding 1865 the Utes of the Utah Valley used the Uinta Basin as a hunting area. A small group of the tribe lived there year-round. The area was also a summer meeting ground between the Utah Valley people and the Yamparika band of Utes who dwelt in the Yampa and White River valleys. The cold of the area, the frequent winter fog, and the limited food resources made the location unsuitable for the more numerous Utes accustomed to wintering at the mouth of the Provo River.

In 1865 the federal government sent O. H. Irish to be superintendent of Indian affairs for the Territory of Utah. A vigorous administrator, Irish moved first to handle the interests of the small scattered bands and then to deal directly with the Utes. He asked all of the Ute bands to meet him at the Spanish Fork Indian Farm on June 6, 1865. In preparing for that event, Irish worked very closely with Territorial Governor James Duane Doty. But as the treaty sessions began, Doty became desperately ill and died. Irish reported to the Secretary of the Interior:

I submitted to him [Doty] a draft of the treaty, which was afterwards accepted by the Indians; and his last assurance to me was, that he had approved of my policy in every respect, and advised me not to be discouraged by the opposition manifested by the other officers of the government, who declared, that rather than associate with Brigham Young on such an occasion, they would rather the Indians than the Mormons, would have the land.

Brigham Young accepted my invitation, a copy of which I herewith enclose, that it may be seen to what extent I committed the interest of the government to his hands; his name appears on the treaty as a witness only, and he acted only in advising the Indians to make the treaty . . . .

The fact exists, however, much as some might prefer it to be otherwise, that he has pursued so kind and conciliatory a policy with the Indians that it has given him great influence over them. It was my duty and policy under your instructions to make use of his influence for the accomplishment of the purposes of government.[33]

For the treaty-making council Irish hired three leading Mormon interpreters, the Huntington brothers and George Washington Bean, and he also invited Brigham Young. Bean appears to have been employed for several months as interpreter and special agent. He worked at the Spanish Fork Indian Farm and "assisted in locating the Uinta Reservation."[34] But his most memorable role was that of interpreter at the treaty negotiations of June, 1865.

Irish had previously written a treaty very much like the treaties concluded in the 1860s. The Indians gave up about half of Utah; the government agreed to provide money, schooling, and farming tools, employ farmers, build a sawmill and a gristmill, and allow the Indians to fish at their accustomed places.[35]

The treaty negotiations graphically exposed the Mormons' Indian policy that had developed in Utah. At the point when the Indians had to decide whether to accept the treaty, Brigham Young addressed them. One of the Huntington brothers translated his speech:

Sanpitch, Sow-e-ett, Tabby, and all of you. I want you to understand what I say to you. I am looking for your welfare. Do you see that the Mormons here are increasing? We have been and calculate to be friends all the time. If you do not sell your land to the Government, they will take it, whether you are willing to sell it or not. This is the way they have done in California and Oregon. They are willing to give you something for it and we want you to have it. If you go to Unitah, they will build you houses, make you a farm, give you cows, oxen, clothing, blankets and many other things you will want. And, then, the treaty that Colonel Irish has here, gives you the privilege of coming back here on a visit; you can fish, hunt, pick berries, dig roots and we can visit together. Kon-osh, San-pitch, Tabby and the rest of you, can come and see me when you please.

Continuing, the Mormon prophet exposed the Mormon attitude about land tenure, and the superior position of the settlers:

> The land does not belong to you, nor to me, nor to the Government! It belongs to the Lord. But our father at Washington is disposed to make you liberal presents to let the Mormons live here. We have not been able to pay you enough, although we have helped you a good deal. We have always fed you, and we have given you presents, just as much as we could; but now the great father is willing to give you more; and it won't make one particle of difference whether you say they may have the land or not, because we shall increase, and we shall occupy this valley and the next, and the next, and so on until we occupy the whole of them; and we are willing you should live with us. If you will go over there and have your houses built and get your property and money, we are perfectly willing you should visit with us. Do you understand that, Kon-osh?
>
> Kon-osh (and others). We do.[36]

One Ute leader, Tabby, in a speech translated by Bean indicated that the Indians wanted to "wait until tomorrow." Tabby concluded, "Let us go back to our lodges and talk and smoke over what has been said to-day. The Indians are not ready now to give up the land; they never thought of such a thing."[37] Tabby's speech only delayed the process until the following day when the Indians accepted the treaty in return for presents given to those leaders who would sign, including Tabby himself.

The U.S. Senate did not accept the Spanish Fork Treaty. The men in Washington were ill-disposed to grant anything to the Mormons. Federal officials and the Mormon leaders had been at odds for many years. Blunders on both sides had led President Buchanan to send an army to Utah in 1857–58 to "reimpose" federal authority. The memories of that encounter remained vivid. In addition, the Mormons had refused to fight in the Civil War. Many senators, in turn, refused to consider any act that might help the Mormons. In spite of high hopes and Irish's careful explanation that Brigham Young had been only a witness to, and not a central figure in, the treaty negotiations, the treaty died in the Indian Affairs Committee of the Senate.

Meanwhile, the Utes felt certain that they had made a good faith treaty with the United States *and* with the Mormons. They waited for the gifts agreed on, and when those goods did not arrive, the troubles between the people of central Utah and the Indians increased.

The Walker War had failed to solve any of the problems between the two peoples. The white residents supposed that a treaty would solve the problems created by starving Indians who resorted to stealing and raiding. The Utes felt that, since the settlers used Ute lands, the Utes deserved a portion of the stock and crops raised on them. If the settlers did not give it freely, the Indians would raid.

In 1864, even before the treaty negotiations, raids began in earnest. Starvation had occurred because the rapid increase of Mormon population in central Utah put pressure on the fish and game used by the Utes. Mormons were not unwilling, as the problem grew, to give charity to the starving. But the white population rose rapidly, and food remained scarce much of the time for all of the frontier residents. A group of disgruntled Indians gathered around a leader named Black Hawk (not to be confused with the Sauk and Fox leader active a generation earlier in the Illinois area). As the Utes' condition deteriorated in the late 1850s and early 1860s, the lack of a coherent policy on the part of either the Mormons or the U.S. government created a situation in which a leader such as Black Hawk could arise.

In Ute tradition "chiefs" did not exist. For example, the leaders of the hunts were appointed only for the duration of that activity. Yet in times of stress or emergency a leader would emerge for the period of need. Black Hawk seems to have risen in response to a popular belief among the Utes that war was the only possible option. He did not appear to have the support of the older Ute leaders. But his ability to attract many to his cause, and many of those from distant points, showed a very widespread desire on the part of the Utes to respond to white encroachment.

Black Hawk. He and his Ute tribe terrorized Mormon Utah in the late 1860s. Courtesy Utah State Historical Society.

The Black Hawk War consisted of a series of Ute raids and responses by the Utah militia, which was still called the Nauvoo Legion from its days in Illinois. Even though no great armies took the field, this became the largest war fought on Utah soil. It had no distinct beginning and ending dates; raids took place from 1864 to 1871.

The Mormons felt the brunt of the war most heavily in the years 1865 through 1867. More than fifty white settlers were killed. Accurate estimates of Indian losses cannot be made, but it would be safe to estimate that several times as many Indians as whites died in the conflict. Women, children, and unarmed victims were killed on both sides. The Mormons lost large numbers of their livestock. Total property losses to the settler communities exceeded $1.1 million. Congress voted no relief or reimbursement, ignoring the memorials of the Utah legislature. The federal government, in effect, left the Mormons alone to fight their frontier war with the Indians.[38]

This war brought George Bean's next mission to the Indians. This time instead of carrying the Bible and the *Book of Mormon*, Bean came in the uniform of the Nauvoo Legion. In 1867 he left his position as probate judge of Utah County to become a lieutenant colonel of cavalry, serving as quartermaster on the staff of General W. B. Pace "in the Sanpete Expedition, vs. Blackhawk & Co."[39]

Tactically the war differed little from others on the American frontier. The Indians raided farms and ranches; the settlers built forts and posted armed guards to defend the stock. When the "generals" of the Nauvoo Legion pursued the Indians to the mountains, the Indians at first defeated them easily from ambush. Black Hawk, who began with about fifty warriors, had three times that many after the original number had been killed, for he was able to attract allies from as far away as Colorado and Arizona. In spite of that success, the Indians met defeat. White numbers and military firepower determined the outcome. At last one of the older Ute leaders, Tabby-to-Kwana (Child of the Sun), led the battered remnant of the Ute people to the Uinta Valley. By 1871 whites had undisputed possession of the Utah and Sanpete valleys of central Utah. The Utes' removal to the Uinta Valley forced them to accommodate more directly to a second white group—officials of the United States government. Although the Utes at times attempted to return to their beloved valleys, they were always escorted back to the Uintah Reservation. In fact, one of Bean's last references to Indians reported:

In 1872 Employed by Lt. George Wheeler U.S. Top'l Surveyor west of the 100th Meridian—as guide and interpreter. Went thru Provo Valley Strawberry Thistle Valley and Sanpete, also served Dr. Dodge and Maj Littlefield getting Ute Indians back to Res'n.[40]

George W. Bean's relationship with the Indians ended at a time when other matters had begun to press upon the Mormon kingdom. Gradually the larger plans of empire building had to be deferred in the face of urgent threats to survival. The federal government had decided to become master in its own house, and federal power in Utah grew throughout the 1870s. At the same time a continental economic empire developed in the United States, and the West began to fill with settlers. The Mormon response became schizoid: the church both tried to develop an insular economic apparatus and hoped to take advantage of the expanding American economy in the West. The attempt at insularity failed. The time when a theocratic oligarch in Salt Lake City could control an isolated kingdom in the mountains had passed. In 1872 the territorial governor outlawed the Nauvoo Legion, which was considered a threat to federal power, but only after the legion had done the fighting and dying in the Black Hawk War. National pressure against polygamy also grew during the decade. After the decision of the U.S. Supreme Court in *U.S.* v. *Reynolds,* which affirmed the federal right to regulate marriage laws in the territories, the Mormons became fugitives, harassed and impoverished. By the 1880s, with coherent central leadership lost, the church abandoned most of its Indian missions. Though some attempts to work with the Indians survived, the fire, the resources, and the organized mission effort did not.

Thus many of the Mormons' endeavors to convert the

Indians ended in frustration. But the same is true for all of the Christian sects that tried to spread their beliefs throughout Indian America. In location after location stories recount the works of Christian missionaries who believed they were contributing an enduring legacy. Perhaps they did, but that legacy has often turned out to be very different from what they intended. In place after place where Europe's children toiled with such diligence, faith, and love, the old native religions remain vibrant. In this failure to supplant traditional beliefs, the Mormon missionary differed but little.

As the activities of George Washington Bean illustrate, however, the system of Mormon-Indian relationships did differ, sometimes markedly, from systems established by other religious groups. The first difference resulted because the Mormons had no professional clergy. Lay members were (and are still) expected to regulate their lives so that males could serve both as an unpaid ministry and as unpaid missionaries. To support this effort, women often had to assume the burdens of wife, mother, and breadwinner at once. In their Great Basin kingdom the burdens multiplied, for the Mormons were also pioneers settling the new Zion. A family might repeat the pioneering process several times, while still carrying out its ecclesiastical duties. Pioneers who moved to Great Salt Lake City might later be "called" by church leaders to colonize first Sanpete and later the Muddy River in Nevada or the Little Colorado River in Arizona. Thus their faith demanded, and they made, great sacrifices.

Second, polygamy imposed burdens not placed on members of other faiths. The nineteenth-century Mormon world required total commitment of all its members. Often single men were sent on missions, but if the father of plural families was called, as many were, the wives and children had to take on the responsibility of maintaining themselves and contributing to support the father's mission as well. Finally, a sense of urgency impelled the mission efforts. Church members believed in "building the Kingdom" and the "the gathering of Zion," a concept that held that the pure in heart would come from the world to their Zion in the mountains.

There was reason for haste because nineteenth-century Mormons expected the millennium to arrive quickly. Each felt it his duty to contribute to the effort to find, convert, and gather up the true believers to Utah before Christ came again in all His glory.

The Mormons, set down in the midst of the wilderness with Indians all around them, soon made some efforts to convert them. Yet, despite the sense of urgency fostered by millennialism, the church's early call to convert and gather up the remnant of Israel, and the belief that Lamanites had a special place in the church, the Indian mission efforts tended to be desultory and of short duration. That raises significant questions. Why should the Mormons send missionaries to such distant places as Denmark, the Sandwich Islands, and even India, but not found a mission in Tooele Valley or on the Uintah Reservation? Why, in spite of theology, did the Indian mission effort falter again and again?

To provide an answer for such questions is very difficult. The contradictions are profound between the Mormons' nineteenth-century theological idealism and historical reality. But one contradiction is stark: The missionaries from Utah produced astounding success in Britain and Scandinavia. Their energies placed in these foreign missions produced bountiful results. But the "Lamanites" next door were not pursued with either the same energy or the same persistence, nor did the natives eagerly seek conversion. The Mormons were able to ignore their own doctrines and heaven-sent orders in their duty toward the conversion of the Indians. Ultimately, their success in terms of Indian converts in the nineteenth century is perhaps less impressive than that of many other religious groups in the American West.

In the main, the Mormon experience with the Indians in nineteenth-century America was not changed by their dogma. The far-reaching changes that their new religion fostered failed to embrace the American Indian community. Nor would their pattern attract the Indians to adopt their ways. Nonetheless, some examples exist of deep and continuing relationships between the Mormons and the Indians. In a few places in Utah, such as near Cedar City, small Mormon and Indian communities lived nearly side by side. Also there exist individual examples of conversion and even in more rare cases inclusions within the Mormon community. With these limited experiences and with the retention of their theological ideals, the Mormons laid a foundation for greater and, in some cases, spectacular successes in Indian missions in the last half of the twentieth century.[41]

As for George Washington Bean, he had been a faithful servant in his church's nineteenth-century kingdom. Early and late in life he was caught up in the system that he served. His journals reflect no hint that he saw any inconsistency in taking Ute lands to build his home. If it troubled his conscience to begin his mission to the Indians by building a fort and planting his garden in the center of their lands, he left no record of his doubts. Such oversights, however, like those made by missionaries of many other faiths, gainsay neither the efforts of the man nor those of his church. He was a builder of houses and temples, a farmer, and a soldier. Although he lost an arm, he went on to serve as a jurist, prosecuting attorney, linguist, guide, and missionary, while fathering thirty children and helping his wives raise twenty-six to adulthood.

Although the process by which the Mormons took the land, built their cities, and established the kingdom often differed from the settlement patterns familiar to much of the West, its results for the Indians were much the same. As elsewhere, when Indian interests conflicted with non-Indian concerns, the Indians were brushed aside. In Utah as in other states, when the Indians became a problem, they were controlled by the army and local militia and then penned on reservations against their will. As in the surrounding areas the Indian population was decimated in Utah. The enervation of numbers does not look very different from the end results in any of the surrounding states of the West, except perhaps New Mexico and Arizona, where a larger percentage of the Indians survived.

The Mormon-Indian mission system was not very effective

in the nineteenth century, but its failures were probably no greater than those of other religious groups. In spite of the many competing varieties of religion, the Indians of the intermountain West, like those in other regions, remained largely committed to their native religions. Even today "foreign" religions often gain acceptance in Indian communities only as a part of a dualistic system in which the foreign beliefs incorporate or coexist with traditional religious preferences. That is not the success that nineteenth-century Mormon missionaries and their counterparts intended, but perhaps it is success enough, for in this the missionary plans represent but one part of a larger attempt at conquest.

The special place of Indians in Mormon theology was special only in belief, not in practice. The details of the history of land appropriation, struggle for resources, Indian removal, and Indian wars make the Mormon system part and parcel of the history of the American West—no better and no worse.

4

Joseph M. Cataldo, S.J.: Courier of Catholicism to the Nez Percés

Robert C. Carriker

There was a time when the most influential Indians in the Pacific Northwest were the Iroquois. Acting as boatmen and fur gatherers to the traders and trappers of the North West Company, they were also bearers of important information about Catholicism, with a new God and a new ceremony. By 1811 this Iroquois impact was noticeable among tribesmen from the interior to the coast. Probably the most influential party was a group of twenty-four who by 1828 had intermarried among the Flathead tribe of present-day western Montana.

In time the Flatheads and other tribes desired formal instructions by a true missionary. They desired a Black Robe who would fulfill the promises they had heard, not the least of which was divine protection from their enemies. Accordingly, a joint party of Flatheads and Nez Percés departed for Saint Louis to seek a missionary. The delegation arrived at the journey's end in October, 1831, after 2,000 difficult miles, but unfortunately, the Catholic bishop was unable to grant their wish.[1]

Ironically, it was the Protestants who energetically responded to the Indians' request for a priest. The Methodists were the first to act, and in 1834, Jason Lee and his nephew Daniel settled among the tribesmen of the Oregon country. The Flatheads sent other messengers to Saint Louis, each time seeking a Black Robe, but in return they only received more

109

ministers, including the Presbyterians Samuel Parker, Henry Spalding, and Dr. Marcus Whitman.

Finally in the summer of 1839 a decade-long frustration bore results for the Flatheads and Nez Percés. A fourth delegation left the mountains for Saint Louis and en route they met their first Jesuit at Saint Joseph's Mission, at Council Bluffs on the Missouri River. This priest, Pierre Jean De Smet, S.J., was in fact the vanguard of a commitment by the Society of Jesus to Christianize the Indians of western America. At the Second Provincial Council in Baltimore in 1833 the American bishops decided that "the welfare of the Indians . . . should be provided for by entrusting their care to the Society of Jesus"; and Pope Gregory XVI approved the recommendation. The Indians' plea was finally answered. Within the following year De Smet was released from his other obligations and took passage in the spring of 1840 with an American Fur Company caravan going to the Green River fur trade rendezvous. From there he made his way to the homelands of the Nez Percé and Flathead Indians, who had waited so patiently these many years.[2]

At the same time in the far-off Old World other events equally pregnant with portent were taking place. On March 17, 1837, while the Flathead and Nez Percé emissaries were en route to Saint Louis on their third expedition, Joseph Cataldo was born in the remote village of Terrasini on the island of Sicily. In due time this man was to take his place as a missionary among the Indians of the Pacific Northwest and for sixty-three years perform his duty to God and man. When he passed to his final reward in 1928, there were few, if any, clergymen in any denomination who could match his commitment to American Indians.

For a man who was resilient enough to survive more than two-thirds of his life in the field as a missionary, Cataldo was a surprisingly delicate young man. He joined the Society of Jesus at Palermo at age fifteen but in two years was released because of tuberculosis. When his health returned six months later he was readmitted to the novitiate, but frailty characterized Cataldo's health for years to come.

In May, 1860, the young scholastic Cataldo was interviewed by the father general of the Society of Jesus, the Very Reverend Peter Beckx, S.J. Cataldo expressed a desire to be a missionary, though it did not matter where. Later that year Cataldo was assigned to theological studies at Louvain, Belgium. Here he also mastered French and requested that his third year in theology be at some location where English was the primary language. It was a fortuitous request, for at that exact time Father General Beckx received an urgent plea from Father Felix Sporanis, S.J., visitor general of Jesuits in America, for more missionaries. Beckx saw the possibilities and ordered Cataldo to take his final year of theology at the Jesuit House in Boston, Massachusetts, and then proceed to the Rocky Mountain Missions of the American Far West.[3]

Cataldo was ordained to the priesthood on September 8, 1862, in Liège, Belgium, and a week later boarded a ship bound for America. Weakened by the oceanic voyage, then buffeted by a blustery New England winter, Cataldo became ill. Doctors diagnosed the deteriorating condition as the final stages of "consumption." Father Sporanis had no place to locate his ill young priest and therefore decided to take Cataldo with him on an inspection trip to California in the hope that it might improve his health. The two men took passage to Jamaica, then made their way across the Isthmus of Panama, and eventually, on May 28, 1863, debarked at San Francisco. Almost immediately Cataldo's health recovered, so there was now no reason to return him to New England for academic requirements that could as easily be completed at Santa Clara College.

Cataldo was blessed with fortunate circumstances, for not only did the California climate improve his condition to the point that he was able to study and pass the order's philosophy and theology exams, but here he also met Gregory Mengarini, S.J., one of the cofounders with De Smet, of Saint Mary's Mission among the Flatheads, the original Jesuit outpost among the Indians of the Pacific Northwest. From Mengarini, Cataldo began to learn the ways of the Indians, the Salish language, and the political situation in the Rocky Moun-

tain Missions both within and without his own order.⁴ This
arrangement, however, was soon to be dismantled by Joseph
Giorda, S.J., superior of the Rocky Mountain Missions.

Giorda required men. Cataldo had been promised to the
missions and now he was needed. The California superior
likewise wanted to hold Cataldo, and he cited his still delicate health as reason enough for keeping him. The matter
was boosted all the way to the attention of the father general
in Rome, and Cataldo himself was queried as to his prefer-
ence. Cataldo wanted to go to the missions. The die was
cast. The father general instructed Cataldo to complete his
studies and then proceed directly to the Rocky Mountain
Missions. Few in California thought Cataldo would survive
the strenuous life in the mountains for more than a year.⁵

Cataldo had some doubts of his own shortly after he arrived
at Vancouver, Washington Territory, in September, 1865,
having taken passage by sea to that port on the Columbia
River. Father Giorda had little patience with his new recruit
and believed that total immersion into the strenuous life was
better than coddling. Cataldo was allowed the luxury of a
riverboat ride as far down the Columbia as Wallula, but from
that point on it was a single day's horseback ride to Fort
Walla Walla for supplies, and then a full week of thirty-
five- to forty-mile days in the saddle north along the Mullan
Road. Giorda spurned lodgings, preferring to sleep in the
open and cook by a campfire.

At first Cataldo was too exhausted to sleep or eat. All the
self-doubts about his health, about his being a liability in the
wilderness, surfaced. His determined heart, however, refused
to falter and by the sixth day out, when they reached the
falls of the Spokane River where camps of Coeur d'Alene
and Spokane Indians were fishing, Cataldo was renewed.
Giorda chided him for an appetite like a wolf's, suggesting
that if he had consumption it was certainly an active con-
dition.⁶ The Indians, however, were blind to this improvement in Cataldo's health and dubbed him "Dry Salmon,"
doubtlessly referring to his still thin body, made taut by hard
work and the exhausting journey.

Joseph M. Cataldo, S.J. An undated photograph believed to have been taken in 1877, when Cataldo was appointed general superior of the Rocky Mountain Missions. Courtesy Oregon Province Archives, Gonzaga University.

Sacred Heart Mission, just east of Lake Coeur d'Alene, was Cataldo's new home.[7] For the next year he studied the Kalispel, or Flathead, language. Cataldo's teacher, Joseph Carauna, S.J., used as his textbook a manuscript prepared by Father Mengarini before he left the Pacific Northwest for California. Cataldo was a willing, and previously tutored, student and so quickly mastered the language.

But a year is a long time for an ambitious young man, and at the end of that time Cataldo was eager to test his ability among the Indians. On his journey to Sacred Heart Mission the previous year Cataldo had been impressed by the Spokane tribe and their apparent earnestness in having a missionary visit them. He now requested his superior's permission to be that man. Giorda reluctantly allowed a stay of one or two weeks, but certainly Cataldo must return before the snows clogged the mountain passes between the falls and the mission.

In several ways this initial excursion to the Indians tested Cataldo's commitment. In the beginning he found the abundant waterways of the Inland Northwest more easily appreciated for beauty than for crossing. Fording the Spokane River, Cataldo got "somewhat scared" and "very wet," perhaps an indication, he thought, that he had kept too busy with studies to the deterioration of his basic trail skills. Even more discouraging, however, was the Indians' reception. The Spokanes were at the falls busy catching salmon, and when Cataldo contacted them they were abrupt in their response: "Do you think you will convert our people in ten days?" they admonished him. "Come some other time and we will be ready to listen to the teachings," they told him, "now we are too busy." Still, the Indians promised that if Cataldo would spend the winter with them on nearby Peone Prairie they would build him a warm cabin, and he could preach to them.[8]

Cataldo was determined to be true to the Spokanes. He returned to Sacred Heart and lobbied incessantly for permission to be allowed to winter with the Indians. Reluctantly they gave him that opportunity, and by November, 1866,

Cataldo was living with the Upper Spokanes in a tent on Peone Prairie a few miles to the northeast of the Spokane falls. It was at once a frustrating, exhilarating, and exhausting experience. Certain headmen turned sour toward Cataldo and would not allow him among them saying that their chief, Spokan Garry, hated Roman Catholics, and though he was away for six months hunting in Montana, he might punish them upon his return. Cataldo compromised the problem by offering to build his own cabin and then burn it upon his departure if it later brought Garry's disapproval. A subchief agreed, and Cataldo spent the long winter months in a small cabin he dedicated to Saint Michael on December 8, 1866.

Cataldo literally worked from sunrise to sunset that winter. A typical day began with an early-morning mass, followed by housekeeping chores, two two-hour classes for children, evening prayers, a sermon, and finally, instructions for adults which lasted until about 11:00 P.M. Though he seemed to thrive on the pace and even felt he was gaining the acceptance of the tribe, it was with some sense of relief that Cataldo received orders in May, 1867, to report to Saint Ignatius Mission in Montana.

When Cataldo arrived in Montana after an eventful seventeen-day journey, he learned that the orders he received were originally intended for another priest but had been directed to him by mistake. Before Cataldo could retrace his steps back across the mountains, another message came in, this one stating that the Jesuits had agreed to Bishop A. M. A. Blanchet's persistent request for them to sponsor a mission among the Nez Percé tribe. Inasmuch as Cataldo did not really have an assignment at Saint Ignatius, he was designated to open this new mission. He spent the summer preparing for the challenge, and in November, 1867, presented himself to the Nez Percé tribe at Lapwai, Idaho Territory.[9]

The Nez Percés had been a party, with the Flatheads, to the original appeal in the 1830s for a priest to live among the western Indians. Captain Benjamin Bonneville, a visitor to the Northwest in 1832, confirmed their sincerity when he noted the presence of "a rude calendar of the feasts and festivals of the Romish Church, and some traces of its ceremonials" among the Nez Percés.[10] De Smet contacted the Nez Percés in 1840 and made many converts, but there was little association between the tribe and the pioneer priest after that.

Slightly earlier, in 1836, the Reverend Henry Harmon Spalding and his wife began their Presbyterian mission among the Nez Percés at Lapwai on behalf of the American Board of Foreign Missions. Spalding had an uneasy time of it. He had to endure the Indians' indifference and sometimes outright hostility, and all the while he was being belittled for his efforts by Asa Smith, a jealous fellow Presbyterian missionary sixty miles away at Kamiah on the Clearwater River. Both of these missions were maintained until 1848, when the events following the Whitman massacre encouraged their closure. The residual effects of the deserted Presbyterian missions, however, still boded ill for Cataldo.

The former mission stations at Kamiah and Lapwai continued to attract Nez Percés. While both of these locations were ostensibly Christian, other bands of the tribe remained secluded in remote areas of the Snake, Wallowa, and Salmon river valleys. Eventually the Christian and "heathen" factions polarized, and each side treated the other as a threat.

The religious variance among the Nez Percés was accentuated by the Treaty of 1855, the tribe's first agreement with the United States. There were no land transfers, but one man had to be acknowledged as a principal chief for administrative purposes of the federal government and when this turned out to be The Lawyer, leader of the Christian faction of Kamiah, a further split in the tribe was inevitable. It finally occurred in 1863 when the government sought a new treaty, this time involving land cessions. Lawyer signed the treaty as chief of the tribe, ceding 95 percent of the reservation, nearly all of it occupied by the "heathens," while the Christian Indians' lands went unaffected. The opposition group, led by Old Joseph and White Bird, returned to their traditional villages in the river valleys anyway, thereby sow-

ing the seed of discontent that would blossom into the Nez
Percé War of 1877.[11]

Church and state may be deemed separate under the United
States Constitution, but that was seldom the case on Western
Indian reservations after the Civil War. In 1862 the Reverend
Henry Spalding returned to the Nez Percé reservation as
superintendent of education. But this time there was an In-
dian agent and he happened to be James O'Neill, a Catholic.
When the Idaho Territorial Legislature moved the capital
from Lewiston to Boise in 1864, O'Neill was, for all practical purposes, free of political constraint. Accordingly, in
September 1865 he dismissed the sixty-two-year-old Spalding.
Bishop Blanchet was, of course, eager to use this opportunity
to place a Catholic missionary at Lapwai. Father Charles
Richard, an oblate of Mary Immaculate, was sent to Lewiston
from Yakima in 1865, and he bought property for a future
church. His efforts to gain entry to the reservation, however,
were constantly thwarted by Lawyer, who was steadfastly
anti-Catholic. Blanchet persevered and in 1867 he persuaded
the Jesuits to take on the responsibilities of the first Roman
Catholic mission among the Nez Percés.[12]

There is some reason to believe that when he sent Father
Cataldo to the Nez Percé agency, Urban Grassi, S.J. the superior of the missions, understood that Agent O'Neill would
make it convenient for his Jesuits to take over the government
day school for Indians. That was not, however, the reality
of the situation. O'Neill was cautious, for there was no great
groundswell for Catholic instruction among the majority of
the tribe. O'Neill asked Cataldo to remain off the reservation
in Lewiston for a few weeks until he could call a council and
encourage tribal approval.

Cataldo understood the problem. His appointment, he felt,
had been made "too late; for the greater number of those
who had been well-disposed towards the faith were now dead,
and hatred of the Catholic religion, infidelity and vice of
every description had fearfully increased among those poor
Indians." Even as the Spokanes had once offered him shelter

if he would come to their camp and then had to be cajoled into living up to their promise, so too he knew that the Nez Percés were reluctant recipients of his services. O'Neill held a tribal council at which he proposed that Father Cataldo assume duties at the school, but predictably, Lawyer was adamant in refusal and the Catholic Nez Percés were impotent to resist his intimidation. Cataldo was advised to remain in Lewiston "until the Indians should become disposed" to receive him well.[13]

In 1868 a small chapel was constructed in Lewiston and consecrated to Saint Stanislaus. Cataldo then invited the Nez Percés to come to him if he could not go to them. To his dismay, few responded. The priest found that old men would not consent to be baptized, and "those who frequented Catholic prayers did not differ from their neighbors, but like them were the slaves of lust, gambling, drunkenness and lying, and some of them were living in actual polygamy." Only the children seemed receptive to the Word of God.[14]

There was hope anew when Dr. Robert Newell became the Indian agent on October 1, 1868, but it soon became clear to Cataldo that Newell too was reluctant to upset the Indian status quo by offering Cataldo an official position while Lawyer remained so opposed to Catholics on the reservation. In spite of this, in 1869, Cataldo did manage to build a small chapel on the north bank of the Clearwater River, about one mile above the agency, on the land of Hair Cut Short, or Stuptup, an Indian sympathetic to the young missionary's plight. Lewiston miners, rather than the timid Catholic Nez Percés, furnished their construction skills for the building, which was named Saint Joseph's Chapel.[15]

The following year Father Grassi recalled Cataldo to Sacred Heart. Cataldo felt that his superior was withdrawing him because he had "met with a few accidents." One such mishap involved falling through a hole in the ice on the Clearwater River, the current nearly sweeping the priest to eternity. And in March, Cataldo suffered a broken leg when his horse fell on him during a tricky mountain traverse near Orofino. "Dry Salmon" of the Spokanes was now "Broken Leg" to the Nez

Percés. But the action taken by Grassi was because of more than these incidents, and Cataldo knew it. Even he had to admit that the "apparent sterility of the mission," did not warrant his full-time presence. Henceforth Cataldo was allowed annual or semiannual visits to the Nez Percés, but took permanent station elsewhere.[16]

Abandonment was not an uncommon device used by the Jesuits to increase Indian ardor for conversion. It was not totally unexpected, then, when the Nez Percés sent an emissary, the only Nez Percé man Cataldo had baptized, saying, ". . . now they are sorry for the past; they beg you to return." What was surprising was that the Indian added, "You must come without delay, if you do not want to lose most of your people, for everyone now at the Agency is a preacher."[17]

Recent developments among the Nez Percés were significant. In 1871 the first of the agents appointed under the Indian policy of President Ulysses S. Grant arrived at Lapwai. Grant's program involved the distribution of the various Indian agencies to religious denominations, and the Presbyterians gratefully accepted assignment to the Nez Percé Reservation. The Board of Foreign Missions recommended John B. Monteith as agent and the Reverend Henry Spalding as teacher, both to be paid by the federal government. Monteith was the son of a pioneer Presbyterian minister, and Spalding had established the original Presbyterian mission among the Nez Percés in 1836 and was about to enter his third term on the reservation. Monteith arrived about the same time as the Yakima evangelist George Waters initiated a Methodist revival among the Nez Percés. Finally, there was Lawyer, who seemed to have less influence in the tribe and was nearly replaced as head chief by a non-Christian. Lawyer deemed it advantageous to support the Presbyterians, but there were now Methodists too, and presently the Catholic Indians sought Cataldo. The reservation was virtually in the throes of several full-fledged revivals.[18]

Cataldo was not immediately free to return to the Nez Percé reservation, but in late April, 1872, while he was visiting Lewiston, the Catholic Nez Percés turned out in large

numbers to convince him of their sincerity. In the next month
he baptized about fifty Nez Percés, revised his itinerary to
visit some villages on Sweetwater Creek, and did everything
among the Indians but remain with them permanently. The
Catholic tribesmen desired a missionary, Cataldo wished them
as his flock, but there was a major roadblock to such an
arrangement: Agent John B. Monteith.

Monteith refused to allow Cataldo to hold meetings in the
agency school or to build a larger church than St. Joseph's.
He even sought to prohibit Cataldo from actually coming
onto the reservation. "This being a Presbyterian Agency and
Mission," Monteith wrote the Commissioner of Indian Affairs
on May 5, 1872, "have I the right . . . to exercise such
control . . . as will enable me to prohibit the teaching of the
Catholic faith?"[19]

Monteith had as a foe, Territorial Delegate Stephen S.
Fenn, and Cataldo had his friends, so the correspondence
against Monteith was vigorous. One detractor attested that
Monteith unfairly pressured the Indians into believing that
"the Great Chief, President Grant, wants them to be Presbyterians." Secretary of the Interior Columbus Delano took
the matter under serious consideration and finally decided
that the Catholics could have a church on the reservation
as long as it was built without government funds. Cataldo
privately believed that "the persecution against the Catholic
Nez Percés had been . . . so evident to the public" that permission was granted "out of shame."[20]

The location for this hard-won church was four miles up
what became known as Mission Creek in a little valley dominated by Chief Slickpoo, a Catholic convert. A fund drive
among Lewiston citizens and miners, plus the Indians themselves, enabled the new Saint Joseph's Church to be completed in September, 1874. Cataldo felt vindicated when
the whites of Lewiston eagerly contributed to the building
of his church. Time and again, he said, he was stopped on
the street and given a donation with the explanation, "It is
not exactly for the sake of the church, nor for the sake of
the Indians, but for the sake of our common American free-

dom." Monteith, the Presbyterians, and the government, people said, must be taught a lesson. According to Cataldo some of his most generous contributors were Presbyterians who were ashamed for the "unchristian behavior" of their own ministers. Perhaps the classic statement came from the frontier citizen who said "Father, this is not for love for the Indians, but for your religion opposed by the [Presbyterian] preachers. If it were for the Indians, I would rather ask you to buy ammunition, and shoot them; yet I want to see them free to practice their religion."[21]

Cataldo was not the first pastor at Saint Joseph's Mission, though he certainly deserved that distinction. Instead, in November, 1875, Anthony Morvillo, S.J., became the resident pastor, and Cataldo moved on to new duties.

In a manner of speaking, the Society of Jesus was grooming Cataldo as the new De Smet. De Smet died in 1873, but even before that date his order sought in another man that same combination of empathy with the Indians plus administrative talent. The Belgian, of course, had founded the Jesuit missions in the Northwest, but after six years in the field he became procurator for the missions from a desk in Saint Louis. Though he did make several more pilgrimages to the West, some at the request of the government, it was from Saint Louis that De Smet continued to supply and fund the Rocky Mountain Missions even when they no longer were a part of the Missouri Province. Cataldo, too, was accepted and respected by the Indians with whom he worked, and his administrative talents were even greater than those of De Smet.

Cataldo's continuing efforts on behalf of the Nez Percés did nothing to lessen his reputation as an administrator. Having won permission for a church on the reservation, Cataldo now agitated for a school. Again the issue was hotly debated in the bureaucratic offices in Washington, D.C., and in November, 1875, the Catholics were granted permission for a school building on the reservation, though again at their own expense.[22]

The final altercation between Cataldo and Monteith was

also the event which shattered the Nez Percé tribe, the War of 1877. The 1863 treaty ceded most of the Nez Percé Reservation to the government for increased cash annuities. Those bands of the tribe whose villages lay in the surrendered area refused not only to sign the treaty but also to obey it. Most notable in this group of headmen was Old Joseph, whose lands lay in the Wallowa Valley of Oregon. Though he was in technical violation of the treaty, the federal government took no overt actions to remove Old Joseph and his followers to the reduced reservation.

Old Joseph passed away in 1871, and to his son Joseph fell the difficult task of easing tensions with the increasing number of whites entering the Wallowa Valley. The Custer massacre of 1876 caused reverberations all across the frontier, and from that time on the nonreservation Nez Percés were heavily pressed to enter the set boundaries of the reservation. In January, 1877, Cataldo was among the Indians of the Nez Percé Reservation when he received an urgent call from near Captain John Creek to baptize a dying man. He was successful in reaching the man before his death, converted some others, and then, feeling confident, continued on to Joseph's band, which was camping in the vicinity. Cataldo knew this band to be "infidels" but friendly to priests. He had a meal with Joseph and later urged him toward Catholicism, but Cataldo made no comment on current political affairs. This was normal, for Cataldo felt that he would compromise his spiritual mission to the Indians if ever he advised them on civil matters. He made it a practice never to make recommendations in temporal affairs.[23]

In February, Cataldo was giving a series of religious services on the Umatilla Reservation, 180 miles east of Lapwai. By coincidence Ollikut, Joseph's brother, was also present, apparently sounding out Umatilla opinions about reservation conditions. Word of these meetings came to Monteith, and on February 28, 1877, he penned a scurrilous letter to the commissioner of Indian affairs, flatly stating that Cataldo "has been trying to influence Joseph against coming on the reserve." This letter was published on April 28, in the *Lewiston*

Teller. Cataldo denied the charges in his own letter to the press on May 5, and the same edition carried an editorial on the matter.[24]

The people of Lewiston overwhelmingly supported Cataldo in his disclaimer of interference in the matter of the non-reservation Indians. But the events of the next month kept Monteith's charge alive. Government-sponsored meetings were held with Joseph in May, promises were made, then broken, and by mid-June there were murders, a pitched battle, and Joseph and his band were in retreat headed for Canada.[25]

For the next two months Cataldo was constantly on the move, "up and down, from Lapwai to Lewiston, and thence north to [Sacred Heart] Mission, and back, in order to reassure both Indians and Whites that there was no danger . . ." of a general Indian outbreak. At first Cataldo reported, "The imagination of some people was so fervid . . ." that it was believed that Joseph and his followers were Catholics, and the mission Indians of the Spokane and Coeur d'Alene tribes were going to join with them and kill all Protestant whites. Later that was seen to be simply not true, and Cataldo was commended for his quick action in communicating with the whites and Indians of the region so that a general misunderstanding was avoided. Cataldo and his fellow Jesuits were also participants in an Indian congress held by General Frank Wheaton near the Spokane Falls in August, 1877, that effectively "tranquillized" both whites and Indians.[26]

The War of 1877 closed the door on Cataldo's hopes for the conversion of the Nez Percé tribe. Some few Indians would be received into the church, but the tribe in general "remained imbittered [*sic*] against the Whites, for their injustice and cruelty, and therefore they hated anything coming from the Whites, and so they also turned against the Christian religion, even those, who had been favorable to our church." In short, Cataldo reflected, "our hopes of converting the whole tribe were shattered."[27]

The Nez Percé experience was a sobering, maturing influence on Cataldo's future relationship with Indians. In the decade he was associated with the tribe their Catholic popu-

lation grew to 300, and two churches were established, one
at Lewiston, the other at Slickpoo on the reservation. There
was satisfaction in these accomplishments, but what Cataldo
saw as the negative, regressive attitude of the Indians after
the War of 1877 seemed to have defeated whatever gains
had been achieved. "What remained for the Missionaries was
to pray for the poor, unfortunate, deceived, robbered [sic]
Nez Percé Indians," Cataldo believed.[28] And for the missions
in general a reevaluation of directions was necessary.

Cataldo's opinion on the condition of the missions was of
paramount importance. On June 15, 1877, while he was in
conference with his superior at Sacred Heart Mission, Cataldo
received two letters. One summarized the actions of Chief
Joseph's warriors with the conclusion that war had begun.
The other letter was from Rome, where on December 27,
1876, the forty-year-old Cataldo had been named the sixth
superior of the Rocky Mountain Missions. Cataldo would now
have an opportunity to redirect the Jesuit presence among the
Indians of the Northwest along the lines of his own beliefs.

Under Cataldo's jurisdiction were forty-three Jesuits, twenty-
three of whom were priests. At first Cataldo used Sacred
Heart Mission as his headquarters, but in 1878 the boundaries
of the Coeur d'Alene Reservation were relocated, and the
mission was left outside the reserve. The Jesuits followed
the Indians to a new location at De Smet, Idaho, and Sacred
Heart was abandoned.[29] Cataldo did not find the location of
the new mission convenient and soon began traveling around
from one to another of the seven mission stations under his
authority.

Though he was encouraged by the modest success of the
missionary effort among the Montana tribes, Cataldo was
generally displeased by the religious attitude of most of the
other tribes within the Rocky Mountain Missions. After the
War of 1877 the Nez Percé tribe was only one example of
a dissipating interest by the Indians in the Black Robes' theology. Cataldo's task was to revitalize that interest.

The original concept of the Rocky Mountain Missions, when
established by De Smet, was that of a chain of "reductions."

First introduced by the Society of Jesus during the 1700s among the Guarani Indians of present-day Paraguay, South America, reductions were interconnected missions operating as a sort of confederation. The emphasis was on education and communal activity, especially in agriculture. The Paraguay experiment lasted a century and a half before it was dismantled by a jealous white population. It then became the model for the Rocky Mountain Missions.[30]

By 1880 it was clear to Cataldo that the dream of a resurgence of the reduction in the Rocky Mountain missions was impossible. True, each of the missions established by the Jesuits was independent, with church, farms, and an Indian camp, and each was also linked with the other missions of the society in the Northwest. But Cataldo's experience as a missionary among the Spokanes and Nez Percés for ten years had shown him some of the hazards of the reduction concept.

The Indians of the Northwest could not rely on agriculture even when supplemented with livestock. It was necessary, as well as traditional, for them to hunt buffalo during one season of the year, dig for camas roots on the prairies at another season, and fish for salmon at the falls in a third period. All of this took them away from the mission environment, and at the same time placed a strain on Jesuit manpower requirements. The result was slow progress by the missionaries to eradicate such problems as gambling, superstition, revenge, and polygamy. By 1880 the Indians were fenced in on reservations and no longer free to travel by the seasons, but the damage was done.

The crux of the matter, as perceived by Cataldo, was that the Indian was originally drawn to the Black Robe by a desire for protection or status or gifts, and he stayed only so long as the "magic" of the ornate Catholic ceremonies, vestments, and symbols could hold his attention. After that he could be sullen, resentful, and unapproachable. The too few Jesuits in the Northwest were just not enough to do the work.

Even more damaging to the goals of the Jesuits was the lack of time. Though slow to explore the Northwest, the white

man was quick to settle it. By the 1860s gold and abundant
farmland brought waves of white men to the region, and there
were railroads in their wake. The Indian had a greater
capacity to learn the sins of Christianity than its blessings,
and the rapid arrival of white pioneers in the Northwest
doomed the reductions. They were effective only in their
element of isolation; amid the turmoil of advancing civilization
they were useless. The Grant peace policy, Cataldo felt, was
the final blow that destroyed the old mission system. Catholic
natives, converted at great sacrifice, were now arbitrarily
assigned to other denominations. Moreover, Catholic clerics
and seminarians, though initially aroused by "feelings of
zeal," soon accepted the situation decreed by the government
and ceased to volunteer for the Indian mission ministry.[31]

Cataldo's recommendation and the direction in which he
thrust the missions of the Rocky Mountains diverted some of
the energies of the society to the white settlers. His experience
in Lewiston, where the whites had been so very helpful on
numerous occasions in the establishment of churches, was
influential. Cataldo made his intentions clear in an open
letter to all provincials and superiors of the Society in America.
"If we do not attend to their spiritual welfare," Cataldo wrote
of the white settlers, "their bad example will so completely
influence the Indians, even the Catholic Indians, that in a
few years they will be entirely lost to the Church and become
infidels."[32] Indians imitated good examples as well as bad,
so a white population imbued with Christian goodness was of
primary importance.

Another way to civilize and Christianize the Indian through
osmosis was in the field of education. Indian and white boys
would be schooled together in a central college. Cataldo was
not unmindful that the money for such a school would have
to come from whites, most of whom would contribute very
little to an institution built entirely for Indians.

This redirection of society commitment in the Northwest
did not mean an abandonment of the Indian missions. As a
matter of fact, Cataldo planned on reopening closed missions,
establishing some new ones, and building several reservation

boarding schools as well as the "prestigious central college" for white and Indian boys. Cataldo hoped to increase his work force by appeals to other superiors, and the Pope, if necessary. He would also recruit Catholic nuns for the schools and develop a special Jesuit residence to train and prepare young American priests in necessary mission skills and Indian languages.[33]

These were grandiose plans, indeed, but the record shows that Cataldo, who remained the superior in the Northwest for sixteen years when the normal term was three, exceeded even his own expectations. The number of Jesuits increased threefold, the mission stations increased from seven to eleven, three orders of nuns came to the inland Northwest, a novitiate was dedicated at De Smet, Idaho, and no fewer than five mission boarding schools for Indians, two prep schools for whites, and two colleges were founded.

Inasmuch as Cataldo did not consider Sacred Heart Mission a usable headquarters, he favored a new site. In 1871, six years after Cataldo first met Indians at the Spokane River falls, white settlers took up residence on the banks. In 1878 they laid out a town called Spokane Falls. The Northern Pacific Railroad was expected to arrive by 1881. This was the location chosen by Cataldo not only for his mission headquarters, but also for his boys' college.

The school was of pressing importance. In 1880 the Methodists founded the Training School of Indian Youth at Forest Grove, Oregon, under the direction of United States Army Captain Melville G. Wilkinson. The Catholic hierarchy resented this institution, saying it took the best Catholic students on the reservations and turned them into Methodists at taxpayer expense. For example, in 1881 seventy-six Indian students were enrolled at Forest Grove, but only sixteen came from Methodist assigned reservations. The following year ninety-one Indians were in attendance, and only fifteen were sent from Methodist reservations. Eventually pressures brought to bear by the Catholic Indian Bureau forced the closing of this school, but in the interim Cataldo ordered that a Catholic academy be established at Saint Michael's Mission, on Peone

Prairie. Twenty-five Spokane Indian students enrolled the first year.[34]

Meanwhile, Cataldo hoped to purchase two half sections of land along the river at Spokane Falls. But the anticipated entrance of the railroad into the town caused such land speculation that he was able to get only one parcel for his college along the river, and another eight miles north on Peone Prairie at Saint Michael's Mission. Cataldo also purchased three city lots on the south bank of the river for a church for whites. On Christmas Day, 1881, Catholic mass was offered before 300 Indians at Saint Michael's Mission; a similar service in downtown Spokane Falls attracted a dozen white settlers. Cataldo's plan of proselytizing both Indians and whites had begun.[35]

Playing both sides against the middle, Cataldo finally got his college. From the bishop of Nesqually [Seattle] Diocese he received congratulations for having bought land "to build an Indian Boarding-School in order to rescue our poor Catholic Indian boys from the hands of the biggoted fellow in Oregon."[36] Cataldo appreciated the laudatory remarks, but he also requested, and received, monetary support from the bishop for his Indian school. Cataldo then sought, and received, financial assistance from the citizens of Spokane Falls who feared that without their input the college might become an exclusive Indian academy. This contrivance was necessary, it seemed, for Cataldo wanted whites to attend his college, because "if we do not insist on our schools, and show the Indians that our schools are good not only for them but also for the whites, within a few years the fruit of forty years of missionary endeavor will be rotted." Construction difficulties delayed the opening of the brick building which was known as Gonzaga College until 1887, but the school was effectively begun in 1882 as part of Cataldo's overall plan.[37]

During the autumn of 1884, while Gonzaga College was still being built, Cataldo attended the Third Plenary Council of Baltimore. Appearing before this deliberative body was a duty rather than a desire for Cataldo, but as superior of the Northwest Jesuits it was necessary. It was also an opportunity. Bishop Aegidius Junger of Nesqually needed more priests, as did Cataldo. The two churchmen laid a plan whereby Cataldo would be requested to accompany Junger to Rome, ostensibly to offer support to a prelate struck with illness, but in reality so that the two could join forces and emphasize to Pope Leo XIII and the Jesuit father general the need for more recruits to staff the mission posts in the Pacific Northwest. So it was that, at the conclusion of the Baltimore Conference, Cataldo proceeded to Italy. The elation of a return to his homeland, however, was twice spoiled when Acting Superior General Anton Anderledy totally rejected Cataldo's appeal, and when Cataldo received a cablegram in Rome informing him that Louis Ruellan, S.J., whom he had left in Spokane as vice-superior of missions, had died on January 7, 1885.

The shock was great. All over his missions the men were either dying or were old enough to die soon. When the father general in Rome saw how deeply upset his Rocky Mountain Mission superior was at this news, he relented and allowed Cataldo a single recruiting trip across Europe. Up to this time the Turin Province of the Society of Jesus had sponsored the Rocky Mountain Missions and since 1854 had been sending its men to America for work in the far-western frontier. But now Cataldo could go to any Jesuit house on the Continent and accept anyone willing and fit for the work. That summer in Italy, France, the Low Countries, and Great Britain provided some thirty-one Jesuits for Cataldo's Indian missions, white churches, and boys' college. Cataldo himself referred to his 1885 trip as "the jump that saved the Rocky Mountain Mission."[38]

Given new life by this young blood from Europe, the Northwest missions prospered. Indian schools and missions were the prime beneficiaries of this transfusion, but hospitals, an orphanage, and another college were also recipients. Even a whole new mission field was opened as the Jesuits from the Rocky Mountain Missions assumed the responsibility for Alaska in 1887. In addition the Sisters of Providence responded to Cataldo's appeal and came to the missions. Two years

later, in 1888, they were followed by the Sisters of the Holy
Names and two years after that by four Sisters of Saint Francis
in Philadelphia. In 1891, Cataldo established a Jesuit novitiate
at De Smet, Idaho. In the future, Cataldo determined, American missionary work would be done by American born and
educated priests. Cataldo always considered the novitiate the
chief contribution of his tenure as superior.[39]

Released from the duties of superior after sixteen years,
Cataldo was not yet ready for retirement. This was fortunate,
since the new superior, Leopold Van Gorp, S.J., needed his
assistance. Cataldo became a troubleshooter for Van Gorp
and his successors, handling difficult situations, prompting
projects where momentum slowed, initiating ideas, and generally serving as a roving visitor or inspector. The first three
years, 1893-96, were spent in eastern Montana on the Crow
Indian Reservation at Saint Francix Xavier Mission.[40]

His next assignment was to the farthest reaches of the
province. When he was superior, Cataldo accepted Alaska as
an extension of the missionary activities of his Rocky Mountain
Missions. Van Gorp was relatively unknowledgeable about
the condition of affairs there, so in 1896, Cataldo was asked
to make a complete inspection of the missions and report
back to the superior. Cataldo passed his sixtieth birthday
during his fourteen months in the northland.

Between 1897 and 1901, Catldo was at Saint Andrew's
School, on the Umatilla Indian Reservation, roughly twelve
miles from Pendleton, Oregon.[41] This was very pleasing to
Cataldo, for he knew these Indians of the Cayuse, Umatilla,
and Walla Walla tribes from his previous experience with
the Nez Percés. He also knew their language, which was
essentially an offshoot or dialect of the Nez Percé tongue.
Best of all, Cataldo was pleased to be in contact once again
with the Nez Percés.

Though disappointed in the Nez Percés after the War of
1877, Cataldo had not forsaken them. As superior he made
certain that Saint Joseph's, at Slickpoo, was staffed, and
he himself made frequent visits. Father Anthony Morvillo
remained at the mission until 1888, and he was succeeded

One month before Cataldo died in April, 1928, the Nez Percé and other tribes met at Saint Andrew's Mission, in Umatilla, Oregon, to pay tribute to Cataldo's diamond jubilee as a Jesuit priest and his ninety-second birthday. Courtesy Oregon Province Archives, Gonzaga University.

by Aloysius Soer, S.J., who stayed on until 1905. Soer, a native of Holland, was recruited by Cataldo on the European trip in 1885 and was much loved by the Indians. Still they tended to gravitate to Cataldo whenever he was near.

Billy Luke, a Nez Percé chief, was sometimes a visitor. From him Cataldo learned of the distressing situation surrounding the Catholic Nez Percés. Cataldo's own plan of broadening missionary duties to include attention to white Catholics had been used by the Nez Percés as an excuse for "slacking and relaxation in their religious duties." And there was the matter of allotment. The General Allotment Act sponsored by Senator Henry L. Dawes was signed into law in 1887. Under its provisions Indian reservations were distributed to tribesmen, generally in lots of 160 acres each, and then the surplus land was sold to the government and opened to general settlement. Allotments were assigned to the Nez Percés between 1887 and 1893, and in 1895 the government opened the reservation to whites, "who literally inundated the country, and entirely drownded the Indians," said Cataldo.[42]

Cataldo believed the foundation of a Catholic school among the Nez Percés would be a proper step to not only their reconversion but also their tribal revitalization. Beginning in 1878 a few devoted Nez Percé families had sent their children several hundred miles north to a boarding school on the Colville Reservation. Later the Coeur d'Alene Mission School became closer and more convenient. But eventually the parents lost heart over the long distances and the absence of their children, and they stopped sending them altogether. Education of the Indians was a cardinal precept of Cataldo's philosophy of bringing the red man to white man's civilization, but the establishment of a school among the Nez Percés, where only about 300 out of a tribe of 4,500 were Catholic, was difficult for even him to justify. The situation was made even more complex by a residual effect of Grant's old peace policy.

The Grant policy had been effectively rescinded in 1877, but for decades thereafter its legacy remained to pollute

Indian affairs. The assignment of reservations to denominations in 1870 began a bitter struggle between Protestants and Catholics over the control of Indian schools. The Nez Percé Reservation, of course, was not spared that conflict. The Protestants used their Indian Rights Association to press Congress for a totally public school system on the reservations, to the exclusion of all religious denominations, including themselves. The Bureau of Catholic Indian Missions countered the proposal, but direct appropriations by Congress for contract schools among the Indians were cut each year from 1896 to 1899 and finally ended completely in 1900. The meaning of this to the Nez Percé children was that if they did not attend a Catholic school funded by independent means they would be forced into government classrooms with all the expected secularism.[43]

For a year Cataldo engaged in a lively correspondence with his superior, now George De la Motte, S.J., and Bishop A. J. Glorieux of the Boise diocese. From August to November, 1901, there were personal visits, consultations among the three, and plans for the all-important fund raising. At last a contract was let to a Lewiston firm, and construction of a Catholic school for Nez Percé children was begun in August, 1902, at Slickpoo.[44]

The opening of the new school in March, 1903, was a proud moment for Cataldo, but one he missed, for he was back in Alaska. For a time he was at Nulato, then he was at Nome. It was a short assignment, however. Partly it was the severe cold that forced the aging Cataldo back to Spokane, but it was also a nagging concern that he had about the worsening condition of the Nez Percés and other tribes of the region. Writing on board a steamer en route to Seattle from Nome, Cataldo suggested to his provincial that "I could be easily sent to the more needy Indian missions," for their wants are great and it is a "grave mistake of those who believe our Indian missions are finished."[45] It was with a feeling of satisfaction that upon his return Cataldo, now beyond his fiftieth year as a Jesuit, was assigned to the Nez Percé Reservation.

Cataldo was deeply moved by the condition of the Nez Percés. The school at Slickpoo was technically open but effectively closed for lack of teachers. Three nuns did all the teaching, cleaning, sewing, laundering, and "prefecting" for the whole school of boys and girls. Without the continuing presence of a school, noted Cataldo, many Indians "have become Protestants in order to be able to change wives, and many others have given themselves to all sorts of vices and are worse than infidels; few remained true Christians." He concluded his report to the provincial: "I saw and heard such spiritual desolation that it made me cry for sorrow."

The old missionary sought help from De la Motte, but he replied that the matter was in the hands of the bishop of Boise. The bishop, however, offered no assistance and seemed in Cataldo's opinion only "to 'unload' himself of his responsibilities." Frustrated, Cataldo made another recruiting trip, this time to Philadelphia and Archbishop Patrick J. Ryan, who had long been a friend to the missions. Cataldo, still persuasive, returned with a dozen postulants to the Sisters of Saint Joseph, with a promise of more to come.[46]

When he turned seventy years of age, Cataldo was sent to San Jose, California, where Holy Family Parish had "great need" of an Italian-speaking priest. They received one who knew Italian plus nineteen other languages including a variety of Indian and Eskimo tongues.[47] Cataldo was clearly being ushered into retirement.

But Cataldo did not remain long in California. In 1908, after only a year's absence, he was needed once more in the Northwest. At first he was an assistant to the young pastor at Saint Mary's Church in Pendleton, but when the pastor died, Cataldo took over. Much of his time was spent among the nearby Indians on the Umatilla Reservation. Then in 1914, Cataldo moved onto the Umatilla Reservation when a replacement was found for him in Pendleton. It was here that Cataldo revised and published his *Jesus-Christ-Nim (The Life of Jesus Christ)* in the Nez Percé language.[48]

The next year Cataldo returned to the Nez Percé mission at Slickpoo for the third and final time. The mission was now run-down. The deterioration had begun in 1905, he noted, when the "Indians had promised to help, but we could no longer count on their promises, especially when they had lost all fervor." Bees inhabited the walls of the rectory, the garden was overgrown, and the once lush orchard was withered.[49] In actuality, the Nez Percé mission did not pull its weight. For all the years of dedication by the Society, the Nez Percé Catholics remained small in number and fluctuating in commitment. To assign to them an eighty-year-old priest, no matter how extraordinary he might be, and no matter how often he would be assisted by brothers and scholastics, was a sign of the situation.

The mission deteriorated even further during Cataldo's loving presence. A disastrous fire in August, 1916, destroyed the convent and school building. Happily the students were still on vacation, and the nuns were at mass, so no one was injured. A group of farmers managed to put up some "sheds" to house the homeless, and while the nuns envisioned this to be only a temporary situation, it was not. It could not have been otherwise, Cataldo appraised the situation, when the provincial himself "seems to have no confidence in the future of this mission," and discouraged the sisters from staying.[50] These same sheds caught fire again in October, 1924, and this time six boys died. In addition, Father Cataldo broke his hip and leg in January, 1924, injuries that effectively crippled him. Though the public response to these tragedies was immediate and generous, and the boy's dormitory was rebuilt with fireproof materials, Father Cataldo was disconsolate at what he considered "the most heart-rendering [sic] of all [my] years on the Indian Missions."[51]

In his efforts to rebuild the Slickpoo mission, Cataldo solicited funds far and wide. It quickly became apparent that his most salable commodity was himself. Potential donors were enthralled by the humility of the ancient missionary who was himself a page out of history. The old man, now able to hobble around only on crutches, became the center of a series of celebrations. Lewiston turned out on February 20, 1928, to celebrate Cataldo's seventy-fifth anniversary as a Jesuit with a mass at Saint Stanislaus Church, which he had established sixty years before. A month later, on March 17, over two thousand citizens joined Cataldo on his ninety-first birthday in Spokane, a city he helped to found.[52]

And then the celebrations were over. Cataldo wanted to return to the Indians. He was driven to Slickpoo, his home. In April he went to Saint Andrew's on the Umatilla Reservation and there celebrated Easter mass. That evening he was taken ill and entered the hospital at Pendleton. He died the next evening. The Indians attended a funeral at Saint Andrew's, and others in Spokane. Father Cataldo was laid to his final rest at Saint Michael's Cemetery, on Peone Prairie, not far from the spot where he had begun his first missionary work among the Spokanes in 1866. Only one life had ended, but several lifetimes of work were finalized.

Retelling the life of Joseph M. Cataldo, S.J., is in many ways less biography than hagiography. Superlatives come easy when describing a sixty-three-year missionary career in a ninety-one-year life span. Cataldo's career included intimate contact with a half-dozen Northwest Indian tribes, the foundation of missions for Indians, churches for whites, and schools for both. He was both a worker in the mission fields and an administrator setting goals. He received his bruises but also his kudos. He was present at the Nez Percé War of 1877, and he saw a city grow up around his Gonzaga College. He did it all—except with the Nez Percés. Cataldo initiated the Jesuit Catholic response to the Nez Percés in 1867, and he remained with them off and on for sixty-one years. In that time Cataldo built churches and schools, jousted with the bureaucracy in both the federal government and his own order, managed to avert a general Indian war, and worked diligently in instructing the natives in Christian doctrine.

But it was not enough. The Nez Percés never exceeded 300 Catholics on their reservation, less than 10 percent of the tribe. When compared with the successes achieved by the Jesuits among the Flatheads, Kalispels, and Coeur d'Alenes, where virtually the entire tribes joined the Catholic faith, the Nez Percé mission effort might be viewed as a failure.

Perhaps Cataldo was correct in 1867 when he said that by the time he arrived among the Nez Percés it was already too late. This was a tribe that had literally begged Catholic authorities in Saint Louis for a priest as early as 1831. Four times they made dangerous journeys halfway across the continent to find a Black Robe. And when De Smet did come to the Northwest, a visit was all they got. Not until twenty-five years later did the Nez Percés actually get their own resident priest. And in that quarter century the Protestants were not idle. Cataldo's assessment was probably true. He was too late: "Those who had been well-disposed toward the faith were now dead, and hatred of the Catholic religion . . . had fearfully increased among these poor Indians."[53]

For the rest of his life with the Nez Percés, Cataldo could never reverse the fact that the tribe was ripe for conversion in 1837 but beyond hope a generation later when he arrived at Lapwai. The rapid dispersal of white men around the Nez Percé Reservation after gold was discovered at Orofino in 1860, and the disastrous reservation policy of the post-Civil War federal government, combined, in Cataldo's view, to forever put him at a disadvantage in dealing with the Nez Percés. The original momentum had been lost by his own society, but after the Civil War factors which Cataldo could not control doomed Catholic activity among the Nez Percés.

By 1871, when the Presbyterian church enjoyed government sanction to convert the Nez Percés, the Jesuits could not compete, all their attributes and resources notwithstanding. Unlike the Protestants, the Jesuits had no families to restrain them, no private property to protect. Moreover, until 1907 the Jesuits of the Northwest were mostly Italians from the Turin Province, with a smattering of other Europeans recruited by Cataldo in 1885. They were not Americans in the eyes of the Indians, not responsible for a repressive United States policy. Cataldo, like his compatriots on other reservations, had at his disposal the resources of his order in the Northwest. There was an organization with a militarylike command structure. A society with worldwide experience, influence, and commitment was indirectly at his command. But still it was not enough to offset the gains made by the Presbyterians and reinforced by the Grant administration's policy.

In a life of successes and challenges Cataldo was deeply frustrated by his results with the Nez Percés. His first two years with them were so barren of accomplishment that he baptized but one Nez Percé man and one Nez Percé woman. Still, in later years Cataldo elaborated on the innate goodness of the tribe. While the adults had not taken immediately to his instructions, the children had, and these youngsters taught their parents to pray. They effectively converted the adults who were subsequently baptized by Cataldo. Cataldo's infectious enthusiasm at one point convinced the father general in Rome that the Nez Percé mission promises "the most valuable results." But by 1905 even Cataldo was disappointed at the degraded condition of the Nez Percés. He reported to his provincial in Turin: "What a change in these people! They were the best of our Indian neophytes, if the Coeur d'Alenes are excluded, and now it can be said that they, the Nez Percés, are the worst."[54] The Nez Percés were never among the "best" in Cataldo's lifetime, but he probably felt better for having remembered that maybe they once were.

There is little dispute that the Indians of the Northwest wholeheartedly loved Cataldo. Whites respected him, and his fellow Jesuits found him "a man easier to admire than to like" with "a surface geniality above a flinty substructure," but Indians and Cataldo were *simpatico*. It was the Jesuit principle of accommodation. The rules of the society allowed its men in the missions to merge themselves into their environment. Adopting the native language was the most important way, but accepting local customs, manners, dress, and mentality was also permissible within bounds.[55]

Even non-Catholic Indians were favorable toward Cataldo. When the Nez Percés under Joseph were captured and placed on a reservation in Indian Territory [Oklahoma], Paul Ponziglione, S.J., of the Missouri Province, visited the tribe. He recorded in his diary that the Nez Percés were timid but that "if you ask them in what religion they believe, they will answer, 'we believe in Cataldo's teaching and that is the only teaching we wish to have.' " The great Joseph himself stated, "Cataldo is my friend, he is a good man, all my people love him."[56]

Cataldo usually tried to work with the chiefs among the Nez Percés. It was in this manner that he placed the first Saint Joseph's Mission on the lands of Stuptup in 1868, and the second church in Slickpoo's valley. The priest was never unmindful that the Indians tended to follow their chiefs. It was this belief, not politics, that brought Cataldo to Joseph's village in 1877, a situation that became ammunition against him when Monteith read more into the visit than religion. To Cataldo it was only courtesy, as well as good sense, to court the approval of the headmen. Such strategy bore big dividends in other tribes of Northwest Indians, but not for him at Slickpoo.[57]

Though other ministers and other denominations may have had more converts than Cataldo in the Nez Percé tribe, none could boast a similar record of success in all aspects of missionary life. Cataldo did not preach merely to expand the numbers of his congregation. He sought a better life for his Indians in education as well as Catholicism.

The "new De Smet" was, in fact, very similar to the real De Smet. Both men deeply affected the character of American Indian Catholicism in the Northwest, both were versatile, dynamic leaders of their Society's men, and at the same time they were compassionate and loving among the Indians who reciprocated in kind. Both were unparalleled formulators of policy and both were action-oriented men. Neither De Smet nor Cataldo left his personalized imprint on a tribe, though certainly Cataldo worked harder in this regard than De Smet. They were generalists. To tally a list of the accomplishments of these two missionaries is to summarize the history of Catholicism in the Northwest during its first century. Like De Smet, Cataldo will be remembered as a founder of the Rocky Mountain missions.

Part Three National Reform Figures

5

Albert K. Smiley: Friend to Friends of the Indians

Clyde A. Milner II

Albert K. Smiley is an important figure not because he worked and lived among Indians in the West, but because he primarily worked and lived among white friends of the Indians in the East. From 1883 to 1912, Smiley hosted and helped organize the remarkably influential Lake Mohonk Conference of Friends of the Indian that were held each autumn at his resort hotel in New York State. Government leaders, major reformers, and proassimilationist Indian spokesmen all made regular appearances at Lake Mohonk. They discussed many issues that affected federal programs toward the western and other Indians, including allotment of the reservations, citizenship for native peoples, civil service guidelines for the appointment of agents, and the termination of government funds to schools controlled by the churches.

Some of these issues, such as the last, took years to resolve, but nearly all the proposals at Mohonk had some impact on public policy and popular opinion. Albert Smiley did not formulate or even directly influence every important proposal that was decided at Lake Mohonk. Nonetheless, his financial resources and organizational efforts created these conferences, and his Quaker heritage gave the conference a distinct form and atmosphere. Smiley's concern for fair treatment of the American Indians may have begun with his upbringing in the Society of Friends, but it reached its zenith

143

when he brought together other friends of the Indians at his Mountain House on Lake Mohonk.

Smiley's active career in Indian affairs had almost no direct connection with any denominational program within the Society of Friends. Instead, his interest in aiding Indians began to take form in 1879, when at age fifty-one he became a member of the federal government's Board of Indian Commissioners. Congress had created this board a decade earlier in 1869. It consisted of ten persons appointed by the president of the United States, who served without compensation. Ideally each member was to be a high-minded, philanthropic citizen not influenced by political pressures. The specific powers of the board were unclear since Congress had authorized "joint control" with the secretary of the interior over the distribution of funds appropriated for the Indians. Although President Ulysses S. Grant had not initiated the legislation that established the Board of Indian Commissioners, his appointment of its first members meant that it would function as part of Grant's reform effort in Indian affairs, his Peace Policy.[1]

One major dimension of this reform centered on Grant's appointment of Indian agents that were recommended by the leading Christian denominations. At first Grant had only wished to experiment with a few agents recommended by the Quakers, but he soon became upset by political maneuverings in Congress over the remaining agencies. He then followed the Board of Indian Commissioners' recommendation that all agencies be awarded to other Christian denominations on terms similar to those held by the Society of Friends.[2]

Throughout the 1870s the churchmen who served as Indian agents received much attention in the halls of Congress, in the offices of the Interior Department, and in the newspapers of the day. This aspect of Grant's administrative program was commonly called his "Quaker Policy" despite its more diverse denominational affiliations. The ten individuals on the Board of Indian Commissioners seemed to reflect, in part, this denominational emphasis. Its members both laymen and clergy came from major Protestant denominations—Epis-

copalian, Presbyterian, Baptist, Methodist, and Congregational. From 1870 until its abolition by executive order on
May 25, 1933, the Board of Indian Commissioners included
at least one, and often two, prominent Quakers. After 1902,
Catholics served on the board, but in its sixty-four-year history the one individual who served the longest term as a
commissioner was Albert Smiley, who remained on the board
from 1879 until his death in 1912.[3]

Surprisingly, Albert Smiley did not participate in Grant's
so-called "Quaker Policy" during the 1870s. Indeed, Smiley
had almost no record before 1879 as a humanitarian reformer
in Indian affairs even within the Society of Friends. By 1879
many Quakers in both branches of the Society of Friends had
worked among the Indians of Nebraska and present-day Oklahoma. These Quakers, either as administrators or as agents,
had become familiar with the problems of the Pawnees, the
Comanches, the Osages, and other Indian peoples. Yet the
Board of Indian Commissioners did not appoint one of these
experienced Quakers when John D. Lang, a Friend from
Vassalboro, Maine, and a member of the Board since 1870,
died in late May. Instead the chairman of the Board of Indian Commissioners, A. C. Barstow, a Congregational banker
from Rhode Island, recommended to President Rutherford B.
Hayes the name of an Orthodox Quaker who also had grown
up in Vassalboro, Maine, and who had become a prominent
educator in Barstow's home community of Providence.[4] It
may be surmised, therefore, that Albert Smiley became a
member of the Board of Indian Commissioners because he
was well known to Lang and Barstow.

In fact, Smiley's nonparticipation in the "Quaker Policy"
of the Grant administration may have influenced Barstow as
well. During the Hayes administration, the nomination of
agents by the churches had come under attack and was being
eliminated by Commissioner of Indian Affairs Ezra A. Hayt,
a former member of the Board of Indian Commissioners.
Hayt's antipathy toward many of the agents approved during
the Grant years had brought him into conflict with representatives of the major Christian denominations, including

the Quakers. In May, 1879, the same month as Lang's death, the Orthodox Friends informed President Hayes that they resigned all further responsibility for the Indian work because of what they considered the unfair dismissal of Agent Hiram W. Jones of the Quapaws and because of the continued harassment of other Quaker agents. The Hicksite Friends who controlled the agencies in Nebraska had experienced the same problems with the commissioner of Indian Affairs but had yet to take similar action.[5]

A. C. Barstow may well have hesitated to nominate any Quaker with experience in government Indian service because of the growing feud between these Quakers and Ezra Hayt. Since Albert Smiley had stayed out of the mainstream of Indian affairs, he had avoided this conflict. Indeed no Indian committee of a Yearly Meeting or any other formal organization among the Quakers had put forward his name. But his unprejudiced position would be tested. As soon as he joined the Board of Indian Commissioners, Smiley's first assignment was to a three-member committee investigating charges against Ezra Hayt.

Whatever the full reasoning behind Albert Smiley's appointment to the Board of Indian Commissioners, it should not be assumed that his previous inactivity meant indifference. As Smiley himself explained in 1888, "I inherited, and have always felt, an interest in the Indian; and when, nine years ago, the President, without my knowledge, put me on the board of Indian Commissioners, it was just to my liking, and I did not decline. I think Mr. Barstow was responsible for my nomination. Since then I have had the opportunity to do what I have desired all my life—something toward the advancement of the Indian."[6]

It may be assumed that Smiley had inherited the nearly legendary Quaker reputation of friendship toward the Indians which helps explain his desire to do something for these native peoples. The Quakers' heritage of social benevolence toward American Indians had become established during colonial Pennsylvania's "Long Peace" which began in the 1680s under the treaty-making of the colony's Quaker founder,

William Penn. It did not end until 1754 with the outbreak
of the French and Indian War. These Pennsylvania Quakers
had certain theological concepts that explain their generally
peaceful and fair treatment of the region's Indians. First,
Friends emphasized the power of God's spirit within the individual. This spiritual Inward Light could be experienced
by any person because Quakers believed that all peoples
were God's children. Second, Friends had established a Peace
Testimony that renounced the taking up of arms and the
fighting of wars. Finally, consistent with their spiritual mys-
ticism and nonconformist pacifism, many Quakers were hesi-
tant to proselytize. They preferred to wait for the workings
of the Inward Light after loving words and honest deeds
had cleared the way for the spiritual awakening of an individual's conscience.[7]

Not all Quakers followed these theological ideals. Evangelically minded Friends of the eighteenth and nineteenth
centuries seemed to practice forms of proselytism, and wars
such as the American Revolution caused some Quakers to
take up arms. Surprisingly few Friends did any benevolent
work among American Indians after William Penn's death.
Still, by the mid-nineteenth century, the peaceful story of
Quaker–Indian relations in colonial Pennsylvania had taken
on a distinctively popular imagery based on representations
of Benjamin West's artistically famous, but historically vague,
painting of *Penn's Treaty with the Indians* (1771). The treaty
motif of a rotund, elderly Penn beneath a great elm with
hand outstretched, the Indians intent on his words had been
reproduced on calendars, medals, trays, candle screens, lamp
shades, bed curtains, bedquilts, cast-iron stoves, various quali-
ties and quantities of crockery and china, and even whiskey
glasses. These items were either used or exhibited in Quaker
and non-Quaker homes on both sides of the Atlantic.[8] In
terms of popular culture they represented either an unofficial
seal for the Society of Friends or an emblem for a Quaker
saint.

Until President U. S. Grant invited the Quakers to serve as
government agents, the Society of Friends had no major pro-

grams among the Indians except a few small missions primarily among the Senecas and Shawnees. Still, Quakers and many other Americans accepted the special reputation of Friends in Indian affairs, and some individual Quakers felt an obligation to act as the nation's moral conscience in matters concerning the Indians. When the spirit moved them, ad hoc delegations of Friends visited Washington to discuss policy reforms with government officials.[9] Albert Smiley's appointment to the Board of Indian Commissioners in 1879 allowed him to continue this Quakerly tradition of advising government leaders as did his later conferences at Lake Mohonk. Yet earlier during the 1870s, Smiley also was informed about the Quaker agents and their work among the Indians. The three major Quaker newspapers, published weekly in Philadelphia but available by mail to any subscriber, were full of letters and accounts of developments at the Indian agencies. The regional Yearly Meetings which were the highest level of formal organization among Quakers of either branch in this period, had Indian committees that supported Quaker work at specific agencies. In 1873, Albert Smiley's younger sister, Rebecca Howland Smiley, was appointed to New England Yearly Meeting's new Committee for the Western Indians. In 1878, Albert Smiley's wife, Eliza Phelps (Cornell) Smiley, joined her sister-in-law on the same committee. Smiley himself, however, never served on this committee.[10]

Nonetheless, Albert Smiley had been an active Friend, if not an active friend of the Indians, before 1879. His parents were members of the Quaker meeting in Vassalboro, Maine, the small community into which Albert and his identical twin, Alfred, were born on March 17, 1828. The Smiley brothers grew up in Vassalboro and were graduated in 1845 from the Oak Grove Seminary, a Friends' preparatory school. In 1848 they entered the senior class at Haverford College, a Quaker school outside Philadelphia. Because of a lack of funds Haverford had been closed from 1845 to 1848, and the twins constituted the entire class of graduates in 1849. They became members of the college faculty the next year. Alfred taught geology, mental and moral philosophy, whereas Albert's courses covered English literature and chemistry.

Their schooling at Oak Grove and Haverford as well as four years on the Haverford faculty helped the Smiley brothers pursue careers as educators. The twins returned to Haverford in 1859 to receive masters' degrees and then moved on to Providence, Rhode Island, in 1860 to take charge of the Friends School (later called Moses Brown School). Albert Smiley served as principal of the Providence Friends School for nineteen years, and Alfred remained associate principal for eight years. He left for Poughkeepsie, New York, in 1868 to begin farming, an enterprise that allowed more time, space, and income for Alfred and Rachel Smiley to raise their six children. Albert and Eliza Smiley had only one child, Annette, who died in 1863 at age five, but a half brother Daniel Smiley, born in 1855, became a surrogate son for them.[11]

The lack of children and the special circumstance of close continued association with an identical twin may have produced both opportunity and influence for the development of philanthropic attitudes in Albert Smiley's life. Certainly the benevolent ideal of the "brotherhood" of mankind can be more readily accepted when one's own brother is so strikingly like one's own self. Similarly, paternalistic instincts frustrated by the tragedy of a child's death and the absence of additional offspring may allow for a generous personal commitment to aid and guide substitute children. Albert Smiley's actions toward American Indians combined both brotherly and paternalistic aspects, but these personal concepts were grafted onto generally held Quaker attitudes about American Indians.

In Providence, Rhode Island, between 1860 and 1879 there can be little doubt that Albert Smiley had become a well-established, or "weighty," Friend. His position was not based on wealth but rather centered on his role as a teacher and principal at the Friends School. In this period among New England's Orthodox Friends no professional clergy existed within the Quaker meetings. Yet these same meetings supported Quaker schools and employed Quakers to teach their children. It may be said that a teacher and principal, such as Albert Smiley, was as close to the status of a full-time professional Quaker as existed among these New England Friends. Not only was such a person expected to be knowledgeable about academic subjects and to carry out certain administrative duties, but also he was paid to exemplify and transmit Quaker values to his students and staff.

Yet his career as an educator had not given Albert Smiley an opportunity to actively pursue the Quakerly tradition of friendship toward American Indians. Only when Smiley changed his career to the unlikely sounding profession of resort owner and operator did the way open for such benevolent efforts. In 1869, Albert Smiley purchased for $28,000 a tract of land that surrounded a small lake in the Shawangunk Mountains near the town of New Paltz, New York. He committed twenty years of his savings, $14,000, to this venture and borrowed the additional $14,000 that was needed. He then persuaded Alfred to sell their jointly owned farm and devote full attention to the resort while he stayed on in Providence for another decade to pay off the $14,000 debt.

The new business flourished in the 1870s under Alfred Smiley's management. An upper-class, educated clientele lodged at the Mohonk Mountain House which was only ninety miles north of New York City. Although many Quaker families stayed at Lake Mohonk, it was not an insular resort for the Society of Friends. As they had done at the Providence Friends School, the Smiley brothers welcomed non-Quakers. Still, the resort hotel operated on Quaker principles. Most striking was the strict temperance maintained at the resort as well as a ban on card playing and dancing. Guests came to Lake Mohonk for the nature walks, the boating, fishing, and horseback riding, all amidst spectacular scenery. In addition visitors enjoyed the morning prayer services, evening hymn-singing and worship meetings on Sunday that were both nondenominational and voluntary.[12] This same religious atmosphere pervaded all the conferences held at Lake Mohonk.

Alfred Smiley opened another resort at a nearby mountain

Albert K. Smiley, ca. 1910, examines a flower from his garden. Mountain House, the main building of the Lake Mohonk resort and site of the Friends of the Indian conferences, is in the background. Courtesy Mohonk Mountain House Archives.

lake, Minnewaska, in the summer of 1879 and gave up managing the Mohonk resort. Albert then moved permanently to Lake Mohonk after resigning his position as principal of the Friends School in Providence. So in the same year Albert Smiley became a full-time resort operator and a member of the Board of Indian Commissioners.

For each brother the success of his resort business would allow for the support of various philanthropies. Albert became better known publicly because of the Friends of the Indian conferences and other gatherings of humanitarian reformers that he organized at Lake Mohonk. Yet the brothers' efforts should be viewed as unified since Alfred, and their younger half brother Daniel, continued to stress the business side of their ventures which often freed Albert to pursue his philanthropic concerns. The three brothers did make money although as their biographer Larry E. Burgess noted, "In reality the brothers were never wealthy in terms of liquid capital, ready money. Friends like the Harrimans, Rocke- fellers, and Carnegies possessed a different type of wealth. While the Smiley resorts did do well financially, the brothers consistently poured their resources back into their businesses and philanthropies." In fact, just as he borrowed money to purchase Lake Mohonk, Albert Smiley willingly borrowed money to support his philanthropic interests whether it was the building of a public park and library in Redlands, Cali- fornia, or the sponsoring of a conference at his New York resort.[13]

The influential Lake Mohonk Conference of Friends of the Indian began as a direct result of Albert Smiley's member- ship on the Board of Indian Commissioners. At the third con- ference in 1885, Smiley explained to the participants the origin of their meeting.

For many years, ever since the organization of our Board of Indian Commissioners, it has been their practice to have a Convention in connection with the annual meeting, in Washington, to discuss Indian affairs generally. To that Convention the secretaries and well-known members of religious denominations have been invited, and they have generally been present, as well as members of Con- gress and others. In these discussions, usually occupying one day, we have always found that the time was short. The pressure of business in Washington was so great that we could not hold people together more than one day, and we have had to adjourn before we were through. So the thought struck me a few years ago that we could give more time to the subject by inviting friends of the cause to this house and having a three-days' conference. I sug- gested the idea to some of my friends and they approved it.

Smiley's next words struck a distinctively Quaker note. Friends meetings, whether the local monthly meeting or the regional Yearly Meeting, tried to act on the consensus of all members. Harmony of decision-making was important to Quakers, and as Smiley explained, "My aim has been to unite the best

minds interested in Indian affairs, so that all should act together and be in harmony, and so that the prominent persons connected with Indian affairs should act as one body
and create a public sentiment in favor of the Indians."[14]

When Albert Smiley attended his first meeting of the Board
of Indian Commissioners on January 8, 1880, he found neither
consensus nor harmony. Instead he found a scandal involving
Ezra Hayt, the commissioner of Indian Affairs. The new chairman of the board, General Clinton B. Fisk, had heard rumors
that Hayt had failed to pursue charges against a recently
resigned Indian agent at San Carlos Agency in Arizona despite ample incriminating evidence. The agent, Henry L. Hart,
owned a part of a silver mine that some of Hayt's friends
apparently planned to buy. Fisk appointed three board members to investigate the charges against Hayt which were now
well known through newspaper stories. One member of the
investigating committee, A. C. Barstow, was a close friend
of Hayt since Hayt's days on the Board of Indian Commissioners; Albert Smiley, another member of the committee,
had just joined the board because of Barstow's recommendation. Smiley served as chairman of the committee and despite the direct and indirect personal connections, the investigation did not whitewash Hayt's actions. All three members agreed in their report of January 31, 1880, that Hayt
should be removed from office. Yet the committee's work
was an anticlimax because Ezra Hayt had been dismissed
from his office by the secretary of the interior two days
before the report was presented.[15]

In the aftermath of the Hayt scandal, that same secretary,
Carl Schurz, asked the Board of Indian Commissioners to
examine more broadly "the conduct of Indian Affairs and the
business methods and management of the Indian Bureau."
Once more a three-member committee was appointed to the
task, but only one appointee was carried over from the previous investigation, Albert Smiley, who again served as chairman. The committee presented its report in April, 1880. It
found that "Indian affairs are now administered with integrity." Nonetheless, the committee suggested the reorganiza-

tion of some of the clerical force and departments as well as changes in the ordering of supplies, especially flour. The committee commended the educational program for Indians at Carlisle in Pennsylvania and at Hampton Institute in Virginia but called for the speedy establishment of more boarding schools on the reservations. Finally, the report concluded that in order to secure "the greatest good for the Indian"

nothing would so aid him, and all associated with him in this good work, as the speedy enactment of the pending bills in Congress providing for lands in severalty for the Indians, the protection and restraint of law, and ultimate citizenship. This much-needed Congressional action secured, the problem of Indian destiny would be of easy solution. The policy of seclusion would soon give way to that of absorption, industrial pursuits take the place of idleness and the chase.[16]

This final passage of the report by Smiley and his two fellow commissioners indicated the direction that they hoped Indian affairs would take. The allotment of reservations along with continued Christian education brought civilization and citizenship among American Indians and led to their absorption into white Protestant American society. Neither the goal of full assimilation nor the means behind the goal — religious education, property ownership, and cultural detribalization — were new ideas. Yet they were carried on into the twentieth century by Albert Smiley and many of the friends of the Indians that he brought together at Lake Mohonk.

Ironically, it could be argued that Quakers had resisted the external pressures of assimilation at times in their own history. Changes had occurred among Friends as a process of acculturation, the establishment of some new cultural patterns through acceptance from within a society instead of transculturation, and the imposition of change from outside, which is what the policy of assimilation meant for Indians. Since its religious origins during the 1640s and 1650s in England, the Society of Friends had been noted as a nonconformist religious movement. The Inward Light and the Peace Testimony were two of many ideas that made Quakers a distinctive "tribe" of radical Puritans. Yet Friends never established the cultural separation from either English or American society that American Indians held as their native birthright. Quakers became too intimately involved with politics and business to be completely separate, and they often interacted with other religious denominations. Despite episodes of apparently insular behavior by some Quaker meetings, Friends never became completely otherworldly in their orientation. Indeed, Quakers often felt an obligation to reform and improve society, not remove themselves from it.[17]

Such an upsurge for social improvement occurred after the Civil War when a remarkably large number of Quaker meetings supported aid and education to the black freedmen of the South and also sustained the work of Quaker Indian agents in the West. Historian Philip S. Benjamin observed that after 1865, "in all their philanthropies, Friends took on the role of guardians of Protestant culture. Ignoring their own beginnings as sectarian critics of the social order and their continued estrangement from many American norms, they attempted to assimilate their charges into the dominant middle-class ethic."[18]

The Quakers' emergence as defenders of middle-class Protestant values occurred because Quakers themselves acculturated some of those values but did not assimilate all of them. Quakers had retained most of their distinctive nonconformist religious principles. The Inward Light and the Peace Testimony still existed, but nonconformist behavior had subsided somewhat, especially plain dress and to a lesser degree plain speech—the "thees" and "thous" of Quakerly conversation. Quakers remained a distinctive people who considered themselves to be within the mainstream of American Protestant society. From this peculiar perspective, Quakers such as Albert Smiley advocated the transculturation of American Indians. Friends had followed the gentler path of voluntary acculturation over two centuries, but Indians were supposed to follow the harder road of imposed assimilation. The fact that Albert Smiley did not see the Quaker pattern of both acculturation and distinctiveness as appropriate for the

Indians demonstrated how much he and like-minded Friends had moved beyond a recognition of their Quaker heritage into the mainstream of humanitarian, Protestant reform.

In the first four months of his service on the Board of Indian Commissioners Albert Smiley had studied closely the operations of the government's Indian Office in Washington, D.C. He also had committed himself to a program of assimilation for American Indians. Yet Smiley had not traveled out into the field and met the government agents or even the Indians on their reservations. In June, 1883, such an opportunity arrived when Smiley and fellow commissioner, General Eliphalet Whittlesey, were sent west by the Board of Indian Commissioners to investigate the 1882 treaty with the Sioux, which had proposed the breakup of the Great Sioux reservation.

The two commissioners' most important meetings occurred not with Indians but with Christian missionaries and with other white visitors from the East. For three days at the Santee Agency, Smiley and Whittlesey held conferences with a group of men that included Philadelphian Herbert Welsh of the Indian Rights Association, Episcopal Bishop William H. Hare, the principal of an Indian boarding school, and Isaiah Lightner, the Hicksite Quaker agent at Santee. Bishop Hare chaired a committee of his fellow missionaries which drew up a statement declaring that the treaty of 1882 was "not just" or "equitable." The statement advocated the division of the Great Sioux reservation into separate reserves for the development of farming among the Indians.[19]

Either at the June 2 meeting or at a final meeting on the evening of June 3, Albert Smiley found the inspiration to issue a verbal invitation to what would be the first Lake Mohonk conference. As he explained eleven years later, "While at the Santee Agency, we met, seemingly by chance, a large number of prominent men interested in Indian affairs; and by common consent we sat in council for three days and discussed the complicated problem connected with the Sioux Reservation. We arrived at valuable conclusions, and agreed to work unitedly thereafter. . . . That council opened

my eyes, and I determined to repeat at Mohonk on a larger
scale the conference which had proved so helpful. I invited
them all to meet at Mohonk the ensuing autumn and promised
to have a large gathering to discuss leisurely the whole Indian question."[20]

Smiley planned to bring together actively concerned east-
erners, such as Herbert Welsh and himself, to meet with
experienced workers, such as missionaries and government
officials, who dealt directly with the Indians. Significantly,
he had not thought to include Indians themselves. In fact
during the 1883 Dakota trip Smiley appears to have held few
meetings with Indian leaders. Instead much time was spent
observing Indian children at school and at church which may
be seen as a benign expression of Smiley's paternalism. At
the Santee agency, for example, Smiley noted with approval
the behavior of the Indian children who attended the agency's
Quaker meeting, but he disapproved of the use of the Dakota
language in the lessons at the American Missionary Association's school.

Only at the Yankton agency did Smiley and Whittlesey
meet with a diverse group of Indian adults, including traditionalists like the old chief, Strike the Ree, and young, white-
educated Yanktons, like William T. Selwin, who taught in a
government day school. The commissioners made note of the
factions that divided the Yanktons, but elsewhere they more
typically noted the names of native preachers such as those
at the Lower Brulé agency and at the Peoria Bottom settlement near Pierre. In general what they said about their visit
to the Cheyenne River agency may have been true at their
other stops, ". . . we saw but few Indians."[21]

The visitors to the Lake Mohonk conference also saw "but
few Indians," and the few they did see and hear were carefully selected to represent the most progressive Indians who
had attended schools and colleges. In short most of the Indians who came to Lake Mohonk served as examples of assimilation and not surprisingly tended to advocate assimilation as well. The first Indian participants did not appear
until 1889. One was an Arapaho, Sherman Coolidge, who

had become a minister in the Episcopal church. The other three were students, one studied law at Yale, the other attended Rutgers, and the third played trumpet and led the musical band at Carlisle. The Yale student, Henry H. Lyman, told the assembled conference, "I came to be instructed, not to instruct you."[22]

From its beginning, even without Indian participants, the Lake Mohonk conferences expected to instruct, rather than be instructed. Although each fall's three-day meeting also served as an official meeting of the Board of Indian Commissioners, the Lake Mohonk conferences had no specific legal power or any established administrative responsibility. Nonetheless, these conferences exerted great influence over the government's policy toward American Indians. The first conference lasted from October 10 through October 12, 1883. Only twelve men attended and the main topic of consideration was the Sioux Treaty of 1882. But from this modest beginning the size and significance of the annual fall conferences grew to include not only government workers and missionaries, but also army officers, leaders of Congress, editors of influential religious and secular publications, presidents of colleges and universities and important teachers, lawyers, judges, and philanthropists. Formal talks by experts led to open discussion and the presentation of opposing views. In general the atmosphere remained agreeable, friendly, and often humorous. Each conference drew up a platform of principles to inform the public, improve government programs, produce new laws, and help bring justice, education, and religion to the Indians. All along Albert Smiley underwrote the expenses of those who were invited to attend. By 1890, 151 "members" were present at a cost of $1,093.40. By 1910, 132 "members" attended, many with their spouses, and the cost had risen to $2,033.33.[23]

Smiley played a more direct role in these conferences than drawing up the list of guests and paying their expenses. He also chose the chairman of each conference. Typically his choice was a leader on the Board of Indian Commissioners, such as the first chairman, Clinton B. Fisk, who served annually until 1890. Fisk was the founder of an educational institution for blacks (Fisk University in Nashville), the vice-president of the Missouri Pacific Railroad, a leader of the Methodist church in New York City and an outspoken prohibitionist. He was followed by Merrill E. Gates, who also replaced Fisk as president of the Board of Indian Commissioners and served as president of Rutgers University and later Amherst College. Gates chaired the conference from 1890 through 1896 and from 1899 to 1901. In 1895 he shared his duties with Lyman Abbott, a Congregational clergyman who had succeeded the famous minister, Henry Ward Beecher, at Plymouth Church in Brooklyn. Abbott also published *The Outlook,* a religious magazine that gave thorough, positive accounts of the Lake Mohonk meetings. He presided at the 1905 conference as well. Philip C. Garrett, a leading Orthodox Quaker philanthropist from Philadelphia and another member of the Board of Indian Commissioners, chaired the 1897 and 1898 conferences. Later chairmen included one of the first two Catholic members of the board, Charles J. Bonaparte, who also served as attorney general under Theodore Roosevelt, and in 1911, James S. Sherman, the vice-president of the United States, who as a congressman had headed the House Committee on Indian Affairs.

A core group of dedicated reformers guided these conferences. In the first decade members of this group included General Fisk, General Whittlesey, Merrill Gates, and Philip Garrett, all of the Board of Indian Commissioners, as well as Lyman Abbott, Herbert Welsh, and Senator Henry L. Dawes of Massachusetts. With the active participation and support of their Quaker host, this group planned the program for each conference. By 1890 a permanent business committee of varied membership evolved out of this inner circle. The committee also guided the direction of each conference, selected speakers, and decided major points of the platform, all before the conference opened. Such planning did limit the scope of each conference, and in later years some participants complained about the lack of attention given to important new issues, like the religious use of peyote.[24]

Although Albert Smiley may have wished to gather a broad and diverse conference of "Friends of the Indian," historian Francis Paul Prucha has noted, "The membership was almost entirely from New England and the Middle Atlantic States. Occasionally an Indian agent or missionary from the West came to report on his work, and frequently Indian students from Carlisle Indian Industrial School were on hand, but proximity to Lake Mohonk seems to have been for many a deciding factor." In addition to the Board of Indian Commissioners, representatives of two major reform organizations, the Indian Rights Association and the Women's National Indian Association, regularly attended. On the whole the conferences were closely knit and harmonious, not only because of the eastern residence and like-minded reform orientation of many but also because of the strong religious orientation of nearly all. Between 1883 and 1900 more than a fourth of the conference members were either ministers and their wives or the established representatives of a religious denomination. Many others represented religious publications or were prominent lay leaders from the churches.[25]

The rhetoric at the Lake Mohonk conferences reinforced this religious unity in an evangelically Protestant tone. Each conference opened with a prayer and closed with a hymn, and much was made of the importance of responsible Christian action. Lyman Abbott told the 1885 conference, "It may be taken for granted that we are Christian men and women; that we believe in justice, goodwill, and charity, and the brotherhood of the human race. At least none of us here desires to break the Ten Commandments nor break down honor and rectitude." The power of a common Christian identity and a common Christian effort impressed Albert Smiley. At the close of the 1890 conference he enthusiastically claimed, "The moment the Christian community gets hold of this work thoroughly, every wrong will be righted and every Indian will be educated." Six years later Smiley stated that great progress had been made in Indian affairs, but that the Christian people of the United States must continue their efforts. He concluded, "As soon as you get the

Indian to become a Christian, you have settled the whole
question in regard to his industry and his morality, and I do
not believe it can be settled in any other way."26

At the time he spoke, Smiley's words reflected the view
of many leading Protestants that Christianization equaled
Americanization for minority peoples such as the Indians.
Smiley himself had not joined the evangelical movement
among Quakers, but he had accepted the mainstream Protestant belief that Christian education and social betterment
went together. In effect Smiley, like other leading Quakers
of his day, believed in a form of social conversion that emphasized Christian values and moral behavior but did not
contradict traditional Quaker opposition to proselytism by
insisting on conversion to the Quaker faith. (The evangelical
Friends of the Midwest and West did insist on such religious
conversion.)

Quaker speakers of both the Hicksite and Orthodox branches
expressed ideas similar to Smiley's when they spoke at Lake
Mohonk. In 1885 and 1886, President Edward H. Magill of
the Hicksite college, Swarthmore, emphasized the need to
break up the reservations and extend citizenship to Indians
as individuals. Magill pointed to the example of William Lloyd
Garrison and the abolitionists. "Garrison kept reiterating one
thing—immediate and unconditional emancipation; with us
it should be immediate citizenship. . . . if we can give immediate citizenship to the vast number of negroes, numbering more than twenty-five to one of the Indians, I am sure it
is safe to give immediate citizenship to the Indians." Magill
felt the power of the ballot would protect Indian rights, although he admitted that "we need to prepare them." In 1886
Orthodox Friend Philip Garrett also called for the end of
tribalism and the breakup of the reservations along with
the granting of citizenship.

Let him [the Indian] lay aside his picturesque blanket and moc-
casin, and clad in the panoply of American citizenship, seek his
chances of fortune or loss in the stern battle of life with the Aryan
races. It will be no hardship, no unkindness to ask this of him. If

civilization is a blessing, then in the name of Christianity let us offer it as a boon, even to the untutored savage. . . . if an act of emancipation will buy them life, manhood, civilization, and Christianity, at the sacrifice of a few chieftain's feathers, a few worthless bits of parchment [i.e., treaties], the cohesion of the tribal relation, and the traditions of their race; then, in the name of all that is really worth having let us shed the few tears necessary to embalm these relics of the past, and have done with them; and with fraternal cordiality, let us welcome to the bosom of the nation this brother whom we have wronged long enough.[27] *AND ARE STILL WRONGING by this statement!*

Such attitudes among Quakers and non-Quakers alike led to the strong support of the Lake Mohonk conferences for legislative programs that called for the allotment in severalty of the Indian reservations. Eventually this policy passed as Senator Dawes's famous General Allotment Act of 1887. Dawes spoke at Mohonk that same year. He felt that "it is not too much to say that there would never have been such a law had it not been for the Mohonk Conference." Yet Dawes warned that the establishment of individual homesteads for Indians and the offer of citizenship along with severalty brought new duties and new obligations for the friends of the Indians. "They [the Indians] do not embrace this new life as by magic, and come out citizens of the United States. We have brought them to this condition . . . and the Mohonk Conference is responsible to-day for what shall take place in consequence of it."[28]

The judgment of most historians has been harsh as to the impact of the Dawes Act on American Indians, especially in terms of their loss of land. Dawes himself came to recognize some of the severalty program's shortcomings. In 1895 he told the Lake Mohonk conference, "Now, what is the matter with this severalty law? It has fallen among thieves, and there have not been enough good Samaritans around to take care of it." Dawes especially regretted the fact that the best reservation lands often seemed to go to white owners, with the Indians being alloted the poorest land. But the work of "thieves" did not convince Dawes or the other attenders at

Lake Mohonk that the ultimate goal of assimilation should
be abandoned.[29]

Three years later Albert Smiley spoke about the inefficiency
and occasional corruption of political institutions. He advocated the eventual end of the government's Indian Bureau
and the immediate abolition of a large number of the Indian
agencies. Sounding every bit the stern Quaker schoolteacher,
Smiley concluded, "I am more and more convinced that Indians should be thrown upon their own resources. There has
been too much coddling, which tends to pauperize them.
Anything which is given to them and not earned is little
valued. Most Indians are capable of taking care of themselves if let alone. Put the Indians on their feet; teach them
to swim by throwing them into the water. When practicable,
I would do away with all rations, but make the Indians work
for their food. I long for the time when all the Indians will
be absorbed in the body politic."[30]

Smiley returned to his hard-line approach in his farewell
remarks to the same 1898 conference. His words revealed
much frustration, but he assured his listeners that more conferences would be held and that "the Indians are worth saving
and that we are going to save them." Yet he had a harsh
plan of salvation.

I say this for the benefit of those who are here for the first time.
I hope that before many years this whole Indian population will
be absorbed into the general civilization of the country, and the
Indians will no longer be either coddled or pauperized by being
shut up on reservations, and having no chance to work out their
own salvation. The best way is to throw them out and make them
swim in deep water—or drown. That is my solution of the question.
There would be a good deal of hardship with it, but it would be
the best thing in the end.[31]

Smiley had in effect advocated saving the Indians not from
drowning but by the threat of drowning. When he repeated
this theme at the 1901 conference, Merrill Gates, the pre-
siding officer, responded, "When you see this state of mind

produced on this man of peace, you can imagine how deep the evils must be."[32]

By 1901 at age seventy-three Albert Smiley had spent over twenty years seeking some solution to the "Indian problem." Much of what he had done could be called good works. Between 1883 and 1895, Smiley had made eight field trips for the Board of Indian Commissioners. His first trip in 1883 had been to the Sioux agencies on the northern plains. A year later between February 15 and April 25, Smiley and General Whittlesey visited agencies in New Mexico, Arizona, and California on a tour of inspection that encompassed more than 8,000 miles of travel.

In New Mexico the commissioners noted that nine thousand Indians lived in nineteen pueblos and were all "industrious farmers and self-supporting." Still the two visitors were disturbed by the pueblo mixture of Catholicism and traditional native worship. They concluded that the Indians "greatly need true Christian education and industrial training." Despite reports of "annual dances with orgies too indecent for description" a dance at Santo Domingo pueblo impressed the commissioners as "more modest and decent than the round dances in our fashionable society." At Acoma the pueblo's spectacular cliff-top location could not be ignored, but Smiley and Whittlesey ignored its cultural and historical significance. They advised a council of the chief men of the village to abandon their location and build houses on individual farms.[33]

The commissioners noted when they visited the Navajos that these Indians resisted sending their children to school and also resisted farming, depending instead upon large flocks of sheep and goats. They concluded that the Navajo reservation was "a very poor country." Toward the end of this trip a special visit to the San Carlos agency in Arizona produced a meeting with a group of Chiricahua Apache prisoners. After conversations with Nai-che-te (a son of Cochise), Kai-te-nay (a son of Victorio), and Geronimo, among others, Smiley and Whittlesey seemed favorably impressed that the Chiricahuas were "the brightest and most vigorous of all the Apaches. If they can be induced to give up their roving and

marauding habits and devote their energies to peaceful in-
dustries they will soon be a prosperous people." In 1907,
Smiley remembered his meeting with Geronimo and attempted
unsuccessfully to have the Apache chief attend a Lake Mohonk conference because as Smiley confessed, "interest in
the discussion of Indian affairs at Mohonk has of late been
declining," and he felt that the presence of "a few of the
really great" traditional leaders might enliven the meeting.[34]

For Smiley the most important part of his 1884 trip involved his visits among the Mission Indians of California.
In 1889, 1890, 1891, and 1894, he did important work for
these Indians as he attempted to protect some of their land
and water claims and helped establish a series of small reservations in southern California.[35] This work had been in-
spired by an 1883 report of the condition of the Mission
Indians, written in large part by Helen Hunt Jackson, the
author of the famous exposé on broken treaties, A *Century
of Dishonor* (1881). Jackson also wrote *Ramona,* a very popular novel on the tragic history of California's Indians, which
appeared in 1884, a year before her death.[36]

By 1890, Smiley was making his winter home in Redlands,
California, along with his brother Alfred and their families.
From this location Smiley not only continued his work among
the Mission Indians, but he also found time in 1895 to travel
to Nevada at the request of the Board of Indian Commissioners to investigate the condition of the Indians living on
the Walker River and Pyramid Lake reservations. His trip
convinced Smiley that he must oppose Senate Bill 99, that
had been introduced by a Nevada senator and endorsed by
both the secretary of the interior and the commissioner of
Indian Affairs.

This bill called for the removal of the 1,100 Walker River
Indians about eighty miles to Pyramid Lake where nearly
1,000 Indians already lived. These Indians were hostile to
the Walker River band and had no room for new residents.
The bill also provided for a $250,000 irrigation ditch forty-
five miles long that would supposedly bring water to the dry
lands of the Pyramid Lake reservation where the Walker

Meeting with Mission Indians at the Mission Inn, Riverside, California, April 27–28, 1908. Among those in the photograph are David Starr Jordan, president of Stanford University; Charles F. Lummis, journalist and organizer of the Southwest Museum; Albert K. Smiley; Frank Miler, master of the inn; and representatives of California Indians. Smiley worked to protect the land and water claims of the Mission Indians of southern California. Courtesy Archives of the A. K. Smiley Public Library, Redlands, California.

River Indians were to settle. Along the course of the ditch the town of Wadsworth, Nevada, and 17,000 acres owned by whites were to be supplied with water before it reached the Indians' lands. Smiley felt, "It is morally certain that the Indians would get no water after the whites are supplied. The proposed ditch will take all the water of the Truckee River, which now irrigates the Pyramid Lake Indian lands. The effect of the bill will be to destroy the farming operations of both bands of Indians, who have been encouraged to improve their lands under the expectation of holding them in perpetuity." The bill also proposed to take the north and west shores of Pyramid Lake, where the Indians did all their fishing. Smiley reported at the 1895 Lake Mohonk conference that the bill had failed in Congress, but he feared that some future Congress might pass similar legislation if the friends of the Indian did not remain vigilant.[37]

Smiley's travels in the desert Southwest and in California helped him understand the diverse problems that confronted distinct groups of American Indians. In 1897 at the Lake Mohonk conference he admitted that difficulties existed in allotting land to all the different Indians.

The Navahoes, for instance, traveled a thousand miles every summer to feed their sheep. They cannot have lands in severalty. The Pueblos, who live in villages, had better stay there. In California there are parts where it would be impossible to give land in severalty. The desert Indians, who live where the thermometer runs up to 125 and 130 degrees in summer, are exceedingly attached to their homes there. There is no land but the desert. They live on mesquite beans, grasshoppers and various things of that kind. What could be done with them? . . . In Nevada the land is of no value without expensive irrigation. If the land everywhere was like that of Oklahoma it could be alloted at once.[38]

At least in a geographic context, Smiley had come to recognize the cultural pluralism of American Indians. In another context, commerce and industry, he advocated basket-making and other native crafts as a way to "stir up the Indians to work." Nonetheless, Smiley had not become a defender of traditional culture. He still clung to the goal of assimilation. As he told the 1903 conference, "I hope to live long enough to see all the Indians made self-supporting citizens, enjoying all the blessings of civilized life that we enjoy. . . . I have mingled with the Indians largely, and have learned to love and respect them, and I hope the time will soon come when they will all be with us as a part of our people."[39]

Quakers had long talked of the Inward Light, that of God in every person, that could bring each individual to God's Truth. This Quaker concept can produce a broad toleration of cultural diversities because of the belief that within every individual there still existed the Inward Light that could awaken the individual soul. But if specific signs of the Inward Light are expected, then the belief can produce an ethnocentric narrowness. In terms of dealing with individual American Indians, Smiley appears to have sought specific signs of assimilation. Although he could be impressed by a Geronimo, Smiley seemed equally impressed by a figure like Frank Modoc, formerly called Steamboat Frank, who had fought against whites in the Modoc War. Smiley met this Indian in the summer of 1884 in Vassalboro, Maine, where Frank Modoc, now a man of peace and a Quaker preacher, had come to study with Friends at the Oak Grove school. He had won acceptance preaching to whites and planned to return to Oregon as an evangelical missionary.[40]

In terms of the Lake Mohonk conference, Smiley carefully screened those Indian guests that he invited. In 1903, Smiley wrote the commissioner of Indian Affairs, William A. Jones, "confidentially" about four Indians, three of whom had made fortunes in the cattle business and one of whom had graduated from Stanford and was a journalist in New York City. Smiley felt that if the Indians in question were "on the right side, [they] would be interesting additions, but if of radical views, they are better left alone." A year later Smiley invited these four Indians, but only John M. Oskison, the journalist, attended.[41]

Other Indians attended the conferences, but not surprisingly they spoke on the "right side" of the assimilation issue. Charles

Eastman, the famous Santee Sioux physician made several major addresses. His general support of Christian training and formal education became clear during his first Mohonk conference in 1890 when he told the members, "My constant prayer was that I might understand the American people— their language, their mode of life and their ways,—that I might be more useful among my own people." Eastman's religious motivation allowed him to voice some effective complaints. In 1895 he condemned denominational competition that merely confused those Indians who needed simple religious instruction. Twelve years later he warned that pushing Indians toward "civilization" might rob them of their sense of religion. Eastman called it "the Great Mystery." But such statements were gentle criticisms. Other Indian speakers at Mohonk advocated more schooling, cutting off rations, taxing Indian lands and putting Indians to work. In 1895, Carlos Montezuma, another educated Indian physician of Yavapai heritage, called for full integration instead of severalty and citizenship. "It is absurd to give him [the Indian] a patch of land and hide him, and expect him to carry on that land like yourself. You must place my daughter and sons with your sons and daughters. As long as you hide them, they can never be civilized like you."[42]

These proassimilationist Indians played a different role at Lake Mohonk from the native converts and preachers that missionaries relied on to influence other Indians. These Indians came to Lake Mohonk to show the white reformers that what they wanted to do could be done. The reformers already believed in assimilation, and their Indian visitors reinforced that belief.

Only at the 1904 conference, did two Indians speak who were not well-schooled manifestations of the assimilationist position, but they still gave a familiar message. Two Comanche men, Nahwats and Periconic, made brief remarks in their native language that were then interpreted for the audience. Chairman Charles J. Bonaparte indicated that the audience would hear "what the interpreter thinks we ought to hear." If the record of the two speeches is accurate, Nahwats and

Periconic strongly favored schooling for the Comanches' children. Nahwats told of the advice given him by a government agent, "Hayward," (James M. Haworth, agent to the Comanches, 1873-78):

There was a man named Hayward, a Quaker, used to be agent for my people way back, and Hayward told me, and it came to pass—he told me that a railroad would go to our country, and we would have to send our children to school. He said that the time is coming when the Indians would have to farm and live like white people. Hayward was an old Quaker; he was our agent, and a good friend to the Indians. I wish I had taken his advice twenty years ago, because then I would have given my children schooling. Now I want to send my children to the mission school or to the government school; I don't want my children to follow the old way.[43]

Although Quakerly advice on education and assimilation may not have changed in nearly a quarter of a century, the direct work of Quakers among the Indians had been greatly reduced. What remained of Quakerly influence in Indian affairs followed the general pattern of what existed before President Grant's Peace Policy. A few schools and missions, nearly all in the Indian Territory, were under Quaker care. Most Friends who felt a concern for Indians tried to influence government officials rather than work among the Indians themselves. Yet some changes occurred for the Quakers. Their missions in the Indian Territory revealed the growing evangelical influence among Friends. Paid ministers now preached to some Indians and conversions to Quakerism were welcomed. Rather than visit Washington in ad hoc delegations, eastern Friends seemed to prefer the nonsectarian Indian Rights Association which lobbied to reform government policies.[44] The efforts of this association showed that these concerned Friends, like the Quakers at Lake Mohonk, had been swept up in the mainstream of humanitarian reform.

For Albert Smiley the conferences at Lake Mohonk became more important than any official Quaker work for the Indians. From 1886 to 1898 he served as a representative of the Orthodox New York Yearly Meeting to the Associated Executive

Committee of Friends on Indian Affairs. This organization had been established in 1870 to help oversee and coordinate the Orthodox Quaker agents in the Indian Territory. By the period of Smiley's service on this committee the days of Quaker Indian agents were over, and the Associated Executive Committee dealt mostly with the few schools and missions under Orthodox Quaker care. Although he kept being appointed as a representative from New York, Smiley did not attend the annual meetings of the Associated Executive Committee from 1889 through 1898, his last nine years as a delegate.[45]

Similarly for Smiley, as well as for the federal government, the Board of Indian Commissioners began to fade as an influential organization after the era of Grant's Peace Policy. By the early 1880s, shortly after Smiley became a member, the board stopped auditing accounts and inspecting supplies and never again exercised financial supervision over the Office of Indian Affairs. The board, and indeed Smiley himself, did continue to visit Indian agencies out in the field, but the Indian office had its own corps of inspectors who made more visits and wrote more detailed reports. The board eventually became an advisory group whose influence over Indian policy lay more through its connections to important reformers and reform organizations than through its unclear relationship to the government's Indian service.[46]

By the turn of the twentieth century the Mohonk meetings had superseded nearly all other functions of the Board of Indian Commissioners. The board had such a small annual appropriation that it could barely afford to publish its yearly report, sustain a secretary in Washington, and hold meetings except for the Smiley-subsidized conferences at Lake Mohonk. By 1911, Albert Smiley felt that the board should be abolished. In a letter to his half brother, Daniel, Albert Smiley stated, "Our Board are [sic] expected to correct abuses in the Indian Service and we have no power whatever." In another letter, Daniel Smiley's wife, Effie Florence (Newell) Smiley told her husband, "Bro. Albert feels that the Mohonk Conference had done the most of the work accomplished in these later years and work which presumably or *apparently* the 'Board' has been doing."[47] From 1890 until his death on December 2, 1912, Albert Smiley attended only seven meetings of the Board of Indian Commissioners that were not held concurrent to the Lake Mohonk conferences. The Board normally met three times a year, first in January in Washington, D.C., then in May in New York City, and finally in October at Lake Mohonk.[48] Smiley's pattern of attendance made its own statement as to how much he valued meetings not attached to his conferences.

For Albert Smiley, his conferences had become his most important way of doing good. In fact Smiley organized other conferences at Lake Mohonk to consider the "Negro question" (in 1890 and 1891) and to advocate international arbitration (1895–1916). He expanded the Indian conferences in 1900 to consider the problems of Puerto Ricans and native Hawaiians. In 1901 the Philippines became a topic of discussion, and in 1904 the title of the conference became "Friends of the Indian and Other Dependent Peoples." Smiley even helped open a western version of the Mohonk Indian Conference in 1908 at the Mission Inn in Riverside, California.[49] The fact that both the arbitration and Indian conferences were carried on after Albert Smiley's death by his surrogate son and half brother, Daniel, demonstrated the importance of this work to other members of the Smiley family.

All these conferences at Lake Mohonk attempted to find solutions to difficult social problems whether in terms of world peace or of race relations. Within each conference Albert Smiley and his guests sought for a unity of purpose and a harmony of planning that would have pleased any traditional Quaker meeting. The active participation of women in the various conferences demonstrated another Quakerly aspect.[50] What is more, after 1901 the inclusion of Catholic representatives in the Indian conferences indicated Albert Smiley's reaffirmation of Friendly toleration toward other religions. This development helped reduce the anti-Catholic expressions that had prevailed among conference participants in the 1890s.

The Lake Mohonk conferences also may have been an influence for change among American Quakers. In the first decade of the twentieth century, two new broadly based gatherings of Friends became well established. Both the Hicksite "Friends General Conference" and the mostly Orthodox "Five Years Meeting of Friends in America" (today's Friends United Meeting) had a purpose and format that resembled the gatherings at Lake Mohonk. In fact James Wood of Mount Kisco, New York, a close friend of Albert Smiley and a regular attender of the Lake Mohonk conferences, helped found the Five Years Meeting and served as its clerk from 1907 through 1912. These Quaker conferences stressed discussion and education about important issues. They might make recommendations, but formal decisions remained with the regional Yearly Meetings.[51]

The Lake Mohonk conferences also used discussion and education to help formulate recommendations on Indian policy. Yet this very process demonstrated some variation from earlier Quaker activities. The ad hoc delegations of Friends who had often visited government officials stood in the Quakerly tradition of speaking religious Truth to worldly power. These visitors tried to stir the conscience of the nation's leaders with their message on Indian affairs. The Lake Mohonk conferences did somewhat the reverse. Political, religious, and reform leaders visited a Quaker resort where they produced their own message on Indian affairs. And their visits bestowed on their Quaker host a great deal of national recognition. Among Quakers only William Penn had held a greater position in terms of national recognition until Smiley's time. And just as Penn's reputation could not be separated from his legendary treaty with the Indians, Smiley's reputation could not be separated from his conferences at Lake Mohonk.

Yet the programs advocated at Lake Mohonk were not exclusively Quaker in their idealism. In fact Albert Smiley and the core group of mostly Protestant reformers that helped shape these conferences began with the same vision of Truth — assimilation. So the annual meetings became a discussion not of that Truth but of the means for establishing that Truth. More often than not these means narrowed down to a consideration of how to improve government programs, educational institutions, and religious missions. The leaders at Lake Mohonk were clearly reformers who rarely questioned the goal of their reforms. They were, in a manner also familiar to the Society of Friends, busily advocating doing good without necessarily questioning the good of what they advocated. Today with historical hindsight the good of assimilation like the good of allotment in severalty can be questioned. The severalty program helped create a massive loss of Indian lands and so helped increase Indian impoverishment. Similarly a loss of cultural identity through assimilation may be seen in many cases as a form of personal, psychological impoverishment. In the twentieth century many Indians would resist the continued erosion of their land holdings, just as they would resist an erosion of their cultural identity.

Well into the twentieth century Quaker leaders in Indian affairs continued to stress assimilation as a goal of Indian policy. Daniel Smiley sounded this theme during his service on the Board of Indian Commissioners from 1913 to 1930 as well as during the last five Lake Mohonk conferences that he hosted from 1913 to 1916 and in 1929. During the administration of a Quaker president, Herbert Hoover, two Orthodox Quakers, Charles James Rhoads and Joseph Henry Scattergood, served as commissioner of Indian Affairs and as assistant commissioner respectively. They also strongly advocated individualism, self-sufficiency, and assimilation for American Indians. Both men attended the final 1929 Lake Mohonk conference. In 1948, as part of a special government commission, Rhoads studied the operation of the Indian bureau. His task force concluded that "assimilation must be the dominant goal of public policy."[52]

So it is not clear that the friends of the Indian who gathered at Lake Mohonk until 1916, if given enough time beyond that period, would have come to question their assimilationist ideals. Certainly these reformers were sympathetic toward the plight of American Indians, but at the conferences few had the opportunity to interact with a diverse range of Indians and consider more fully the gentler path of acculturation. Before 1916 a full and positive appreciation of the cultural and racial diversity of American society had not taken hold. In many ways the friends of the Indian at Lake Mohonk could not escape their own homogeneity when they advocated assimilation for the Indians.

If a new and better day had dawned for the American Indian after 1916, then perhaps the Lake Mohonk conferences could be judged a great success. Certainly the conferences wanted that day to dawn, but because it did not, the accomplishments of the friends of the Indian, and of Albert Smiley in particular, must be viewed in more modest terms. They had brought to the Indian problem a spirit similar to progressivism through emphasis on the exposure of corruption and an advocacy of social responsibility, both of which were combined with a strong sense of Christian idealism. Most significantly, they sought improvement even if they did not always accomplish it. Such good efforts and sad frustrations are familiar elements in histories of many missionary endeavors. Although the Lake Mohonk conferences were not missions out in the field, they tried to create a conversion that did not succeed. In effect the conferences could not convert all federal policies and all American Indians to what they considered a "better way." Nonetheless, even at his last conference in 1912 a little more than a month before his death, Albert Smiley continued to advocate an earnest effort. In his closing remarks he reminded the conference, "Everyone of you is a magnet drawing other people. All of you are missionaries in this world. You need not go to China to be a missionary—you can right at home stir up sentiment."[53] Certainly Albert Smiley had exemplified his own advice, for at his home on Lake Mohonk he had been a good friend to friends of the Indians.

6

"Straight Tongue's Heathen Wards": Bishop Whipple and the Episcopal Mission to the Chippewas

Martin N. Zanger

The broad outlines of Bishop Henry Benjamin Whipple's career as an Indian policy reformer—his advocacy of honest administration and "enlightened" policy reforms—are well known.[1] During the 1862 Santee Sioux uprising he rose to national prominence for courageously advocating that Indians loyal to Minnesotans be rewarded for their faithfulness and that the outbreak's long-range causes in Indian-white relations be examined. He spent the next four decades as a leading Christian spokesman for Indian reform. Since scholars have paid less attention to his direct religious contacts with the native Americans in his Minnesota diocese, there will be no attempt here to chronicle Whipple's national reform career nor his simultaneous work with the Sioux. The contrivance of ignoring his considerable involvement with that tribe permits a more detailed analysis of the less familiar Episcopal experience with the Chippewas (or Ojibwas). Avoidance of specific analyses of government policies, treaty negotiations, and the like allows concentration on the missionary-Chippewa relationship.

Illness forced young Henry Whipple to drop out of Oberlin College after a year. He worked in the family business in upstate New York, dabbled in Democratic politics, and finally in the late 1840s decided to study for the ministry. Ordained an Episcopal priest in 1850, Whipple served Rome, New York. Even at this stage of his ecclesiastical career he equated

177

Henry B. Whipple, Bishop of the Protestant Episcopal Church in the U.S.A., Courtesy, Science Museum of Minnesota, Saint Paul, Minnesota.

cleanliness and godliness, requiring a poor family of German immigrants to improve their personal hygiene as a condition of continued aid. This early emphasis on "respectability" and the distinction between the deserving poor and those unworthy of assistance carried over into his attitude toward Indians. Those native people who tried to resist either of the "evils" (introduced vices or aboriginal beliefs) deserved sympathy and encouragement.

Experience in setting up a "free church" parish in the working-class southside of Chicago gave Whipple a feel for ministering to the downtrodden. He found that even among the "most brutal lives there were traces of God's image left," an opinion he also carried on to his Indian concerns. In Chicago in 1859, Whipple learned that he had been named bishop of Minnesota.[2]

In the fall of that year the new bishop journeyed to the Chippewa settlement at Gull Lake as part of a swing through the far reaches of his diocese. Accompanied by James Lloyd Breck, the missionary at Saint Columba Mission, Whipple was shocked at seeing wigwams filled with half-starved Chippewas in "pitiable condition." The sight of mothers scraping the inner bark from pine trees to feed their children appalled him. Breck had founded the mission seven years earlier, left it to the care of Ebenezer S. Peake, and went on to start another at Leech Lake. Within a year Chippewas, who he claimed had been drinking, roused him in the middle of the night and ordered him to abandon the mission. Reasoning that "he could gain no honor for his Master by allowing himself and family to be murdered by drunken savages," he left. Years later Leech Lake Chippewas told Whipple that their agent had belittled the differences between religions and encouraged them to drive away missionaries they disliked.[3]

From the time of that Gull Lake visit to his death in 1901, Whipple devoted himself consistently to the Chippewa cause as he interpreted it. By the 1860s the attitudes the bishop had begun to formulate from his initial contacts with the Indians of Minnesota had crystallized into his Indian ideology: a catalog of ideas, experiences, notions, beliefs—some

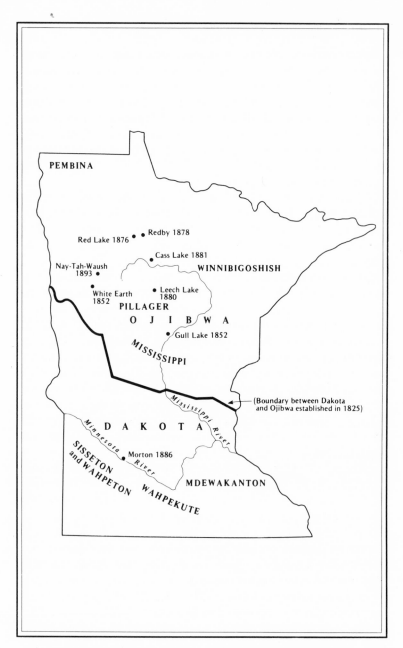

Episcopal missions among the Ojibway in Minnesota

misconceptions, others accurate; some derived from direct observation, others through hearsay—by which he judged Indian people and what constituted a proper relationship of non-Indians with them. This ideology changed only insignificantly over time. Similarly, many of Whipple's assumptions were generalized ones about Indian character, and even Indian religion, which had scant regard for tribal differences. These undifferentiated ideas affected the bishop's involvement with the Chippewas.

Whipple's papers reveal that he was no dilettante in Indian affairs, especially during the 1860s and 1870s. Policy-reform schemes, the appointment and behavior of federal Indian agents, questions about removal, treaty analyses, land cessions, annuities, timber and water resources, alcohol, "civilization" and education proposals, and, of course, missionary work are just some of the topics within the scope of his enormous correspondence. Whipple corresponded with sympathetic people on the Indian reform scene—members of the Indian Rights Association, the Board of Indian Commissioners, the Indian Commission of the Protestant Episcopal Church, and like-minded do-gooders, as well as Sioux and Chippewas themselves. Moreover, he constantly lobbied with those who could directly influence the course of Indian policy, that is, the commissioners of Indian Affairs, army officers, secretaries of the interior, congressmen, the president, and Minnesota political leaders.

Whipple's published writings and letters reiterate his twin concerns for the physical and spiritual well-being of the Indians of Minnesota. He relentlessly sought justice and honesty in Indian affairs, frequently decrying the degraded conditions on the reservations of his state. He was outraged by the injustices Indians suffered from those who would profit from the "Indian business" and by the indifference, incompetence, and even malevolence of government officials. Yet even at their nadir of degradation, Whipple did not despair in his belief that the Chippewas and the Sioux would respond positively to missionization by metamorphosing into "useful Christian citizens."

Sharing the view of reformers of his day, Whipple subscribed to an assimilationist approach to Indian peoples. "Heathens" who had been corrupted by contact with the worst elements of Euro-American culture, the Indians were innately decent human beings fully capable of "civilization." In his opinion the process simply required fair treatment and acceptance by Indians of the values of Christianity and acquisitive capitalism. Believing as he did, the bishop stressed the urgency of missions, vocational education, agricultural training, and the adoption of the style of dress and other manifestations of the majority culture.[4] The attempt to apply these ideas to Chippewa communities eventually expended an enormous amount of Episcopalian energy.

The Chippewa villages of Minnesota underwent a major transformation in the last half of the nineteenth century. With the onset of land-cession treaties and the general absence of warfare, the kinship-based social structures of larger villages like Leech Lake began to break down. Reservation politics and relations with the United States now revolved around power centers outside the warrior groups. The result was a more particularistic society in which "factions crystallized around . . . medicine cult groups, drum societies, church groups, [and] local and tribal councils." Land cessions and bitterly contested decisions about timber and water use exacerbated internal factional divisions. Latecomers to the area, the Episcopal missionaries either found Chippewa politics an unfathomable "Chinatown" or, perhaps worse, presumed to understand its inner workings when they were often naïvely incorrect.

Ethnohistorians who have examined the Chippewa fur trade and prereservation periods have pointed out that traders, agents, and missionaries met with mixed success when they attempted to intercede in Indian social and political life. The latter two especially tried to use economic inequality between Indian and non-Indian as a way of forcing acculturation, while traders simply emphasized the utility of trade rather than status differentiation and thus stressed the more Indian-like values. However, induced scarcity, particularly control of distribution of food, helped traders undermine the Chippewa communal structure. The missionaries had a similar goal.[5] While they desired Chippewa cultural adjustment to their concept of the model Christian Indian, Whipple and the Episcopalians who worked with him ironically used the time-honored device of bolstering the power of favored Indians. They attempted to enhance the prestige and influence of Christian Indians who remained in their communities. Sometimes missionaries were even called on to protect those who had opted for Christianity from their non-Christian kinsmen.[6] Gifts (ranging from fishnet twine to warm coats) dispensed to them, either directly or through native missionaries or sympathetic agents, could then either be kept or redistributed by them. Presumably this resulted in an accretion to convert and missionary power. That it meant a sort of double standard when these same missionaries worked to strip from band leaders the right to redistribute annuities seemed not to bother Whipple and his associates.[7]

One way the bishop of Minnesota tried to keep in touch with affairs in the Chippewa communities in his diocese was by visitations. Nearly every summer of his long episcopate he visited Chippewas residing on the major reservations at Red Lake, White Earth, and Leech Lake, as well as small bands and settlements. On several occasions he oversaw the fall annuity distributions. Whipple also received regular reports from lieutenants such as Enmegahbowh (John Johnson), an Ottawa Episcopal deacon and later priest, and Joseph Alexander Gilfillan, Episcopal missionary to the Chippewas. Their letters and conversation covered a wide range of subjects from acculturative progress and resistance of traditionalists to timber frauds, machinations of traders, and corruption of agents. These two men, and others (Indian and non-Indian), were the bishop's eyes and ears in the Chippewa communities. He in turn translated their parochial complaints and squabbles and pleas for money, clothing, agricultural equipment, and the like into formal requests to Indian service officials, politicians, and donators of funds for mission work who could affect Chippewa lives.

Within his diocese, Bishop Whipple's periodic visits to Chippewa country gave him some feel for his potential constituency. An avid fisherman who carried his own backpack on portages, he covered hundreds of miles of north woods by canoe each season. In one detailed journal of an early visit to Red Lake Chippewas, Whipple describes how he and his Christian and non-Christian companions talked about their religious beliefs around their campfire and in Indian villages. On one such occasion Enmegahbowh tried to use to his advantage the fact that he struck a number of Chippewas as a cross-cultural curiosity. Shaugenash, for example, told him, "When I see you and hear you talk, I can't believe you were ever wild Indian and wear breech cloth — you so unlike us. I can't believe that you was ever as we are." The Ottawa missionary replied that only the religion of Christ made him different. "I was once as your are," he preached, "but when the Great Spirit gave me little light, I followed it and more came and it made me all I am." The bishop drew on a simple analogy of his trip to Red Lake. Starting out, though he could only see a short distance, he would have been foolish to turn back before reaching his objective. Should you be shown a little way by teachers of the white man's religion, he told Shaugenash, "go, and God will show you more." To this the Chippewa fell silent, and the often optimistic Whipple reported that "he seemed very thoughtful."[8]

Several incidents on Whipple's visit to Gull Lake Mission during the Civil War illustrate his approach to the proselytization and pastoral care of Indians. He found nine Christians at the mission — the wives of White Fisher and of Minogeshik; Manitowaub and William Superior and their wives: Susannah Roy; and two elderly Chippewas baptized as Abraham and Sarah. Enmegahbowh read a service, and the bishop preached through an interpreter, confirmed several Indians, and spent a few days visiting wigwams into which, from time to time, he reported in standard missionary rhetoric, "gleams of light penetrated the darkness." A mother requested that Kitchemedewiconaye (the Great Blackrobed Priest) preside at the burial of her child and asked him to have a lock of her baby's hair made into a cross memento. Whipple commented that he had never heard a sweeter service than that sung in the Chippewas' "musical tongue."

The bishop ministered to physical as well as spiritual needs of the Chippewas as he made his rounds. Just as doling out presents was a means of gaining their respect and confidence, so too was relieving the bodily suffering of Indians, say, by pulling a sore molar. He hoped that his kindness would in turn smooth the way for the Christian message. Indeed, the bishop learned from a dentist friend in Chicago how to pull teeth to equip himself to provide this often-requested service. His new skill with forceps gave Whipple, as he put it, "the feeling that I possessed a new means of reaching the hearts of my red children."[9]

On his early visits to their villages Whipple tried out evangelical techniques on the Chippewas from which he never deviated, though he refined them over the decades. Usually in his entourage were Christianized Indians who could serve as living testimonial models for prospective converts, engaging them in casual conversation and deftly criticizing the Medicine Lodge and what they viewed as other negative features of Chippewa society. One night, lying in his tent shrouded in mosquito netting, the bishop overheard William Superior, a Gull Lake Christian, imploring Shaugenash and another "wild Indian" to embrace Christianity. Superior attested that he was happy and confident that if he continued "walking in the way" he would "reach the Great Spirit's home beyond the grave." Shaugenash was inclined to try but thought it difficult without a resident missionary. Like many other Indians he also wondered why, with one Bible, the white man had so many religions. In this exchange Superior also stressed what may be termed the "vanishing red man theme." That is, Indians everywhere, particularly where they have been exposed to the Gospel, were "dying off very fast, . . . because they will not obey the Great Spirit."[10]

In a similar vein Whipple seldom lost an opportunity to chastise the Chippewas for what he regarded as their social degradation and for clinging to pagan ceremonies. He preached that "disease & death were destroying their people, that adultery & drunkenness were the twin deadly sins," for which they would receive God's punishment. The Grand Medicine Lodge, Whipple told the Chippewas, was a "folly" which "deluded their people, that they had no word of God & no story of His Son, no message of mercy, no knowledge of home beyond the grave—that they practised on the credulity of their people." Conversations with Enmegahbowh had convinced Whipple that increased drinking and women falling prey to "the one deadly sin of their sex" were by-products of poverty and Euro-American contact. In this instance several elders agreed that their bands had been sinking into deeper poverty since losing their lands and their game and were becoming dependent on annuities. Despite avowing their intent to become Christians, they agreed that they had little chance of success unless Whipple provided them with a teacher.

On his first visit to Red Lake, Whipple preached to Chippewas crowded into the missionary's house a sermon typical of his approach to unconverted Indians. Impressed by the slit ears, ornaments, and dress of his audience, the bishop noted his "strange Congregation . . . would have been grotesque if less solemn." He tried to convey a number of simple messages in his long sermon. He had made the arduous trip to speak to them as father to children. After having created man as holy, the Great Spirit promised him happiness in exchange for obedience. But when the devil whispered otherwise, foolish man listened and sinned. Hence all men of whatever color have "a dying body and a dark heart"; all societies have graves; all humans are brothers. He then described the sinless home of the Great Spirit, the miracle of the Virgin Birth, Christ's Crucifixion, and the meaning of Christ as a mediator and the source of salvation. Then, after explaining the necessity of repentance, faith, and baptism, the bishop concluded (according to his sermon notes) as follows:

Have now told you way to Heaven—it is for you to say whether you will go or not—You will say all not plain—true—but you can

begin—Great Spirit gives more light to all who ask it—pray—
Keep praying day—avoid firewater—if you begin I promise you in
Name of God, He will help you and lead you to Heaven—All
seemed deeply interested.

Following the sermon the Red Lake headman, Madwaganonint (One Who Has Spoken), gathered his elders and spoke
with Whipple about impending land-cession matters. The
Red Lakers they represented intended to sell their land, but
because they feared that they would end like their unfortunate brothers farther south, they asked Whipple's assistance
in securing a fair treaty. As for Whipple's religious message,
these Chippewas, who already had missionaries in their midst,
cordially avoided any statements which could be called a
commitment to the Christian faith. At the same time they
certainly did not close the door on an increased Episcopal
acculturative presence among them. Madwaganonint said that
what they had understood of the sermon was "pleasant."
He hoped someday to have the bishop send a teacher and
build a school. "The Indian is like a blind man," he said.
"He cannot see, for he has no teachers. When you come you
will be welcome and we shall send you word about the
Missions."[11]

Speaking for himself, Madwaganonint said: "I think that
the trail you have brought into my country is a good trail;
those who have walked in it have not come to harm. I do
not say that I will walk in it. I do not know it. I shall always
be glad to see you and will listen with open ears to the
words you speak." Over the years the Red Lake leader gradually shifted from this early uncommitted though open-minded
stance. Whipple thought him "dignified in bearing as one of
a kingly race," and the two men built a relationship of mutual
respect. When Whipple began lobbying in Washington in
support of those Chippewas who sought acculturative features, such as schools and houses in their treaty agreements,
Madwagononint began to visit him regularly. They also corresponded through the black-Indian trader George Bonga. They
talked at length about religion as well as treaty provisions.
Finally, perhaps feeling he owed his friend something for

his efforts, Madwaganonint told Whipple: "I want your religion for my people; I can see it; it is good. I like it for two reasons. I hear that when you plant a mission you *stay*. You are patient and *make the trail plain*. Your church cares for little children. *I like it!*"[12]

In setting up Saint Antipas Mission at Red Lake, the bishop sent two young Indian missionaries, Frederick Smith and Samuel Nabicu, the son of Shadayence, a prominent Medicine Lodge figure. A regular attendant at their worship services, Madwaganonint received instruction, confirmation, and baptism. He even stood by at the chancel rail to make sure that others of his band kept their promise to be confirmed. By the 1880s, when his village consisted entirely of Christians, Madwaganonint publicly thanked Episcopalians for choosing a bishop "whose heart was large enough to have room . . ." for his people.[13]

Whipple's account of this notable conversion raises a number of important questions. What, more precisely, comprised Madwaganonint's constituency? How large was his band? To what extent did Chippewas at Red Lake or elsewhere ostracize them? In becoming at least nominal Christians, how many renounced their native religion? Extensive analysis on the Chippewa conversion process needs to be done before these kinds of questions can be answered.

The man responsible for a good many of these conversions, a man upon whom Bishop Whipple's native ministry to the Chippewas most relied, was an Ottawa, Enmegahbowh, Christianized John Johnson. A detailed examination of Enmegahbowh's career yields valuable clues about how Whipple and his Episcopal associates operated among the Chippewas. His own reminiscence glosses over details of his early "heathenism" and experience in the Grand Medicine Lodge. An Anglican minister visited the family's wigwam in Canada and persuaded his parents to allow their son to attend school with his sons. Enmegahbowh ran away after three months, but during that time he learned to read and improved his English. In later years he regretted having truncated his schooling.

Enmegahbowh (the Reverend John Johnson). An Ottawa Indian, ordained an Episcopal priest by Bishop Whipple in 1867, he became Whipple's Ojibwa interpreter and a primary informant on life in their communities. Courtesy Science Museum of Minnesota, Saint Paul.

"I might have been a greatly educated man," he mused, "and would have been a greater help to my people."[14]

Local missionaries then persuaded Enmegahbowh's parents to allow him a trial stint as a missionary at Sault Sainte Marie. Though initially his parents tried to dissuade him by saying that "heathen cannibals" awaited him, Enmegahbowh accepted the call and never saw his forebears again. He taught school at L'Anse for two years, after which time his superiors urged him to commit himself to more intensive missionary work. An awareness of his limited education made him reluctant because he felt ill-prepared to answer "heathen arguments." "I know that some of them are strong," he said, "and make strong proof in favor of heathen religion, and of the Grand Medicine Lodge."

After four more years of eastern schooling, Enmegahbowh declined the opportunity, as he put it, to attend college for fear that the study of the languages of dead heathens would not prepare him to work among living ones. While he was isolated for about ten years in the Mississippi headwaters Chippewa country, Enmegahbowh's facility in English left him. At the insistence of the influential chief Hole-in-the-Day (Pakwane-ki-sik), Enmegahbowh spent a lonely year in his village teaching a few children. In the course of that year he grew steadily more disheartened when Hole-in-the-Day's frequent raids yielded Sioux scalps. He fled to the American settlements, "tired of living with heathen."

En route to Ottawa kinsmen in Canada, Enmegahbowh married a relative of Hole-in-the-Day and Strong Ground, a respected Grand Medicine Lodge man at Rabbit Lake. The woman's parents consented to the union only on the condition that the couple not leave Chippewa territory during their lifetime. Enmegahbowh then broached the sensitive question whether the parents would allow baptism of their daughter before marriage. He was told: "We have given you our only child to protect and to make happy. If your Christian baptism would make her happy do what would be for her good." Enmegahbowh at first feared that members of his mate's Medicine Lodge would oppose the baptism, but they attended the ceremony. Moreover, as soon as he had killed a moose he claimed that his new in-laws accepted him as a worthy provider for Charlotte. The significance of this marriage is problematical. It may indicate a calculated strategic marital alliance with families prominent in the most important Chippewa religious institution, or it may simply signify tacit Chippewa acceptance of Christianity as an addition to, rather than a replacement for, their existing belief system.

Still plagued with feelings of personal inadequacy, Enmegahbowh thought seriously about abandoning the missionary field. When learned white men left the country in discouragement, he remarked, how could he and his wife accomplish anything? While his "wicked heart" urged him to quit, he remembered his vow to Charlotte's parents. When horrendous storms twice threw back his eastbound ship, Enmegahbowh saw it as a parallel to the story of Jonah: God's punishment for leaving his task undone. He later wrote that, having "exhausted my wicked efforts to leave my heathen people, I returned to live and die with them."

According to his story, upon returning to the village at Sandy Lake, Crossing Sky and his people received Enmegahbowh warmly. Although they pleaded with him not to desert them, and he found them "favorably inclined to give heed to the strange story of the life of the Great Spirit," he traveled the seventy miles to his wife's village at Rabbit Lake, where the non-Christian women built them a comfortable wigwam.

First-hand knowledge of the intricacies and esoteric rites associated with the Midewiwin, said Enmegahbowh, proved "a help during my missionary work when my heathen people have confronted me with questions as to why the Christian religion is better."[15] Already familiar with a native medicine society virtually indistinguishable from the Chippewa rite, a missionized Ottawa like Enmegahbowh could deal effectively with those who still participated in this religious institution. Talking with a Grand Medicine Lodge member, Enmegahbowh revealed his former acquaintance with "all its secrets" and dismissed them as "foolish lies to deceive the people and get gain." His Chippewa listener apparently agreed with this economic view, saying, "But all my life I have been a Medicine Man and this is my only way to get my living—What can I do for I am old"?[16]

Ordained an Episcopal deacon in 1859, Enmegahbowh was tending the Saint Columba Mission at Gull Lake when Bishop Whipple arrived in Minnesota. Enmegahbowh shared with fellow missionary James Lloyd Breck the joy of having brought old Wagemaweshkong (Grand Medicine Brother) into "Christ's flock of Ojibways." Writing from Saint Columba, Enmegahbowh reminded Breck why conversion of this particular man was considered such a coup. He had told the Ottawa missionary that he had already given up his children "to be numbered with the Christian Ojibways. . . ," that they were doing well (indeed, they were learning catechism in Enmegahbowh's home), and that they could soon expect to find him kneeling beside them in church. Moreover, Enmegahbowh noticed a behavior change which he interpreted as a favorable sign; the old man had stayed away from "whiskey city" all summer. But most significant, Wagemaweshkong had been one of the leading *midé,* or Medicine Lodge "priests," "the only one that have [sic] any way opposed the Missionaries and the Christian religion here."[17]

As relative newcomers to the field, just how well did the Episcopalians and their bishop understand Chippewa religion and its broader cultural context? Enmegahbowh probably had a firm grasp of Chippewa and Ottawa cosmology, as did some of the other Indian converts. The knowledge of priests like Gilfillan or Peake was less detailed and accurate, perhaps only partly because of the language barrier. Gilfillan, for one, became fairly proficient in the Chippewa language. Chippewa traditionalists, like other practitioners of native or nativistic amalgam religions, used protective means to guard their institutions. Anthropologist Ruth Landes refers to "the secrecy that curtained off knowledge of the Midéwiwin."[18] Thus Episcopal religionists displayed no shortage of ignorance and misinformation regarding Chippewa beliefs.

Another source of distortion stems from the tendency of missionaries to look for useful analogues to Christian tenets in the native world view. For example, in his summation of Chippewa religion Whipple saw hope for Christianizers in that these people had neither atheist nor idolator among them, believed in an afterlife, and had "a tradition of one Supreme God whom they call 'Kitchemanido'—the uncreated, or the kind, cherishing Spirit."[19] Of course, this explanation fails to recognize Christian intrusions already long incorporated into Indian beliefs by Whipple's day. Indeed, such a syncretic process may well explain the elevation in status of Kicci-manito, the primary spirit.[20]

Whipple reports other elements of Chippewa religion more accurately. His descriptions of burial practices and the Indians' conception of the soul and its passage into the afterlife are fundamentally sound. One anecdote he cherished concerns a dying Christian Indian who testified to his friends of his new faith and urged them to make themselves ready to join him in the afterworld. Hearing this, the medicine men left the village, returning two weeks later, their faces blackened in mourning. They gathered the villagers and related the following story:

We have had a fast. . . . The Great Spirit showed us the spirit world. Our friend that died is in great trouble. We found him wandering alone in much sorrow. He told us that when he went to the white man's heaven an angel asked him who he was and he said, "I am a Christian Ojibway." The angel shook his head and replied, "This is a white man's heaven; we have no Ojibways here. There are Happy Hunting-grounds for Ojibways; go there!" He went to the Happy Hunting Grounds, and an angel at the gate asked him who he was. "I am a Christian Ojibway," he answered. The angel shook his head, and said: "The Ojibways are all Medicine-men. Christians never come here. Go to the white man's heaven." My friends, our brother has lost the trail. He gave up the religion of his people, and he must forever wander alone.[21]

Variants of this story of "double discrimination" occurred for decades in the Great Lakes area, where non-Christian Algonkian speakers apparently used them to combat the spread of an alien religion.[22] "Such stories," comments Robert F. Berkhofer, Jr., "had a profound effect in discouraging converts." Why would Bishop Whipple care to reiterate a tale potentially so critical of missionary efforts? Such a colorful example of native resistance may serve to deflect criticism about the lack of Christian progress and at the same time glorify the converts made in the face of formidable opposition. Finally, Berkhofer suggests, this sort of didactic tale addressed the alienation of converts because it "symbolized in vivid terms the plight of the Lord's stepchildren caught between two cultures."[23]

Whipple was not complimentary when discussing the Grand Medicine Lodge. His description was garbled. He mixed shamanism, curing rites, and vision quests. "Medicine men" were, in his view, mere charlatans who profited from Chippewa gullibility. "They make great gain out of the people," wrote the bishop, "and are their counsellors in peace and war." Obviously the overriding reason for his hostility arose from the fact that these men were "bitter opponents of Christianity." Once they were established as influential archpagans, however, it followed that to win over one of them was a remarkable triumph.

Shadayence was a case in point. Whipple presented this "venerable Medicine-man," his Alexander Coppersmith, as "the most cunning antagonist [he] . . . ever had among the Indians." His conversion supposedly came through the example of his son. A short stay at Andrews Hall, Whipple's Indian school at Faribault, Minnesota, had evidently left an imprint on the younger Shadayence. After an interlude during which the young man worked in lumber camps, Whipple recruited him as a candidate for holy orders. By 1880 he was organizing a "young men's praying band" at White Earth Reservation who not only worked there but proselytized the Chippewas of the Pillager band at Leech Lake who had not yet "taken the faith." According to Whipple, when the elder Shadayence witnessed his son preaching, "it so touched his heart that he became a Christian." Indeed, he was said to have trekked seventy miles through snowy woods "to tell the

heathen among his people of the joy that had come to him."[24]
Shadayence told Whipple that he thought of nothing but his
new religion:

I have cast far away behind me my old Grand Medicine, for ever,
always I think on and pray to the Lord; that thought fills my
mind. When I hear the Medicine drum beat I am exceedingly
grieved and angry. Come, my friend, assist me by your good advice
to attain the object I am living for; namely to save my soul.[25]

The significance of this sort of cross-generational conversion
is elusive. Was it genuine? Did the elder Shadayence possess
an adequate comprehension of Christian theology, one that
would have satisfied most Episcopal clergymen? Did he, in
fact, totally reject his former beliefs? To what degree may it
have been feigned conversion designed to elicit tangible
rewards from the dominant society? Was it a syncretic
mechanism which allowed individuals to preserve, albeit in
modified form, Chippewa cultural integrity? Whipple offers
no clues specific to this case. He claimed that he had a
thousand times answered the question, "Do Indian converts
remain faithful to their Master?" His usual response emphasized the recency of exposure to Christianity. Then he turned
on his questioner with, "Did you ever know of a white man,
with fifteen hundred years of civilization at his back, who
was not a model of Christian propriety?"[26]

Among the other notable Chippewa converts claimed by
Bishop Whipple and his "Spirit Man," Enmegahbowh, were
Monogeshik and Nebuneshkung. Their stories conform more
closely to standard conversion patterns. No Indian faces, said
the man they called "Straight Tongue," "are . . . imprinted
more clearly on my heart."[27] Enmegahbowh's detailed account
of Nebuneshkung's conversion is instructive. He was Hole-in-
the-Day's "head soldier." According to the Ottawa missionary,
when Hole-in-the-Day proposed to have nothing to do with
the missionary "but to go on with their heathen religion,"
Nebuneshkung disagreed forcefully. He reportedly pleaded
for toleration:

No, no; let the Missionaries come among us; and let them teach and do their duty. Let us try them with unprejudiced minds. If we find anything to the disadvantage of our people, then it will be time to say to the Missionaries that we do not want their Services amongst us.

His argument prevailed, and Enmegahbowh had entree to his band.

Discussing with Nebuneshkung the fate of his "fast sinking" people before the onslaught of "a higher class of Nation," Enmegahbowh pressed him as a leader to state his plans for their future. The chief allegedly expressed love and pity for his people, but his plans did not extend beyond the crafts of war. The missionary told him that a more efficient defense than the "warclub and scalping knife" was to listen to his instruction about the Great Spirit and the afterlife. Nebuneshkung responded with a version of the story of the medicine man who converted to Christianity only to be denied admission to both the great hunting ground and heaven. He concluded:

... for this [reason], as well as the instructions received of my fathers, I hope I shall never turn to a praying man. But, at the same time, I shall not prevent Missionary [sic] from entering into our country, and if my people want to become Christians, I shall not prevent them, nor discourage them; but as to myself, I hope I shall never be one. I am too much of a man to stoop down so low like a woman; and besides, to cut my long hair locks would be a disgrace to myself and my standing.[28]

At the time of the Chippewa removal to White Earth in the late 1860s, the followers of Hole-in-the-Day and Nebuneshkung confronted one another in a tense scene. Nebuneshkung led his caravan of four hundred past angry fellow Chippewas to the reservation. Until Hole-in-the-Day's assassination four months later, Enmegahbowh feared to join them. For several years the missionary held services in Nebuneshkung's home and the homes of others in the village. Finding the chief alone one day, Enmegahbowh told him it was his duty to "stand up among his brethren, and . . . openly renounce his heathenism; that this was the only hope and salvation of his people." Ultimately convinced that even as a

warrior with "blood on his hands" he was acceptable, Nebuneshkung agreed to convert, but he explained that like
readying himself to go into battle he needed time to prepare
fully. Finally, after more exhortation and soul-searching, Nebuneshkung came to Enmegahbowh to announce:

If the Great Spirit has so big a love for poor Indian, surely Indian
ought and must give back big love. . . . Now, dear brother . . .
to be true to return my big love to the GREAT SPIRIT, I brought
this scissors, to have you cut my hair locks which I shall throw away
for ever.[29]

The symbolic renunciation of his warlike ways was traumatic.
Nebuneshkung swiveled his head wildly to see if anyone
watched his braids being cut off. Enmegahbowh tactlessly
told the shorn man that he reminded him of a baboon he had
seen at Barnum's Museum in New York.

News of the symbolic haircut spread fast. The next Sunday
curious Christian and non-Christian Chippewas gathered
early to witness the baptism. Baptized as Isaac H. Tuttle,
Nebuneshkung testified that he was prepared to lead his
people "to do battle in the cause of God." He met his first
test of faith on the way home. A member of the Medicine
Lodge called him foolish and cautioned him to "retract his
new religion" or lose his influence with his people. Others
taunted him with derisive laughter and called him "squaw."
Chief Tuttle, as he now preferred to be known, averred that
his faith was unshakable. Here the bishop's version adds
that back in his lodge the chief cried for the first time in
his life. His Christian wife, whose role in all this Enmegahbowh's account ignores, consoled him. "Can't you be as brave,"
she pleaded, "for Him who died for you as you were to
fight the Sioux?" He vowed to try, and the bishop later observed that he had "never known a braver soldier of the
cross."[30]

Tuttle's faith apparently helped him through a family crisis
in the summer of 1873, when both his fourteen- and eighteen-
year-old sons (both Christian, and one preparing for missionary work) died. Before the year was out, Tuttle too was

on his deathbed. His last request was to have his principal
men and others of the community share his last communion.
Then he uttered his last words to them, a message of Christian conformity Enmegahbowh might just as well have written himself:

My advice to you all is, be true, be firm, and be earnest to your
calling, and, as long as you are true to our FATHER, fear nothing.
Attend to your family prayers, and be punctual to your public
Services. Never stay from Public Worship, unless you are sick; and,
above all, love GOD with your hearts. I am going home to the
GREAT SPIRIT, and there I shall be waiting for you all. Love our
poor Missionary. Assist him to talk to our poor brethren.

Clearly Enmegahbowh took great pride in his conversion
of Nebuneshkung. "Here . . . is another big Indian witness
for the love of Jesus," he wrote. His example could, believed
the missionary and his bishop, help convince skeptics. Enmegahbowh wanted the story broadcast to those "Palefaces . . .
who have their doubts of an Indian becoming truly Christian,
that Indian [sic] can love Jesus with all his heart and can
be happy as well as your Palefaces who love Jesus."[31] The
"striking contrast" illustrated in Nebuneshkung's metamor-
phosis from "savage cruelty" to "obedience of the faith" provided inspirational material for Episcopal publications aimed
at supporters of missions. The *Spirit of Missions* reprinted
Whipple's maudlin letter reporting his death. The bishop
praised him as a fierce, brave warrior who, though "he stood
aloof from the religion of Christ" for years, fearing conversion would weaken his political power, finally gave in and
became gentle and childlike. "He was most happy," said
Whipple, "when leading others to the Saviour."[32]
    The Mille Lacs leader Minogeshik (baptized Edward Wash-
burne) adopted Christianity after his wife had converted, and
he led a number of his band into the faith. He revered
Whipple. By his testimony Christianity brought him solace
and helped him endure, perhaps even escape, as an individual
some of the drastic changes being wrought on his people.
The timber frauds, removals, factionalism, and other suffer-

ings affected him deeply. "I should not be an Indian," he said at one council session, "if I did not feel the wrong done unto my people; but I am a man who has started on a journey. The place I want to reach is the home the Great Spirit had made for me. If I let myself be angered by things which happen on the way, I may lose the trail."[33]

Minogeshik's motives and conversion pattern seem to fit Wilcomb Washburn's assertion that Christianity "helped the Indian accept the poor place the white world offered him and helped him overcome the rage and despair he might otherwise have felt because of his inability to prosper in that world."[34] Before categorizing a particular Indian in this way, one would have to know whether or not the convert desired prosperity on the terms offered by acquisitive capitalism. Again in Minogeshik's case, as in most others involving Whipple and his associates, not enough evidence exists to permit us to measure the degree to which Episcopal Christianity displaced, paralleled, or added to his native beliefs.

Episcopalians claimed other prominent Chippewas as trained deacons, ordained priests, and converts. At White Earth, Chief Wahbonaquot had his followers perform a three-act skit of the coming of Christianity for a visitor, the Reverend Lord Charles Harvey. After having Chippewas portray the aboriginal "free-born native American," the chief had a "wretched-looking Indian" pull a bottle of *ish-ko-te-wabo* (firewater) from under his tattered blanket. It was displayed as "the gift of the white man," and it accounted for this Indian's degraded state. At this point, said Wahbonaquot, "we hated white men, and we would not listen to his [sic] words." In the third scene the Chippewas encounter a "pale-faced man who sought neither trade nor anything else." The chief told his people to open their ears because he may have been sent by the Great Spirit. They listened and took his message to heart. To illustrate the resulting transformation, as the chief clapped his hands, there appeared "a manly young Indian clergyman in clerical clothes, . . . and by his side a gentle woman in a neat gray gown." Thus a cross-cultural transformation had taken place. The chief's pantomime demonstration showed his sincerely held view of the birth, death, and rebirth cycle of his people's history and their future course. Whipple educated and ordained Wahbonaquot's son, the Reverend Charles Wright, who served Leech Lake in the 1890s. Enmegahbowh's son, the Reverend George Johnson, whom Whipple called a gifted preacher, died before his father.

Among other converts Whipple claimed to have baptized a "hereditary chieftainness" at Sandy Lake in the 1860s. When Whipple reached her, she had just lost her baptized daughter and was hearing voices telling her to get ready for the Great Spirit's call. A chief of the Turtle Mountain Pembina band told Whipple that he had gone on a sort of modified vision quest in the woods to try to talk to the Great Spirit but "could not take a hold of His hand." Evidently he meant that previous missionary efforts had failed to reach him. Hearing the "new message" of the Episcopalians by going to sit at the feet of their "spirit man," Enmegahbowh, and by long talks with Whipple, this man turned into a devout keeper of the "praying day."[35]

Conversion may be narrowly defined as a spiritual turn toward Christian righteousness and faith. As measured by looking at those Chippewas who "found it rather easy to confine their Christianity to Sunday mornings," conversions must be judged less successful, even by Episcopal standards, than by a definition subsuming the whole range of acculturation work.[36] Such work placed special emphasis on education. Throughout his career Bishop Whipple held an abiding interest in Indian education. In addition to sponsoring much of the missionary educational effort among the Minnesota Chippewas, he stayed current with national developments in vocational education at Carlisle Indian School, Hampton Institute, Tuskegee, and reservation schools all over the West.

In Minnesota, when Whipple or his missionaries identified an especially promising young Indian catechist, they recommended separation of the boy from the contaminating influences of an Indian environment. This usually meant finding the means to send him to boarding school at Faribault. Enmegahbowh's own children apparently fit this category. Although he missed their assistance and was lonely for them, he feared what might happen to them if they did not get some "English education." Because one boy had already grown too fond of hunting, Enmegahbowh resolved to "get him away from our people."[37] Because isolation in a boarding school was not feasible for large groups, Episcopal missionaries advocated establishment of government regional schools and ultimately "smaller schools . . . under Indian teachers in every village in their Bands."[38]

Education was only the most obvious of the items in the civilization agenda. Like other self-styled friends of the Indian in the late nineteenth century, Whipple saw detribalization as a necessary part of the Christianizing process. Kinship affinities and the band-level political structure must be broken down before thoroughgoing Christian acculturation could occur. In recognition of his efforts to secure a fair settlement for the Chippewas, President Lincoln appointed Whipple to a three-man board of visitors to attend the annuity payments of the Mississippi and Pillager bands. They were to determine whether treaty provisions were being properly carried out. Whipple's report for the board criticized distribution of annuity goods by bands, because it gave "the opportunity for unworthy chiefs either to withhold a portion . . . for their own use or to bestow them on their favorites." Instead of this method, which acknowledged and even enhanced the traditional redistribution powers of Chippewa leaders, Whipple advocated allocation to families on a per capita basis.[39] In a private addendum to the report board members warned that dangerous consequences would follow if the government persisted in trying to appease recalcitrant and hostile Chippewas like Hole-in-the-Day by increasing his annuity support.[40]

Along with detribalization Whipple's lieutenants also favored an isolation strategy. Indians ought to be concentrated in one spot, one wrote, in order to "break up the tribal arrangement, and subject them to a few simple [tenets] or rules; and fence them off from Whiskey-men. Then we might have hope to giving them the blessings of the Gospel."[41] Quarantining Indians in this way, however, required a resident priest. When the Reverend Mr. Peake became an army chaplain, Enmegahbowh, as deacon, took charge of Saint Columba Mission at Gull Lake. Because there was no priest within a hundred miles, communion could be given only on Whipple's visits. Finally the bishop obtained for Enmegahbowh a dispensation in Greek and Hebrew, and he passed his examination for ordination to the priesthood. The bishop was overjoyed that "his red children could receive regularly the Christian's Bread."[42]

During the difficulties known as the "Hole-in-the-Day Uprising," Enmegahbowh and his few converts had to leave Saint Columba Mission. After their gardens were destroyed by dissidents and the church was wrecked and ransacked, some Christian Chippewas accompanied Enmegahbowh to Crow Wing, where many Chippewas gathered to separate themselves from their "hostile" brethren. Other Christians scattered, having reverted to hunting and fishing. These actions of Hole-in-the-Day's band and others amounted to an anti-Christian reaction extending beyond a protest against government policies.[43] This would explain the virulence with which Episcopal missionaries interpreted Hole-in-the-Day's actions. They depicted this band as reprobates, usurpers of leadership, representing a throwback to the worst traits of the wild Indian. They condemned some of the government's efforts to placate this protest, instead frequently calling for more violent means than the Indian Office was willing to sanction. Frustrated missionaries thus found it more comfortable to characterize Hole-in-the-Day's rebelliousness as the work of an essentially evil individual rather than to see it as a predictable native factional response to unfair treaties, forced acculturation, and other repressive measures. To explain the movement otherwise would have required an unacceptable admission of failure.

According to Whipple's informants, the "wily chief" Hole-in-the-Day had conspired with Little Crow, leader of the dissident Mdewakanton Sioux, to launch a coordinated attack on the settlements in 1862.[44] Episcopalians repeatedly took credit for a bright spot during these otherwise upsetting events.

Christian Indians and "friendly Indians, who had been influenced by the missionaries," were instrumental in thwarting the alleged plot. Enmegahbowh had a "faithful messenger" warn Fort Ripley and then fled the Gull Lake mission himself. All night he dragged a canoe bearing his wife and children down Gull River. Two of the children later died from the ordeal and exposure. Naturally, Whipple made good use of this heroic story in his fund-raising efforts for his missions.[45]

The turmoil in the Chippewa country in the 1860s profoundly disappointed some Episcopal missionaries. Following a flight for his life, the loss of two children, and the destruction of his mission, Enmegahbowh fell into deep depression. Temporarily quartered in a tent, he held Chippewa language services every Sunday. "I have been down hearted & much discouraged," he wrote, "every thing present look darks [sic]." Manitowaub, formerly one of the prized converts, had even discarded his "civilize[d] dress and put on a piece of cloth between his legs," to become a leader of Hole-in-the-Day's rebels. After this apparent reversion in Manitowaub's behavior, Enmegahbowh claimed he had never put much faith in the man's professions of Christianity. The Reverend Mr. Peake, on the other hand, praised Manitowaub for having protected the Bible from Chippewa looters at Saint Columba.[46] Another convert, William Superior, who accompanied Enmegahbowh to the fort with his family, announced that he would never return to live among the Chippewas. Enmegahbowh agreed with this reaction; he urged the visiting commissioner of Indian affairs to separate such "well disposed & civilized Indians from the wild ones—and make them a separate settlement and . . . show them every encouragement."[47] Peake hoped that the "demonstrations" of the "rowdy sect of Pillagers" would yield a treaty which would remove the "roving" Indians, leaving Saint Columba as the focus for a community of mission Indians.[48]

Among other leaders who appeared at Fort Ripley to disassociate their bands from Hole-in-the-Day and the Pillagers were Bad Boy and Shaboshkung. They told Commissioner

Dole that they wished to withdraw to their own reservation and that they hoped to have Enmegahbowh come to them as "instructor and missionary." Both Sandy Lake and Mille Lacs Chippewas supposedly sought the Ottawa missionary, while Peake preferred that the pair return to Saint Columba when the disturbance subsided. When he finally inspected the devastated mission some months after his departure, a saddened Enmegahbowh reported that his former "flocks" looked "much cast down." Even the non-Christians unanimously asked him to return, one man offering as inducement a hundred bushels of potatoes. Because he believed there were still "true Christians" at Gull Lake who felt remorseful about recent events and desired his return. Enmegahbowh was willing to do so if the bishop concurred.[49] In the months that followed, however, the missionaries—Peake, Gear, Enmegahbowh—and apparently, Whipple, vacillated on the question of whether or not a return to Gull Lake was possible or even desirable.

For some months following his ignominious ouster from Saint Columba, Enmegahbowh, destitute and despondent at Crow Wing, searched for an outlet for his missionary zeal which would be acceptable to the Chippewas and to his Episcopal superiors. Without a paid position he would have to "shoulder a gun" to hunt for the winter. He was evidently still persona non grata at Gull Lake, where the mission lay in ruins. A year after his departure Gull Lakers refused to allow his family access to their maple-sugar camps. Enmegahbowh even feared for his life.[50]

Through Whipple's influence and his kinship ties by marriage, Enmegahbowh found temporary work when he accompanied a Chippewa treaty delegation to Washington. Whipple stayed in touch with such negotiations through a network of informants that included Minnesota Senator Henry M. Rice and trader George Bonga.[51] Enmegahbowh functioned as a bilingual intermediary and tour conductor. He preached en route and in other ways attempted on behalf of his Episcopal patron to counter what he called "Romanist" influences on the Indians. He sought, with some success, to persuade the band representatives with whom he traveled to invite him to live among them and to agree to settle down and live "in the man[n]er of the whites."[52] His rambling letters to the bishop are filled with complaints about the unfair tactics of "drunken half-breeds & interpreters," of the "papist pursuasion" [sic] in the competition to win support, or at least an invitation, for a missionary. But in the process Enmegahbowh made Episcopal views known to the commissioner of Indian affairs and other policymakers. Although the issue of subsidized missionaries remained unresolved, this particular negotiation provided for a board of visitors to oversee the subsequent application of treaty provisions in Minnesota. Enmegahbowh most likely reinforced government and Chippewa inclinations to appoint Bishop Whipple to that board.

Dabbling in intersocietal political negotiations undermined Enmegahbowh's effectiveness as an Episcopal evangelist. As late as a year after the 1863 Washington trip opponents threatened to kill him if he traveled to Mille Lacs and other Chippewa settlements. Feelings ran high against those who had cooperated in the latest treaty-making venture, and Enmegahbowh found himself pilloried by leaders antagonistic to the agreement. It took him years to regain a modicum of respect as a missionary among some disgruntled bands. In the meantime he continued to decry the debauchery and homicide among the Chippewas which he said resulted from "the poisonous water." He conducted a Sunday school at Crow Wing, worried about being drafted to fight in the South ("where the niggers are"), wondered whether Indians were actually the wicked descendants of Cain, begged for a worthwhile assignment, and pondered his future.[53]

A good bit of the "wickedness" that disturbed Enmegahbowh, Whipple, and others involved in mission work related to Indian drinking and drunken behavior. They wrote about it often. Conversely, they spoke of the pure Indian, uncontaminated by the white man's manufactured drug," who "drank no devil's spittle to burn away his brains."[54] Renunciation of strong drink, like changes in hairstyle, dress, and mode of subsistence, indicated a visible shift to the ideals of Christian civilization. Enmegahbowh judged an old Sandy Lake leader, who had been under instruction for several months and who had baptized Henry Benjamin in honor of the bishop, ready for church membership because he was "truly penitent for his wicked acts and promises never more to use the *fire water*."[55] Gear and Enmegahbowh frequently reported on Chippewa drinking habits, noting an upsurge in alcohol-related deaths and violence during the stressful period after a delegation's return from Washington treaty negotiations.[56] Seldom did missionaries try to ascertain the sociopolitical ramifications of increased levels of drinking and intratribal violence. To deny widespread alcohol misuse, lethal or nonlethal, by any cultural standards is to ignore a substantial corpus of historical data. Yet the missionaries' preoccupation with the subject lends credence to the conclusion that "the abuse of alcohol became a convenient explanation for the Indians' condition and their nonacceptance of Christianity."[57]

Most of Bishop Whipple's correspondence with frontier bishops, missionaries, and teachers is concerned with evaluating Episcopal missionary endeavors and securing financial support for them. Thousands of letters from individuals and church group contributors detail the level of support he was able to win for his Indian missions. Beyond the smaller cash or in-kind donations the bishop adeptly and substantially tapped the purses of philanthropists in such families as the Vanderbilts, the Leas, and the Shattucks, many of whom he knew personally. In the early years of his episcopate Whipple was eager to recruit and adequately pay missionaries attuned to the rigors of a frontier (or even exclusively Indian) ministry. Because neither local frontier parishes nor the Episcopal church Board of Missions could underwrite these efforts, Whipple had to cultivate eastern benefactors assiduously.

In the internal Episcopalian dispute between high and low churchmen over the proper level of ritual and degree of rigidity in liturgy, Whipple comes off as nominally a high churchman. Though evangelicals attacked his "Romishness," he regarded doctrinal polemics as secondary to the clergy's duty to "preach Christ crucified." In the realm of Indian missions, even fellow Episcopal communicants were divided over church affairs on their reservations. At Cass Lake in the late 1880s, Tombey (William Johnson), described as a lesser chief, and Little Gnat requested a change in clergymen assigned to them. The other Episcopal Chippewas, "getting wind of their request, asked that no change be made"; they approved of their pastor. On another occasion twenty-six Chippewa and mixed-blood church members sent a petition asking Whipple to ordain Indian missionaries Frederick Smith and Charles Wright so that they could administer communion.[58] At other times Episcopal Chippewas let their bishop know in no uncertain terms whether or not they approved of their government agents. Often they were critical of them, though occasionally, as in the case of the two chiefs who said, "All the time the Romanist party are running down our agent," they complained of nefarious pressures on them from rival Roman Catholic factions.

Episcopal missionaries, too, sharply criticized government policies and the schemes of traders. Enmegahbowh commonly railed against "the black nigger," his epithet for trader George Bonga, while the acerbic priest Ezekiel G. Gear kept up a steady flow of comments to his bishop. Upon the turnover of agents to the Chippewas, for example, he remarked:

The rogues will have things their way now. The former [agent] I understand thinks the Indian Department a very corrupt Institution. How this thought crept through his brain, blanched with the frosts of sixty winters, I have no means of knowing.[59]

Like observant consuls in a foreign land, these men tried to pass on useful intelligence to the bishop, and like most other intelligence corps, they had misperceptions, biases, and delusions about the people they observed.

Unlike some of his subordinates, Whipple stressed ecumenism and the similarities among Protestant groups ranging from Scandinavian immigrant to Presbyterian churches. He downplayed interdenominational rivalries. Frequently he had high praise for Quaker work on behalf of Indians, and he respected the American Board of Commissioners for Foreign Missions.[60] Though competition with Catholics for converts and administrative control of the Minnesota Chippewa reservations made them the major rivals of Episcopalians, underlings such as Enmegahbowh and Gilfillan carried on much of the overtly bitter contest with Catholic priests.[61] Gilfillan accepted information from Catholic traders that Red Lake was ripe for Episcopal efforts because the Medicine Lodge had "died out" and the Congregational minister was inactive, but he bristled when "Romanists" spoke too confidently of taking over an agency.[62] Whipple generally stayed above the fray. He had a cordial, if formal, relationship with Archbishop John Ireland of Saint Paul, and although he claimed that the Episcopalians had reached more full bloods among the Turtle Mountain Chippewas in North Dakota than had their Catholic competitors, he acknowledged the sincerity of Catholic concern for these former residents of his diocese.[63] Occasionally, however, as in this entry from his Red Lake diary, his skepticism about what he thought were shallow Catholic missionary methods rose to the surface:

Among my listeners was a woman who said, "a few years ago, I was baptized, the Priest gave me a Cross & some beads—he told me to look at the Cross & count the beads & I would be a good Christian—" She said she lost her Cross and beads and has forgotten it all now—Alas! for the defective teaching of Rome.[64]

Whipple shared with other contemporary Indian policy reformers, whatever their religious persuasion, a strong faith in the civilizing influence of private property. Indians "must have rights of property," he wrote, "and then with lessons of the Gospel, we shall make them a civilized & Christian people."[65] He envisioned that as the detribalization process advanced, the Chippewas would be concentrated on the White Earth Reservation. Calling it the "handsomest country" he had ever seen and noting that it was the last remnant of Chippewa-owned land in Minnesota suitable for agriculture, Whipple presented a grand design to make it the focal point for Episcopal missionary efforts. Before long he was confident that these efforts were paying dividends. When he confirmed a class of thirty-eight there in 1871, it gladdened him to meet "only two painted savages." It also encouraged him to find other signs of progress at White Earth; the Chippewas he thought reverent, and a number of full bloods worked in a reservation sawmill.

In his long national crusade to preserve the shrinking Chippewa land and resource base, Whipple never lost sight of his ultimate goal. While the federal government had allowed the Episcopal church virtually full control over its agency at White Earth since the early 1870s, one of his biggest fears was that "deviling" parties would pressure the "civilized" Chippewas to sell part of the reservation by threatening to deal with the "blanket Indians" if they resisted. Through the last quarter of the nineteenth century the bishop used all of his political influence to protect his civilization plan. Enlisting the aid of the Indian Rights Association, in part by exploiting his connections with its Episcopal leadership, he wrote of the Minnesota Chippewas:

For 24 years I have labored and prayed for this poor people. When I began they were the most helpless and degraded men. Hundreds of them are now living as civilized men. All the other scattered bands feel that their only hope is to follow the example of the Indians at White Earth.[66]

Episcopal missionary self-appraisals of accomplishments are probably more instructive for what they reveal about the missionaries themselves than for any reliable descriptions of native communities. The Reverend Joseph A. Gilfillan's evaluation of 1873 of the Episcopal experiment at White Earth is characteristic. In religion he was satisfied that the Gospel had "seized hold of these Red men." He readily accepted it as fact when White Earth chiefs spoke to him of the frequent family prayers intoned in Chippewa homes. Their regular attendance at Sunday church services also attested to it. Chippewas sometimes even had to be crammed into Enmegahbowh's church, which held about three hundred worshipers. In those services the priest discerned a "devoutness and fervency of spirit." The Indians' attentiveness, deportment, and relish for hymn singing impressed him. In summer months Chippewas who came for morning services often milled around the church, "usually without anything to eat," until the 5:00 P.M. service. "Sometimes," wrote the priest, "Enmegahbowh takes them out a little flour—there are many heavy drains upon him—and they bake cakes of it under the trees to appease their hunger." Samaritans also doled out parcels of secondhand clothing from eastern Episcopalians.[67] As Robert F. Berkhofer remarked, ". . . probably not a few . . . converts gathered about the mission to share the 'loaves and fishes' more than the blood of Christ."[68]

Gilfillan contrasted Chippewa freedom from the vices of drinking, stealing, swearing, and Sabbath breaking with the prevalence of those sins among lumberjacks and other frontier whites. The material progress of the White Earth community also seemed to keep pace with supposed advancements in conduct. Nearly all lived in Chippewa-built log houses. Gilfillan cited favorable statistics on crops raised and acreage under cultivation. Although a shortage of livestock hindered progress, church leaders sought remedies. As Gilfillan noted, "Bishop Whipple and some friends bought a number of cows and presented one each to some of the most deserving families."

The priest thought the White Earth Chippewas were proud of their improvement. Whether speaking of housing, clothing, thrift, furniture, or crops, the chiefs commonly harangued their people about the contrast between themselves and "the wild or blanket Chippewas who have not yet adopted the habits of Civilization." Gilfillan claimed that Christianity even transformed their personalities; it "modified and mellowed them, . . . changed the very expressions of their faces."

Since his arrival at White Earth, Gilfillan had spent much of his time preparing three young Chippewas for the ministry. Kadawabide (Frederick Smith), Babinap (Peter Parker), and Kakagewigun (Milton Lightner) were learning English as Gilfillan studied the Chippewa language. The priest singled out Smith as a model Christian student, and he told Episcopalians that these men comprised "the future Enmegahbowhs, to take his place when he shall have finished his noble work." A scholarship from the Indian Committee of the Episcopal Board of Missions, grants from the Society for the Increase of the Ministry, and direct cash gifts sent by Whipple supported these young men and their families. Gilfillan hoped readers of the *Spirit of Missions* would contribute funds for their education. Because he expected the Otter Tail and Pembina bands, numbering some four hundred individuals each, to join about seventy Gull Lakers at White Earth in a few months, the priest knew that he would need these Christian-trained Chippewas to evangelize the newcomers and to shield them from Medicine Lodge forces.[69]

If the enduring attraction of the Medicine Lodge provided constant competition for Catholic and Protestant missionaries at the beginning of Whipple's episcopate in midcentury, another nativistic religious movement posed additional problems for them late in the century. In actuality, missionaries may have confused the ghost dance with another religious complex introduced from the West, the drum dance. In either case participation in one ceremony seldom meant that an Indian had renounced others. Chippewa individuals took part in both Medicine Lodge and drum dance activities with no feeling of inconsistency.[70] On the other hand, Chippewa infatuation with these dances proved somewhat ephemeral. It would be useful to know more precisely how many lapsed Christians returned to the fold, how many remained apostates, and, indeed, how many never considered themselves to have left the fold. When about fifty Sioux emissaries brought their revitalization movement to Chippewa country, Gilfillan described the ideological invasion as a major setback for decades of Episcopal progress:

They went wherever we had missions and schools. The strange dances which they brought caught like wild-fire; many of the Christians renounced Christianity for the new Sioux dance, and there was only a remnant of men and women, in our White Earth, Wild Rice River & Leech Lake Churches, who were not carried away by it. Many even of Dr. Breck's old Christians of nearly 40 years standing, and who had been our leaders for years, left the Church for the Sioux dance. It was like a desolating wave. . . . some communities have given themselves up almost wholly to Sioux dancing, and do little else. Neither farming nor the religion of our Savior, have the slightest attraction for them.[71]

Veteran missionaries saw what were by their criteria disturbing evidences of cultural retrogression in these years, the cumulative effect of habitual reliance on annuities, a decline in farming, deep-seated distrust of American promises, and bitterness over the loss of land, timber, water, rice, fish, and game resources all caused Chippewas to lean toward the "heathen party," a faction which desired "neither the white man or his religion, nor anything of his."[72] At the least this development suggests a superficial commitment to Christian ways by many Chippewas, a veneer that the new pan-Indian beliefs challenged with some spectacular initial successes.

Until his death in 1901, Bishop Whipple built his solid reputation for work with the Chippewas on the basis not of pastoral care or on numbers of successful converts or even on his own religious work, but of action in what he deemed to be their best interest. In this respect he shared with most other reformers of his day a commitment to the Christian acculturative model. Self-styled "friends of the Indian" were cultural imperialists who damaged Chippewa cultural integrity in a variety of ways which we are only beginning to understand. The respect the bishop earned among many Chippewas and virtually all well-intentioned Americans derived from his lobbying efforts on behalf of Indians. At times he was a self-appointed spokesman listened to by Indian policymakers and reformers because he voiced opinions with which they already agreed. He said what they wanted to hear, but unlike many of them, he could bolster his position by drawing upon his first-hand experience with Indians.

Sometimes unwittingly, Whipple performed as an intercultural intermediary, carrying out the wishes of one faction or the designs of a trader like his friend George Bonga. He believed himself more neutral and benign. As he reminded a belligerent and suspicious Flatmouth in 1873, "I am not a servant of the Great Father; I am the servant of the Great Spirit."[72] Yet he was still a servant with an acculturative ax to grind. Once they had established their credentials for honesty among both Indians and non-Indians, Whipple and his Episcopal forces were able to get at least a wider, if not more receptive, audience for their brand of Protestantism.

The Chippewas of Minnesota, then, responded to Episcopal missions in a variety of ways. There are instances where they used force or the threat of violence, as in the chasing of missionaries off their lands. Some opted for conversion, which in itself had a range of meanings. Others disputed Christianity by engaging in what some scholars have called "Indian theological criticism." Syncretism, the adaptation of elements of Christianity on Chippewa terms, provided another means of cultural survival, as did revitalization whether predominantly Christian or native in its form.[73]

Because the Midéwiwin itself was a nativistic response amalgamating ancient rites and beliefs with elements from external social and economic forces, many a Chippewa conversion was simply an alternative survival step beyond that amalgam. The proportionate admixtures of native and introduced features varied along a wide spectrum from one individual convert to another. It is doubtful that most Chippewa converts knowingly committed "ethnocide" in opting to incorporate more Christian elements into their lives. Many of these people were certainly experiencing community decline. For some, conversion proved a successful adaptation. For others, their behavior reveals a sort of anomic receptivity to change. Just as the missionaries' approach was not monolithic, neither was the Chippewa selection process; they often chose carefully within, as well as among, denominations. In the exercise of that choice nonreligious motives, unrecognized by the missionaries, frequently entered into their decisions.

An atomistic Chippewa social structure may have increased the range of individual responses to Christian intrusions. In some instances both missionaries and Indians revamped the system of reciprocity or gift giving fostered by the fur trade to reinvigorate the spiritual lives of those Chippewas who embraced Christianity. What is remarkable about the Chippewa experience with Episcopal missions, and other missions as well, is that, whether they accepted Christianity (even if only slightly modified on their terms) or rejected it, they maintained their strong sense of spirituality.[74] As Donald L. Fixico, a commentator on an earlier draft of this chapter put it, "Insecurity of the Chippewa psyche allowed the Episcopal religious system to tap the spiritual power of Chippewa life." The struggle either to resist the alien religion or to build a Chippewa Christian church heightened the Chippewas' religiosity and enhanced their thinking and rethinking about their relationship to the Great Spirit.

Notes

1. Angie Debo, *The Rise and Fall of the Choctaw Republic* (Norman: University of Oklahoma Press, 1934), pp. 23-24, 34-41. See also J. Leitch Wright, Jr., *The Only Land They Knew* (New York: Free Press, 1981); R. S. Cotterill, *The Southern Indians* (Norman: University of Oklahoma Press, 1954); Verner W. Crane, *The Southern Frontier, 1670-1732* (Ann Arbor: University of Michigan Press, 1929); Patricia Dillon Woods, *French-Indian Relations on the Southern Frontier, 1699-1762* (Ann Arbor: UMI Research, 1980); Arthur H. DeRosier, Jr., *The Removal of the Choctaw Indians* (Knoxville: University of Tennessee Press, 1970), pp. 18-37.

2. The standard histories of the American Board of Commissioners for Foreign Missions (hereafter ABCFM) are Rufus Anderson, *Memorial Volume of the First Fifty Years of the American Board of Commissioners for Foreign Missions* (Boston: Board, 1861); William E. Strong, *The Story of the American Board: An Account of the First Hundred Years of the ABCFM* (Boston: Board, 1910). Particularly helpful is Clifton Jackson Phillips, *Protestant America and the Pagan World* (Cambridge, Mass: Harvard University Press, 1969).

3. The relationship of civilization to the Gospel message is documented in Robert F. Berkhofer, Jr., *Salvation and the Savage: Analysis of Protestant Missions and American Indian Response, 1787-1862* (Lexington: University of Kentucky Press, 1965), pp. 1-15, 33. Early in his career Cyrus Byington embraced the New England perspective. "Where does society appear to better advantage than in New England? Why not introduce as many of the precious customs, practices & principles of our fathers, as possible?" he wrote. See Mary Elizabeth Young,

215

Redskins, Ruffleshirts, and Rednecks (Norman: University of Oklahoma Press, 1961), p. 24. See also Robert T. Lewit, "Indian Missions and Antislavery Sentiment: A Conflict of Evangelical and Humanitarian Ideals," *Mississippi Valley Historical Review* 50 (June, 1963): 39-40; Francis Paul Prucha, *American Indian Policy in the Formative Years* (Lincoln: University of Nebraska Press, 1970), pp. 211-24; James D. Morrison, *Schools for the Choctaws* (Durant: Choctaw Bilingual Education Program, Southeastern Oklahoma State University, 1978), p. 23; Phillips, *Protestant America,* p. 65.

4. William B. Morrison, *The Red Man's Trail* (Richmond, Va.: Presbyterian Committee on Publication, 1932), pp. 41-42, 47-48; Debo, *Rise and Fall,* p. 42. Although named for John Eliot, the noted Puritan missionary, the name of the station is consistently spelled "Elliot" in the pages of the *Missionary Herald.* The best study of Cyrus Kingsbury is Arminta Scott Spaulding, "Cyrus Kingsbury: Missionary to the Choctaws" (Ph.D. diss., University of Oklahoma, 1974).

5. Morrison, *Schools,* p. 24; *Missionary Herald* 18 (November, 1832): 373.

6. Cyrus Byington, *Grammar of the Choctaw Language,* ed. D. G. Brinton, M.D. (Philadelphia: McCulla & Stavely, 1879), Introduction. The only survey of Byington's life is Harriet Daniel Leake, "Sounding Horn: A Biographical Study of Cyrus Byington, Missionary to the Choctaws" (Master's thesis, University of Tulsa, 1972). See also *Missionary Herald* 18 (January, 1822): 5.

7. *Missionary Herald* 17 (October, 1821): 311; ibid., 18 (January, 1822): 5.

8. Ibid., 17 (September, 1821): 294.

9. Ibid., 17 (December, 1821): 381. See also 18 ibid., (April, 1822): 108. For an excellent discussion of the purposes of boarding schools see Berkhofer, *Salvation and the Savage,* pp. 35-43.

10. *Missionary Herald* 19 (April, 1823): 116. Some of the names were not all that pronounceable—Samuel Postlethwaite, for example.

11. Ibid., 18 (January, 1822): 7. See also Morrison, *Schools,* p. 25.

12. Berkhofer, *Salvation and the Savage,* pp. 25-26; Morrison, *Schools,* p. 25. See also *Missionary Herald* 18 (April, 1822): 103.

13. *Missionary Herald* 18 (December, 1822): 377-78; ibid., 19 (April, 1823): 115; ibid., 19 (July, 1823): 203; ibid., 19 (August, 1823): 252; ibid., 25 (December, 1829): 376.

14. Ibid., 19 (April, 1823): 115; ibid., 19 (September, 1823): 285; ibid., 22 (January, 1826): 3.

15. Ibid., 25 (June, 1829): 186; ibid., 25 (October 1829): 321; ibid., 23 (July, 1827): 213-14.

16. Ibid., 23 (September, 1827): 280; ibid., 25 (January, 1829):

11; ibid., 25 (October, 1829): 321; ibid., 25 (December, 1829): 376.

17. Ibid., 25 (October, 1829): 321; ibid., 25 (November, 1829): 347-48.

18. Morrison, *Red Man's Trail*, p. 48.

19. *Missionary Herald* 25 (September, 1829): 280; see also ibid., 24 (September, 1828): 282; ibid., 25 (October, 1829): 321; *Annual Report of the ABCFM, 1835*, pp. 93-94.

20. *Missionary Herald* 25 (September, 1828): 283; ibid., 26 (August, 1829): 283; ibid., 30 (December, 1834): 450.

21. Ibid., 25 (April, 1829): 121; see also ibid., 25 (October, 1829): 381; Morrison, *Schools*, p. 29.

22. *Missionary Herald* 25 (October, 1829): 321.

23. Ibid., 25 (November, 1829): 347; ibid., 26 (November, 1830): 348. See also Sophia Byington to Anselem and Rebecca Nye, July 23, 1829, Byington Papers, Thomas Gilcrease Institute of American History and Art (hereafter GI), Tulsa, Okla. This collection contains the corpus of Byington's original papers. Typescripts of the collection, plus some original letters, are available in the Indian Archives of the Oklahoma Historical Society (hereafter OHS). The Manuscript Division of the University of Arkansas Mullins Library has a small selection of the Gilcrease typescripts.

24. *Missionary Herald* 25 (December, 1829): 383, 384.

25. Ibid., 26 (January, 1830): 11; ibid., 29 (January, 1833): 24; see also *Annual Report of the ABCFM, 1832*, p. 104.

26. DeRosier, *Removal of the Choctaw Indians*, pp. 47-69; Debo, *Rise and Fall*, p. 42; see also Grayson B. Noley, "The History of Education in the Choctaw Nation from Precolonial Times to 1830" (Ph.D. diss., Pennsylvania State University, 1979).

27. *Missionary Herald* 24 (December, 1828): 380; Sophia Byington to Mother, September 9, 1828, Byington Papers, GI.

28. Jesse O. McKee and Jon A. Schlenker, *The Choctaws: Cultural Evolution of a Native American Tribe* (Jackson: University Press of Mississippi, 1980), p. 70.

29. *Missionary Herald* 19 (January, 1823): 9; see also James D. Morrison, *Seven Constitutions* (Durant: Choctaw Bilingual Education Program, Southeastern Oklahoma State University, 1977), pp. 23-24.

30. *Missionary Herald* 23 (September, 1827): 280; ibid., 25 (March. 1829): 153; ibid., 25 (December, 1829): 377; Morrison, *Seven Constitutions*, pp. 24-27; W. David Baird, *Peter Pitchlynn: Chief of the Choctaws* (Norman: University of Oklahoma Press, 1972), p. 25.

31. *Missionary Herald* 25 (November, 1829): 348-49; see also DeRosier, *Removal of the Choctaw Indians*, pp. 100-105; *Missionary Herald* 25 (December, 1829): 385; ibid., 26 (May, 1830): 257.

32. Cyrus Byington to Spencer Byington, January 25, 1829, Sophia Byington to Anselem Nye, July 23, 1829, Byington Papers, GI; see also *Missionary Herald* 26 (January, 1830): 21.

33. *Missionary Herald* 26 (May, 1830): 157.

34. Ibid., 26 (August, 1830): 252-54; see also Baird, *Peter Pitchlynn*, pp. 36-38; *Annual Report of the ABCFM, 1830*, p. 85; Young, *Redskins, Ruffleshirts, and Rednecks*, pp. 28-30.

35. *Missionary Herald* 26 (December, 1830): 385; DeRosier, *Removal of the Choctaw Indians*, pp. 121-28.

36. *Annual Report of the ABCFM, 1831*, pp. 80-81, 83; *Annual Report of the ABCFM, 1832*, p. 104.

37. *Missionary Herald* 27 (January, 1831): 9; ibid., 27 (September, 1831): 285; ibid., 29 (January, 1833): 24.

38. *Annual Report of the ABCFM, 1832*, p. 99; Debo, *Rise and Fall*, pp. 65-66, 77-79.

39. Cyrus Byington to Anselem Nye, October 1, 1833, Cyrus Byington to Sophia Byington, June 19, 1834, Byington Papers, GI; see also Cyrus Byington to Sophia Byington, October 22, 1832, Byington Papers, GI; *Missionary Herald* 29 (November, 1833): 425.

40. Cyrus Byington to Sophia Byington, July 23, 1834, October 15, 1834, March 20, 1835, Byington Papers, GI; *Missionary Herald* 30 (December, 1834): 453-55; ibid., 31 (January, 1835): 24-25.

41. Cyrus Byington to Anselem Nye, June 29, 1836, Byington Papers, GI; *Missionary Herald* 33 (January, 1837): 21.

42. Spaulding, "Cyrus Kingsbury," p. 175; Cyrus Byington to Sophia Byington, September 29, 1847, Byington Papers, GI; *Annual Report of the ABCFM, 1839*, p. 140.

43. *Missionary Herald* 32 (March, 1836): 110; Debo, *Rise and Fall*, p. 62.

44. Morrison, *Schools*, pp. 77-79; *Annual Report of the ABCFM, 1848*, pp. 288-89.

45. Cyrus Byington to Brother, August 20, 1852, Byington Papers, GI; Cyrus Byington to Sophia Byington, December 12, 1852, Byington Papers, Indian Archives, OHS; see also Joseph Henry to J. D. Lesley, May 16, 1870, no. 740, American Indian Manuscript Collection, American Philosophical Society, Philadelphia, Pa.

46. Morrison, *Schools*, p. 79; *Annual Report of the ABCFM, 1848*, p. 246; *Annual Report of the ABCFM, 1856*, p. 198; Earnest Trice Thompson, *Presbyterianism in the South: Vol. 1, 1607-1861* (Richmond, Va.: John Knox Press, 1963), p. 449.

47. Morrison, *Schools*, pp. 73-76.

48. Ibid., pp. 90-93; Baird, *Peter Pitchlynn*, pp. 64-65.

49. Minutes, December 12, 1842, October 10, 1843, ABCFM Mis-

sionaries, Choctaw Nation, Hotchkins Collection, Historical Foundation of the Presbyterian and Reformed Churches (hereafter HF), Montreat, North Carolina (microfilm).

50. Cyrus Byington to Lucy Byington, September 24, 1844, December 20, 1844, Byington Papers, GI.

51. Morrison, *Schools*, pp. 201-02; Minutes, May 6, 1853, ABCFM Missionaries, Choctaw Nation, Hotchkins Collection, HF.

52. Debo, *Rise and Fall*, pp. 61-62. This conclusion may be over optimistic. A recent statistical study has shown that 49 per cent of Choctaw heads of households were unable to read or write any language in 1900. The collapse of the school system in the decade following the Civil War may account for the illiteracy at the turn of the century rather than reflecting negatively on the nature of instruction before 1860. See Lance Weisend, "Accumulation of the Choctaw and Comanche Indians: A Quantitative Study of the Family, 1900" (Master's thesis, Oklahoma State University, 1982).

53. Anderson, *First Fifty Years*, pp. 321, 322.

54. Spaulding, "Cyrus Kingsbury," pp. 191, 214; *Constitutions, Treaties, and Laws of the Choctaw Nation, 1847* (reprint, vol. 14; Wilmington, Del.: Scholarly Resources, 1973), pp. 20, 32, 37, 60.

55. *Annual Report of the ABCFM, 1848*, p. 89. For Byington's attitude see Cyrus Byington to Spencer Byington, December 29, 1831, Cyrus Byington to Sophia Byington, November 6, 1856, Byington Papers, GI; Courtney Ann Vaughn, "Job's Legacy: Cyrus Byington, Missionary to the Choctaws in Indian Territory," *Red River Valley Historical Review* 3 (Fall, 1978): 14-16. How Presbyterian missionaries in Indian Territory as a whole approached the slavery issue is discussed in William G. McLoughlin, "Indian Slaveholders and Presbyterian Missionaries, 1837-1861," *Church History* 42 (1973): 535-51.

56. Spaulding, "Cyrus Kingsbury," p. 198; Morrison, *Schools*, pp. 169-71, 177-79, 208-209, 213-14; John Edwards to J. L. Wilson, Edwards Papers, Indian Archives, OHS; S. Orlando Lee to Commissioner of Indian Affairs, March 25, 1862, in Annie Heloise Abel, *The American Indian as Slaveholder and Secessionist* (Cleveland: Arthur H. Clark Co., 1915), pp. 75-79; *Annual Report of the ABCFM, 1840*, pp. 63-64; *Annual Report of the ABCFM, 1843*, p. 67; *Annual Report of the ABCFM, 1844*, pp. 66-68.

57. An objective treatment of the controversy is found in Lewit, "Indian Missions and Antislavery Sentiment," pp. 39-55.

58. *Annual Report of the ABCFM, 1848*, pp. 97-102. For Byington's views see Cyrus Byington to Sophia Byington, July 1, 1848, Byington Papers, GI.

59. *Annual Report of the ABCFM, 1848*, pp. 102-10.

60. Cyrus Byington to Sophia Byington, October 10, 1851, October 16, 1851, Byington Papers, GI.

61. Cyrus Byington to Sophia Byington, October 7, 1852, October 28, 1852, Byington Papers, GI; daily entries, September 6, 22, 24, October 26, 28, December 1, 1852, Journal of Cyrus Kingsbury, 1852-53, and sketch of Simon Harrison, Hotchkins Collection, HF.

62. Cyrus Byington to Sophia Byington, August 4, 1851, August 9, 1851, December 12, 1851, October 10, 1851, Byington Papers, GI.

63. Lewit, "Indian Missions and Antislavery Sentiment," pp. 51-53; John Edward to G. W. Wood, February 27, 1856, Edwards to S. B. Treat, October 9, 1856, Edwards to G. W. Wood, February 19, 1857, Treat to Brethren, July 27, 1859, John Edwards Papers, Indian Archives, OHS. For the work of the General Assembly Board see McLoughlin, "Indian Slaveholders and Presbyterian Missionaries," pp. 542-46; *Historical Sketches of the Missions Under the Care of the Board of Foreign Missions of the Presbyterian Church in the U.S.A.* (Philadelphia, Pa.: Women's Foreign Mission Society, 1886), pp. 27-29.

64. Kingsbury et al. to Walter Lowrie, February 15, 1860, box 10-1, no. 73, American Indian Correspondence, Presbyterian Historical Society (hereafter PHS), Philadelphia, Pa.; *Historical Sketches,* p. 29.

65. Cyrus Byington to Walter Lowrie, January 12, 1860, box 10-1, no. 56, American Indian Correspondence, PHS. Although the letter is dated 1860, internal evidence makes it certain that it was written in 1861.

66. Cyrus and Sophia Byington to George and Lucy Dana, April 29, 1854, Byington Papers, GI; William G. McLoughlin, "The Choctaw Slave Burning: A Crisis in Mission Work Among the Indians," *Journal of the West* 13 (1974): 113-27.

67. Cyrus Byington to J. L. Wilson, April 16, 1860, September 6, 1860, box 10-1, nos. 99, 167, American Indian Correspondence, PHS; Morrison, *Schools,* pp. 177-78, 213-15.

68. Minutes, September 14, 1861, Session of the Indian Presbytery, Hotchkins Collection, HF.

69. Sophia Byington to Brother, May 8, 1851, Byington Papers, GI.

70. Cyrus Byington to Lucy Byington, August 19, 1846, Byington Papers, GI.

71. Cyrus Byington to Sophia Byington, August 9, 1851, Sophia Byington to Sister, April 15, 1852, Cyrus Byington to Sophia Byington, October 6, 1851, Byington Papers, GI.

72. Cyrus Byington to Lucy Dana, January 10, 1853, Byington Papers, GI.

73. 1 Cor. 1:30. See minutes, March 31, 1864, Session of the Indian Presbytery, Hotchkins Collection, HF.

74. Anderson, *Fifty years,* p. 259; Constitution of the Choctaw Nation, 1860, art. 7, secs. 4, 19, in Morrison, *Seven Constitutions,* pp. 115, 117.

75. Anderson, *Fifty Years,* p. 303.

76. Quoted in Spaulding, "Cyrus Kingsbury," pp. 267, 268.

CHAPTER 2

Acknowledgment: This chapter could not have been completed without the invaluable assistance of two persons. Walter N. Vernon, Jr., a noted historian of Oklahoma Methodism, whose father served churches in western Oklahoma in the early 1900s, generously lent microfilm, photocopies, and notes he has gathered in his impressive survey of research materials; no words of thanks could be sufficient. Patricia Jorgensen typed the manuscript, handling obscure notations and ridiculous deadlines with valor and grace.

1. Sidney H. Babcock, "John Jasper Methvin, 1846-1941," *Chronicles of Oklahoma* 19; no. 2 (June, 1941): 113. Basic biographical sketches are provided in the Babcock article and in Sidney Henry Babcock and John Young Bryce, *History of Methodism in Oklahoma . . .* (Oklahoma City: By the authors, 1935), pp. 231-40; Leland Clegg and William B. Oden, *Oklahoma Methodism in the Twentieth Century* (Nashville, Tenn.: Parthenon Press, 1968), reprints Methvin's obituary from the *West Oklahoma Conference Journal* (1941) on pp. 288-90; C. E. Nisbett, "John Jasper Methvin," *Encyclopedia of World Methodism,* ed. Nolan B. Harmon (Nashville, Tenn.: United Methodist Publishing House, 1974), 2:1595.

2. John Jasper Methvin, "Reminiscences of Life Among the Indians," *Chronicles of Oklahoma* 5 (June, 1927): 166.

3. Babcock and Bryce, *History of Methodism in Oklahoma,* p. 23.

4. Much of the background provided in these paragraphs is discussed in the first chapter of Clegg and Oden, *Oklahoma Methodism.*

5. Ibid., p. 28.

6. For a list of the schools, see Clegg and Oden, *Oklahoma Methodism,* pp. 28-29.

7. Minutes, Indian Mission Annual Conference, 41st session, October 20-25, 1886.

8. *Our Brother in Red* 4, no. 4 (December, 1885): 1.

9. Minutes, Indian Mission Annual Conference, 41st session, October 20-25, 1886.

10. Ibid.

11. Babcock, "John Jasper Methvin," p. 114.
12. Report by J. O. Shanks and J. F. Thompson, in Minutes, Indian Mission Annual Conference, 42d session, October 12-17, 1887 (manuscript). Also published in *Our Brother in Red* 6, no. 8 (October 22, 1887): 2.
13. J. J. Methvin, "Work Among the Wild Tribes," *Methodist Review of Missions* 14, no. 4 (October, 1893): 204. An edited version of the same article reappeared in *Methodist Review of Missions* 21, no. 1 (March, 1901): 533-36.
14. J. J. Methvin to Babcock, August 5, 1931, published in Babcock, "John Jasper Methvin," p. 115.
15. Methvin, "Reminiscences," p. 169.
16. Mildred P. Mayhall, *The Kiowas,* 2d ed. (Norman: University of Oklahoma Press, 1971), pp. 106, 108. Much of the following summary of Kiowa culture and history is dependent upon Mayhall's book, an introductory overview of Kiowa ethnohistory. Virtually all historians, including Mayhall, are in turn dependent on James A. Mooney's classic interpretation of Kiowa calendars: *Calendar History of the Kiowa Indians,* Smithsonian Institution, Bureau of American Ethnology, 17th Annual Report (Washington, D.C., 1895). Anthropologists also have relied upon cultural descriptions by missionaries: Thomas C. Battey, *The Life and Adventures of a Quaker Among the Indians* (Norman: University of Oklahoma Press, 1968; originally published 1875); John Jasper Methvin, *Andele, or the Mexican-Kiowa Captive* (Louisville, Ky.: Pentecostal Herald Press, 1899). Alice L. Marriott, *Kiowa Years: A Study in Culture Impact* (New York: Macmillan, 1968), discusses effects of white contact. Books on Kiowa folklore include Alice Marriott, *Saynday's People: The Kiowa Indians and the Stories They Told* (Lincoln: University of Nebraska Press, 1963); Wilbur S. Nye, *Bad Medicine and Good: Tales of the Kiowas* (Norman: University of Oklahoma Press, 1962); Elsie Parsons, *Kiowa Tales,* American Folklore Society, Memoir no. 22 (New York, 1929).
17. Mayhall, *The Kiowas,* pp. 307-15.
18. Battey, *Life and Adventures,* p. 4.
19. Ibid., p. 314.
20. The most widely available description of the Baptist effort, Isabel Crawford, *Kiowa: Story of a Blanket Indian Mission* (New York: Fleming H. Revell Co., 1915), narrates life at the Saddle Mountain mission from 1896 to 1906.
21. Report by Agent E. E. White, in *Fifty-seventh Annual Report of the Commissioner of Indian Affairs . . . , 1888* (Washington, D.C.: Government Printing Office, 1888), p. 97. John J. Methvin, *In the Limelight: Or, A History of Anadarko and Vicinity* (Anadarko, Okla.:

By the author, 1925), pp. 84-85. Milton A. Clark, "Work Among the Kiowa and Comanche Indians," *Western Methodist,* August 15, 1907, p. 4; Mayhall, *The Kiowas,* p. 307.

22. Methvin, "Work Among the Wild Tribes," p. 205.

23. J. J. Methvin, in *Our Brother in Red* 6, no. 19 (January 14, 1888): 3.

24. *Woman's Missionary Advocate,* February, 1893, p. 235.

25. J. J. Methvin, "Work Among the North American Indians," in *Missionary Issues of the Twentieth Century: Papers and Addresses of the General Missionary Conference of the Methodist Episcopal Church, South . . .* (Nashville, Tenn.: Executive Committee, 1901), p. 455.

26. Clegg and Oden, *Oklahoma Methodism,* p. 15.

27. Walter N. Vernon, in *One in the Lord: A History of Ethnic Minorities in the South Central Jurisdiction, the United Methodist Church* (Oklahoma City: Commission on Archives and History, S.C. Jurisdiction, UMC, 1977), p. 29.

28. Methvin, "Work Among the North American Indians," p. 455.

29. Report by J. J. Methvin in *Sixty-first Annual Report of the Commissioner of Indian Affairs . . . , 1892* (Washington, D.C.: Government Printing Office, 1892), p. 390. Frederick Norwood includes a brief discussion of women associated with the Methvin mission in "American Indian Women," *Women in New Worlds: Volume II,* ed. Rosemary Skinner Keller and others (Nashville, Tenn.: Abingdon Press, 1982), pp. 185-87.

30. Report of an address by J. J. Methvin to the Women's Board of Missions, published in the Fort Worth *Daily Gazette* and reprinted in the *Woman's Missionary Advocate,* July, 1891, p. 8.

31. Report by Mrs. M. B. Avant in *Woman's Missionary Advocate,* November 1890, p. 140.

32. *Woman's Missionary Advocate,* September, 1894, p. 72.

33. Ibid., June, 1893, p. 364. Samples of other mentions of "camp work" in ibid.: August, 1890, p. 16; September, 1890, p. 86; July, 1891, p. 8; December, 1891, p. 176; January, 1892, pp. 204-205; March, 1893, p. 271; May, 1893, p. 334.

34. Methvin, "Work Among the Wild Tribes," p. 207.

35. Methvin, "Reminiscences," p. 179. See also the brief description of a revival at New Hope Seminary, p. 167.

36. Mayhall, *The Kiowas,* pp. 149-54.

37. For a provocative, introductory portrayal of this contrast, see Barre Toelken, "Seeing with a Native Eye: How Many Sheep Will It Hold?," in *Seeing with a Native Eye,* ed. Walter H. Capps (New York: Harper, 1976), pp. 15-17.

38. Methvin, *In the Limelight,* p. 88.

39. Ibid.

40. Ibid.

41. Letter from Acting Commissioner of Indian Affairs to Charles E. Adams, April 25, 1890; "Kiowa-Methvin Institute," Indian Archives Division, Oklahoma Historical Society.

42. Mrs. M. B. Avant, in *Woman's Missionary Advocate,* August, 1890, p. 45.

43. J. J. Methvin, in *Woman's Missionary Advocate,* September, 1894, p. 74.

44. *Woman's Missionary Advocate,* April, 1892, p. 305.

45. Eugenia Mausape, T-37 (35:200), *Duke Indian Oral History Collection* (Norman: University of Oklahoma, American Indian Institute, 1972). Reproduced on microfiche, Greenwich, Conn. Johnson Associates, 1981.

46. Ibid. See also interviews with Guy Queotone, T-637 (37:212), and Ethel Howry, T-78 (27:154).

47. Mayhall, *The Kiowas,* p. 140.

48. Methvin, "Work Among the Wild Tribes," p. 205. Methvin here is referring to mission efforts in general, but the remarks are applicable to the school.

49. Robert F. Berkhofer, Jr., *Salvation and the Savage: An Analysis of Protestant Missions and American Indian Reponse, 1787-1862* (Lexington: University of Kentucky Press, 1965).

50. Guy Queotone, T-637 (37:212), in *Duke Indian Oral History Collection.*

51. Ethel Howry, T-78 (27:154) in *Duke Indian Oral History Collection.*

52. Mrs. M. B. Avant, in *Woman's Missionary Advocate,* August 1890, p. 46.

53. Methvin, in *Woman's Missionary Advocate,* December 1891, p. 176.

54. For instance, in the January, 1894, *Woman's Missionary Advocate,* p. 211, Methvin wrote: "I sigh for two or three more ladies like Miss Brewster. She is an inspiration to the other missionaries here, as well as a benediction to the Indians."

55. *Woman's Missionary Advocate,* January, 1892, p. 204. See also ibid., December, 1891, p. 176.

56. Methvin, "Work Among the North American Indians," p. 454.

57. Ibid.

58. Ibid.

59. Ibid., pp. 453-54.

60. Methvin, "Work Among the Wild Tribes," p. 206.

61. J. J. Methvin, "The Western Tribes and Our Work Among Them,"

Western Methodist, May 9, 1907; Methvin, "Reminiscences," p. 178.

62. Methvin, "Western Tribes."

63. T-37 (35:200), *Duke Indian Oral History Collection.*

64. Cecil Horse, T-27 (34:191-2), *Duke Indian Oral History Collection.*

65. Angie Debo, *A History of the Indians of the United States* (Norman: University of Oklahoma Press, 1970), p. 113.

66. Howard L. Harrod, *Mission Among the Blackfeet* (Norman: University of Oklahoma Press, 1971), p. 21.

67. T-138 (35:200-201), *Duke Indian Oral History Collection.*

68. For example, see Methvin, "Western Tribes." "There is an Indian woman here who speaks seven different languages, English, French, Spanish and four of the Indian tongues. She says sometimes in a crowd she hears some of these curious people saying unseemly things about her, thinking that she is nothing but a poor ignorant Indian, and she turns to them, and thanks them in the language which they are speaking for their compliments. The astonishment it produces makes the old lady shake with laughter as she tells about it."

69. Clegg and Oden, *Oklahoma Methodism,* p. 91.

70. R. Pierce Beaver, ed., *The Native American Christian Community: A Directory of Indian, Aleut, and Eskimo Churches* (Monrovia, Calif.: MARC, 1979), p. 363.

71. Some of the following comments are borrowed from two of my previous publications: "Thomas Fullerton's Sketch of Chippewa Missions, 1841-1844," *Methodist History,* January, 1979, p. 108; "Evangelization and Acculturation Among the Santee Dakota Indians, 1834-1864" (Ph.D. diss., Princeton Theological Seminary, 1977) pp. 78-81.

72. Wade Crawford Barclay, *The History of Methodist Missions* (New York: The Board of Missions and Church Expansion of the Methodist Church, 1949), 1:318-57. William R. Cannon, "Education, Publication, Benevolent Work, and Missions," in *The History of American Methodism,* ed. E. S. Bucke (New York, Nashville: Abingdon Press, 1964), 1:586-99.

73. Barclay, *History of Methodist Missions,* vol. 1, p. 203.

74. Milton A. Clark, "Work Among the Kiowa and Comanche Indians," *Western Methodist,* August 15, 1907, p. 4.

75. *Woman's Missionary Advocate,* January, 1895, p. 207.

76. Ibid.

77. For instance, Guy Queotone attended the Institute for six or seven years and then returned as an adviser. T-637 (37:212), *Duke Indian Oral History Collection.*

78. Quoted by Vernon, *One in the Lord,* p. 27.

79. Methvin, *Andele,* p. 181.

80. See Vernon, *One in the Lord,* pp. 27-29. Clegg and Oden, *Oklahoma Methodism* pp. 283-92.

81. Methvin, *Work Among the "Wild Tribes,"* p. 204.

82. Methvin, "Reminiscences," p. 176.

83. Ibid.

84. Ibid., p. 177.

85. Methvin, *Our Brother in Red* 6, no. 2 (September 15, 1888): 7.

86. *Woman's Missionary Advocate,* March, 1891, p. 270.

87. Methvin, "Reminiscences," p. 177.

88. Ibid., p. 178. *Woman's Missionary Advocate,* September, 1894, p. 73.

89. *Woman's Missionary Advocate,* May, 1895, p. 335.

90. Ibid., September, 1895, p. 76.

91. Ibid., July, 1891, p. 8.

92. Methvin, "Reminiscences," p. 167.

93. Cecil Horse, T-27 (34:191-2), *Duke Indian Oral History Collection.*

94. *Our Brother in Red* 7 no. 2 (September 15, 1888): 7.

CHAPTER 3

1. Leonard J. Arrington and Davis Bitton, *The Mormon Experience* (New York: Alfred A. Knopf, 1979), p. 146.

2. Ibid.

3. Ibid.

4. Sidney E. Ahlstron, *A Religious History of the American People* (New Haven and London: Yale University Press, 1972), pp. 502-503.

5. Arrington and Bitton, *The Mormon Experience,* p. 146.

6. Ibid.

7. Ibid., pp. 145-46.

8. This phrase was coined by Perry Miller for the book, *Errand into the Wilderness.*

9. Howard Christy, "Open Hand and Mailed Fist: Mormon-Indian Relations in Utah, 1847-1852," *Utah Historical Quarterly* 46 (Summer, 1978): 228-29.

10. George Washington Bean, "Autobiography," in Latter-day Saints Historical Department, Salt Lake City, Utah, p. 12 (hereafter LDS Historical Department).

11. For ethnography see Anne M. Smith, *Ethnography of the Northern Utes,* Papers in Anthropology no. 17 (Sante Fe: Museum of New Mexico Press, 1974); *Ute Ways* (Salt Lake City: Uintah-Ouray Ute Tribe, 1976); Fred A. Conetah, *A History of the Northern Ute People*

(Salt Lake City: Uintah-Ouray Ute Tribe, 1982).

12. Ibid.

13. Ibid., p. 13.

14. Ibid., p. 14.

15. Solomon Nunes Carvalho, *Incidents of Travel and Adventure in the Far West with Colonel Fremont's Last Expedition* (New York: Derby and Jackson, 1856), p. 193.

16. Ibid.

17. Ibid.

18. Ibid., pp. 193-94.

19. *Latter-day Saints Millenial Star* 16 (September 9, 1854): 563-65.

20. "A Blessing upon the head of George W. Bean setting him apart to his Mission among the Lamanites, given by W. Woodruff and A. P. Rockwood in the Seventies Council Hall, April 22, 1855," in LDS Historical Department.

21. Bean, "Autobiography."

22. Journal of Aroet Lucious Hale, n.p., in LDS Historical Department.

23. Ibid.

24. Jack Rice, Maurine Frank, John Alley et al., *Nuwuvi' A Southern Paiute History* (Reno: Intertribal Council of Nevada, 1976), p. 13.

25. The most complete description of a settlement mission is presented in Charles S. Peterson, *Take Up Your Mission: Mormon Colonizing Along the Little Colorado River, 1870-1900* (Provo, Utah: Brigham Young University Press, 1973).

26. Communication was obviously poor. Thomas D. Brown in his *Journal of the Southern Indian Mission* admonished himself: "You are not sent to farm, build nice houses and fence fine fields, not to help white men, but to save the red ones, learn their language, and you can do this more effectually by living among them as well as writing down a list of words, go with them where they go, live with them & when they rest let them live with you feed them, clothe them and teach them as you can, & being thus with you all the time, you will soon be able to teach them in their own language, they are our brethern, we must seek them, commit their language, get to their understanding, & when they go off in parties you go with them. This, I call no fort, a new settlement will be made south west of this, but with you new houses and farms is not the first thing, but their language—their language—to know all their language, *I find Dymock, Geo. Bean & other interpreters much deficient in understanding what they say.* Learn their language perfectly, and help yourselves in labor only to live, a room or two in the building may be necessary for headquarters." [Italics mine.] *Journal of the Southern Indian Mission: Diary of Thomas D. Brown,* ed. Juanita Brooks (Logan, Utah: Utah State

University Press, 1972), pp. 29-30.

27. Arrington and Bitton, *The Mormon Experience,* pp. 212-13.

28. For the only major source on the White Mountain Expedition see Clifford L. Stott, *Search for Sanctuary: Brigham Young and the White Mountain Expedition* (Salt Lake City: University of Utah Press, 1984).

29. Norman Furniss, *The Mormon Conflict* (New Haven, Conn., and London: Yale University Press, 1960).

30. Stott, *Search for Sanctuary,* p. 217.

31. Bean, "Autobiography," p. 18.

32. *Deseret News,* September 28, 1861.

33. *Report of the Secretary of the Interior, 1862,* pp. 160-61.

34. Bean, "Autobiography," p. 19.

35. For a more complete treatment of this subject, see *Report of the Secretary of the Interior, 1862.*

36. National Archives Record Groups, 75, Unratified Treaties File (Ute).

37. Ibid.

38. Hubert Howe Bancroft, *History of Utah* (Salt Lake City, Utah: Bookcraft, 1964), p. 633.

39. Bean, "Autobiography," p. 19.

40. Ibid.

41. In a speech delivered at Snowflake, Arizona, President Spencer W. Kimball said that more than 20,000 Navajos are Latter-day Saints today. *Navajo Times,* July 27, 1978, p. A-16. The *Navajo Times* of March 1, 1979, p. B-14, reported that there were at that time 45,000 Indian Mormons, and that 20,000 of them were Navajos.

CHAPTER 4

For her assistance in the accumulation of research materials for this chapter, I wish to thank Sharon Prendergast, of the Crosby Library, Gonzaga University.

1. Gilbert J. Garraghan, S.J., *The Jesuits of the Middle United States* (New York: America Press, 1938), 2:238. By the middle 1830s "Black Robe" was being used by the Indians of the Oregon Country to mean any Christian minister. But when the Protestant missions in the interior of the Oregon Country closed in 1847, the predominance of Jesuits in the area gave the title exclusively to them. It is today universally considered a synonym for a Jesuit missionary. Thomas E. Jessett, "Origin of the Term 'Black Robe,'" *Oregon Historical Quarterly* 69 (Spring, 1968): 50-56.

2. Hiram M. Chittenden and Alfred T. Richardson, *Life, Letters and Travels of Father Pierre-Jean De Smet, S.J., 1801-1873* (New York: Francis P. Harper, 1905), 1:25ff. In 1841, DeSmet was named superior of the Rocky Mountain Mission by the Missouri Province superior of the Society of Jesus. He remained dedicated to this mission field until 1846, when he was reassigned to Saint Louis as procurator for the Missouri Vice-Province. Joseph Joset, S.J., took DeSmet's place as superior of the six residences in the Rocky Mountain Missions.

3. The Missouri Vice-Province of the Society of Jesus, established in 1830, was responsible for the missionary activity in the vast, undefined "Oregon Country," which they termed the Rocky Mountain Missions. In 1851 the father general detached the Rocky Mountain Missions from the Missouri Jesuits and the region in the west became known simply as the California and Oregon Missions. This arrangement left the missions without support, so in 1854 the Turin Province (Italy) assumed responsibility for them as dependencies. In 1858 the California and Oregon Missions separated from each other, though not from the Turin Province. Henceforth each had separate superiors, and the Oregon Missions once again were referred to as the Rocky Mountain Missions.

4. Mengarini, an Italian by birth, joined the Society of Jesus in 1828 and came to America in 1840 to serve in the missions. His facility with languages, medicine, and music made him an especially valuable missionary. He was with DeSmet in the journey of 1841 and stayed at Saint Mary's Mission until it closed in 1850. His efforts in the Flathead tongue received wide acclaim from Indians, fellow Jesuits, and linguists. See Gregory Mengarini, S.J., *Recollections of the Flathead Mission,* ed. Gloria R. Lothrop (Glendale, Calif.: Arthur H. Clark, 1977).

The Whitman massacre had a tremendous impact on the Catholic missions, especially since the Reverend Henry Spalding charged that the Jesuits masterminded the Indian attack on the Whitman Mission on November 29, 1847, when fourteen whites were killed. Spalding went so far as to have the inscription "She always felt that the Jesuit Missionaries were the leading cause of the massacre" included on his wife's tombstone. In 1849, Joseph Accolti, S.J., was named the superior. A year later Saint Mary's Mission was ordered closed because the missionaries were being harassed by whites and Indians in the vicinity. Accolti protested. He felt that the Indians were intimidating the missionaries. Another priest wrote, "Our Fathers in China have more to fear from the sword of the Mandarin, still they stand firm." In addition, the society was in a dilemma over whether to concentrate manpower in Gold Rush California or the Indian Northwest. Garraghan,

Jesuits in the Middle United States, 2:385; Clifford M. Drury, *Henry Harmon Spalding: Pioneer of Old Oregon* (Caldwell, Idaho: Caxton Printers, 1936), p. 361.

5. *Woodstock Letters*, 21:429; "Cataldo Autobiographical Notes," Oregon Province Archives of the Society of Jesus (hereafter OPA), Gonzaga University, Spokane, Washington.

6. C. A. Hawkins, "Father Cataldo, S.J.," (manuscript, 1930), Cataldo Collection, OPA, p. 18. George F. Weibel, S.J., "Rev. Joseph M. Cataldo, S.J., Jubilarian, A Short Sketch of a Wonderful Career," *Gonzaga Quarterly* 16 (February 20, 1928). Also published in *Salem Catholic Monthly* in 1928, 1, no. 5:9-12, 18-23; no. 6:11-15, 21-22; no. 7:11-15, 19-20, and reprinted as a pamphlet, March 15, 1928. Hereafter the pagination from the reprint is cited. The change in spelling from "Spokan" to "Spokane" took place over years of white influence. For purposes of regularization the present-day spelling is used throughout this chapter.

7. The first mission among the Coeur d'Alene Indians was established in 1842 by Nicholas Point, S.J., and was named Saint Joseph. It was along what is now called the Saint Joe River. In 1846 a new mission was built farther along the Coeur d'Alene River and called Mission of the Sacred Heart. It is the first permanent building in the state of Idaho and today is enclosed in a state park. In 1878 the working mission was removed to De Smet, Idaho, where it remains even today staffed by Jesuit missionaries.

8. Laurence E. Crosby, *"Kuailks Metatcopum" (Black Robe Three-Times Broken)* (Wallace, Idaho: Wallace Press-Times, 1925), pp. 12, 5. This privately printed publication was also offered in Italy as C. Testore, trans., *Kuahilks Metatcopnim: le memorie di un Vest Enera* (Venice, 1935).

9. Weibel, "Cataldo," p. 11; [Joseph M. Cataldo, S.J.], "Autobiography of Kauilks Metatcopnin," *Jesuit Missions* published in 1927, 1, no. 1:13-14; no. 2:33-34; no. 3:53-54; no. 4:75-76, 78; no. 5:95-96; no. 6:114-116, 54.

10. This was evidence of the activities at Fort Walla Walla of the trader Pierre C. Pambrun, a devout Catholic. Washington Irving, *The Adventures of Captain Bonneville* (New York: P. F. Collier, n.d.), 3:291, 340.

11. See Allen Slickpoo, *Noon Nee-Me-Poo (We, the Nez Perces)* (Lapwai, Idaho: Nez Perce Tribe of Idaho, 1973); Deward E. Walker, Jr., *Conflict and Schism in Nez Percé Acculturation: A Study of Religion and Politics* (Pullman: Washington State University Press, 1968); Clifford M. Drury, *Chief Lawyer of the Nez Perce Indians, 1796-1876* (Glendale, Calif.: Arthur H. Clark, 1979); Alvin M. Josephy, Jr.,

The Nez Perce Indians and the Opening of the Northwest (New Haven, Conn.: Yale University Press, 1965).

12. Erwin N. Thompson, "Joseph M. Cataldo, S.J., and St. Joseph's Mission," *Idaho Yesterdays,* 18 (Summer, 1974): 19; Drury, *Chief Lawyer,* p. 270.

13. Joseph M. Cataldo, S.J., "The Nez Percé Indian Mission," Cataldo Collection, OPA. This manuscript was dictated to Michael O'Malley, S.J., a scholastic, in 1905. It was subsequently published in *Lewiston Catholic Monthly* in 1922, 5 no. 9:17-20, 24; no. 10: 17-21; no. 11:18-20; no. 12:13-14; 6 no. 1:12-16; no. 2:15-16, 23). "Historia Domus," 1901-15, St. Joseph (Slickpoo) Collection, OPA, entry for June 7, 1905. See also [Joseph M. Cataldo, S.J.], "Sketch of the Nez Percés Indians," *Woodstock Letters,* 1880, 9:43-50, 109-18, 191, 199; 1881, 10:71-77, 198-204.

14. [Cataldo], "Sketch of the Nez Percés Indians," p. 46.

15. Ibid., p. 45. Three Catholic miners from Lewiston donated their services for a few days to help Cataldo. The Indians "owing to the invectives" made against Cataldo by "one of Lawyer's adherents,"were reluctant to participate in the project. Cataldo, "The Nez Percé Indian Mission," pp. 3-4. See also for this period Michael O'Malley, S.J., "Mission Career of Father Cataldo, S.J." and Michael O'Malley, S.J., "Northwest Blackrobe: The Missionary Career of Father Joseph Cataldo, S.J.," (manuscripts), O'Malley Collection, OPA.

16. Previously, on Cataldo's trip to Saint Ignatius Mission after his winter with the Spokanes in 1867, his horse stumbled, and the priest injured his leg. Cataldo walked with a limp, but his leg was not really broken. Fortunately, when Cataldo did truly break his leg, he was found by two Indians who took him back to Orofino, where he spent forty days in recuperation. Cataldo, "The Nez Percé Indian Mission," pp. 6-8.

17. [Cataldo], "Sketch of the Nez Percés Indians," p. 47; Burns, *Jesuits and the Northwest,* p. 370.

18. Drury, *Chief Lawyer,* pp. 263, 274; Kate C. McBeth, *The Nez Percés Since Lewis and Clark* (New York: Fleming H. Revell Co., 1908), pp. 77-81. Spalding was with the Nez Percés as a missionary from 1836 to 1847; and as a superintendent of education on the reservation from 1862 to 1865. See also Peter J. Rahill, *The Catholic Indian Missions and Grant's Peace Policy, 1870-1884* (Washington, D.C.: Catholic University of America Press, 1953).

19. John Monteith to E. P. Smith, May 5, 1872, Office of Indian Affairs, Letters Received, Idaho Territory, National Archives Microroll 234.

20. Charles Ewing to Secretary of Interior, October 28, 1873, ibid.; Weibel, "Cataldo," p. 19; [Cataldo], "Sketch of the Nez Percés In-

dians," p. 115.

21. Cataldo, "The Nez Percé Indian Mission," p. 12; Weibel, "Cataldo," p. 19. Slickpoo was a corruption of Zimchiligpusse. The seven-acre plot on which the church stood was carried in the agency books as a "donation" by the Catholic Nez Percés.

22. Cataldo insisted that the Treaty of 1863 provided carpenters for the benefit of Indians, and his Catholic school building applied. Monteith refused to supply lumber and nails and also attempted to prevent white workers from Lewiston from being available to the Catholics. [Cataldo], "Sketch of the Nez Percés Indians," p. 192; Thompson, "Cataldo and St. Joseph's Mission," p. 23.

23. Burns, *Jesuits and the Northwest,* p. 373, says, "In all his actions and writings, this neutrality was Cataldo's inflexible position, both with White men and Red." Cataldo was not unaware of the political situation, and he also knew that Monteith was eager to discredit him.

24. *Lewiston Teller,* April 28, May 5, 1877, microfilm copy, Idaho State Historical Society. A rebuttal of Monteith's charges by Congressional Delegate S. S. Fenn in the *Congressional Record,* 45th Cong. 2d sess. (May 2, 1878), pp. 3141-43 refers to the "infamy of Monteith," and the "base and slanderous chargers . . . against Reverend Father Cataldo . . . ."

Cataldo met Ollikut again in April. The Indian hinted at becoming a Catholic, but he wanted first to know more from Cataldo about "the injustice of the Government in dealing with the Indians of the Wallowa Valley." Cataldo could only encourage him to come into the mission at Slickpoo. [Cataldo], "Sketch of the Nez Percés Indians," p. 75; Cataldo, "The Nez Percé Indian Mission," p. 17.

25. Burns, *Jesuits in the Northwest,* pp. 376-78, covers the Council in May with Joseph. Cataldo was in attendance. General Oliver O. Howard was somewhat piqued at Cataldo's neutrality, since he was led to believe by Monteith that the Jesuit had great power among the Indians. Howard wanted Cataldo to join the government side and scolded Cataldo that " 'neutrality' was, in my judgment, equivalent to positive opposition."

26. Ibid., pp. 59, 405-20, is comprehensive on the subject of Cataldo during the Nez Percé war. Burns, a Jesuit and a historian, believes Cataldo's extensive peace efforts were motivated by a fear that the entire tribe would be destroyed and with it his own considerable effort. He wished to limit the war not necessarily for the sake of pacificism but for the extensive commitment he and the Society had made toward the tribe. Wilfred P. Schoenberg, S.J., a Jesuit historian, believes that Cataldo and the other Jesuits who worked for peace in 1877 did so "in part to convince Washington that the Catholic missionaries were

not traitors and that they could be trusted despite the abuses heaped upon them as a result of Grant's Peace Policy." This was necessary, he speculates, because "it was a period when religious and racial labels were taken too seriously," and the largely Italian immigrant clergymen had something to prove. Wilfred P. Schoenberg, *Paths to the Northwest, A Jesuit History of the Oregon Province* (Chicago: Loyola University Press, 1982), p. 112.

A testimonial letter of thanks was signed by over one hundred white citizens of the region and presented to Father Cataldo. It is in the Cataldo Collection, OPA. Only Mark H. Brown, *The Flight of the Nez Percé* (New York: G. P. Putnam's Sons, 1967), p. 50, still incorrectly views Cataldo as a possible conspirator in the Nez Percé war.

27. Cataldo, "The Nez Percé Indian Mission," p. 19.

28. Ibid.

29. See Edmund R. Cody, *History of the Coeur d'Alene Mission of the Sacred Heart* (Caldwell, Idaho: Caxton Printers, 1930).

30. Burns, *Jesuits and the Northwest,* pp. 41, 48-50.

31. [Cataldo], "Sketch of the Nez Percés Indians," p. 49.

32. Joseph M. Cataldo, S.J., to Very Reverend Provincials and Superiors of the Society of Jesus in America, April 4, 1879, Provincial Papers, OPA.

33. Cataldo Correspondence, 1879-81, in ibid.

34. Schoenberg, *Paths to the Northwest,* p. 118.

35. *Woodstock Letters,* 1889, p. 358. See also Joseph M. Cataldo, "Spokane Mission: Indian and White, 1865 to 1886" (132-page manuscript), Cataldo Collection, OPA.

36. Aegidius Junger to Joseph M. Cataldo, October 31, 1881, Provincial Papers, OPA. See Wilfred P. Schoenberg, S.J., *Gonzaga University, Seventy-five Years, 1887-1962* (Spokane, Wash.: Gonzaga University, Press, 1963), for all facets of the foundation of Cataldo's college and the growth of Spokane.

37. Joseph M. Cataldo to Peter Beckx, December 17, 1881, trans. Gerard Steckler, S.J., Gonzaga University Collection, OPA. See also Weibel, "Cataldo," pp. 23-25; Hawkins, "Father Cataldo, S.J.," pp. 85-90.

38. An excellent summary of Cataldo's European trip in 1885 is Lucia Ahern, "The Long Harvest: The Life of Joseph M. Cataldo, S.J." (Master's thesis, Nebraska State Teachers College at Peru, 1958), chap. 13, "The European Recruiting Tour." Ahern translated many letters written by Cataldo in his native Italian. Seventeen of the recruits came to America with Cataldo; fourteen departed when their studies were completed. Eight were Italian, thirteen were French, four were German, one each came from Holland and Belgium, and the final four

were American scholastics picked up along the way. Cataldo also accepted donations in the amount of 30,000 francs.

39. Weibel, "Cataldo," pp. 28-31. Cataldo, like many other Catholic Indian missionaries of the period, received generous financial help from the sizable inheritance of Katherine Drexel, founder of the Sisters of the Blessed Sacrament.

40. Cataldo was very troubled by the Crow Indians. He feared that they had "committed some great sin," for they seemed to be in the "power of the devil." But after just six months at Saint Francis Xavier Mission, Cataldo had achieved such success that his associate wrote that "the Indians would have destroyed the mission . . . if the Lord had not been served by Father Cataldo." Letter of Father Andreis to the Scholastics of Chieri, January 11, 1894, in *Lettre della Provincia Torinese* (1900), trans. Lucia Ahern, pp. 87-88, Cataldo Collection, OPA.

41. Father L. Courardy, a Belgian priest, was assigned to the Umatilla reservation in 1875 by the bishop at Portland. He left in 1888, and the Jesuits took over, not because they were eager to add to their number of missions but because no other agency could assume the responsibility. Saint Andrew School was built in 1889-90. Letter of Father Joseph Cataldo to Reverend Father Provincial, February 13, 1900, in ibid., pp. 199-206.

42. Cataldo, "The Nez Percé Indian Mission," pp. 23-24. The allotments were made by Alice Fletcher, assisted by Jane Gay. See E. Jane Gay, *With the Nez Percés: Alice Fletcher in the Field, 1889-92*, ed. Frederick E. Hoxie and Joan T. Mark (Lincoln: University of Nebraska Press, 1981).

Five churches, four Presbyterian and one Catholic, were allotted 160 acres each. The Catholics also opted to buy 160 acres more from the federal government at three dollars an acre. Two Jesuits also took out patents for homesteads, giving the mission an additional 320 acres, or a total of over 600 acres. St. Joseph (Slickpoo) Collection, OPA.

43. Letter of Father Joseph Cataldo to Reverend Father Provincial, February 13, 1900, in *Lettere della Provincia Torinese* (1900), p. 206. See Francis Paul Prucha, *The Churches and the Indian Schools 1888-1912* (Lincoln: University of Nebraska Press, 1979).

44. Cataldo, "The Nez Percé Indian Mission," p. 24. Father Soer, who was then resident at Saint Joseph Mission, begged from his relatives and friends in Holland $2,000 for the school plus $480 to pay the government for the additional 160 acres.

45. Letter of Father Joseph M. Cataldo to Reverend Father Provincial, September 9, 1903, in *Lettere della Provincia Torinese* (1904), pp. 93-94.

46. Letter of Father Cataldo to the Reverend Father Provincial, January 23, 1905; ibid., 1907, p. 107; Cataldo, "The Nez Percé Indian Mission," p. 24.

47. Crosby, *Kuailks Metatcopun,* p. 15; Rev. J. M. Cataldo, "Early Inland Empire Indians Spoke Four Basic Languages," *Spokane Spokesman-Review,* May 15, 1925. Presumably Cataldo's experience among the Italians of San Jose was more peaceful than in 1903 when "he made a great effort to awaken among the Italian population of Spokane their sleeping religion." A "capitano" was murdered, and three days later his assailant was struck down, leaving a total of twelve orphans and two widows behind. Cataldo refused to permit a Catholic burial for either man, and he nearly started a riot. Letter of Joseph Crimont to the Fathers and Brothers of Alaska, January 1, 1904, in ibid. (1907), p. 89.

48. Joseph M. Cataldo, S.J., *Jesus-Christ-Nim (The Life of Jesus Christ)* (Portland), Ore.: Schwab Printing Co., 1915).

49. Letter of Father Cataldo to the Reverend Father Provincial, January 23, 1905, in *Lettere della Provincia Torinese* (1907), p. 107; O'Malley, "Northwest Blackrobe" and O'Malley, "Mission Career."

50. "Historia Domus," 1916-27, St. Joseph (Slickpoo) Collection, OPA, entry for April 19, 1919; Cataldo, "The Nez Percé Indian Mission," p. 25.

51. Weibel, "Cataldo," pp. 35-36; [Cataldo], "Autobiography," *Jesuit Missions,* p. 116.

52. The Cataldo Collection, OPA, has a large collection of newspaper clippings, congratulatory cards, and memorabilia from these celebrations.

53. Cataldo, "The Nez Percé Indian Mission," p. 12.

54. Rev. Joseph M. Cataldo, "Little Nez Percé Children Taught Elders to Pray," *Spokane Spokesman-Review,* May 13, 1925; Burns, *Jesuits in the Northwest,* p. 372: Letter of Father Cataldo to the Reverend Father Provincial, January 23, 1905, in *Lettere della Provincia Torinese* (1907), p. 107.

55. Burns, *Jesuits in the Northwest,* pp. 372, 38-40.

56. Garraghan, *Jesuits of the Middle United States,* 2:562-63. The original diary is at the Pius XII Library, Saint Louis University. See also Ponziglione in *Woodstock Letters,* 1879, 1880.

57. Sue McBeth, who came to the Nez Percés in 1885 as a Presbyterian missionary, believed that "no real progress could be made until tribal relations were broken up" and the power of the chiefs destroyed. Her conversions among the Indians exceeded those of Cataldo. McBeth, *The Nez Perce Lewis and Clark,* p. 220.

CHAPTER 5

For their aid and advice during my research, I wish gratefully to acknowledge Jane Rittenhouse Smiley, of Lake Mohonk, New York; Larry E. Burgess, of the A. K. Smiley Public Library, Redlands, California; and Barbara Curtis, of the Quaker Collection, Haverford College, Haverford, Pennsylvania.

1. Paul Stuart, *The Indian Office: Growth and Development of an American Institution, 1865-1900* (Ann Arbor, Mich.: University Microfilms International Research Press, 1978, 1979), pp. 60-63.

2. Clyde A. Milner II, *With Good Intentions: Quaker Work Among the Pawnees, Otos, and Omahas in the 1870s* (Lincoln: University of Nebraska Press, 1982), pp. 2-4.

3. National Archives (hereafter NA), Record Group (hereafter RG) 75, "Minutes of the Board of Indian Commissioners" (hereafter BIC), 1869-1915 (manuscript entry 1381); ibid., 1869-1933 (typescript, entry 1382). A complete list of BIC members appears at the end of vol. 3 of entry 1382.

4. NA, RG 48, Records of the Secretary of the Interior, Appointments Division, members of the BIC, letter sent by A. C. Barstow; *Friends Review* 32 (1878-1879): 681, obituary of John D. Lang.

5. Milner, *With Good Intentions*, pp. 190-91. The best study of the Hicksite-Orthodox schism among American Quakers which began in the 1820s is Robert W. Doherty, *The Hicksite Separation: A Sociological Analysis of Religious Schism in Early Nineteenth Century America* (New Brunswick, N.J.: Rutgers University Press, 1967).

6. *Proceedings of the Sixth Annual Meeting of the Lake Mohonk Conference of the Friends of the Indian* (hereafter LMC), 1888, p. 30. These proceedings were published separately by the conference each year and were regularly reprinted in the annual reports of the BIC.

7. Excellent studies of the early history and theology of Quakerism include Hugh Barbour, *The Quakers in Puritan England* (New Haven, Conn.: Yale University Press, 1964); and Peter Brock, *Pioneers of the Peaceable Kingdom* (Princeton, N. J.: Princeton University Press, 1968).

8. Ellen Starr Brinton, "Benjamin West's Painting of Penn's Treaty with the Indians," *Bulletin of Friends' Historical Association* 30 (Autumn, 1941): 99-131.

9. Rayner Wickersham Kelsey, *Friends and the Indians, 1655-1917* (Philadelphia: Associated Executive Committee of Friends on Indian Affairs, 1917).

10. Minutes of New England Yearly Meeting of Friends, 1856-1879. Quaker Collection, Haverford College, Haverford, Pa. (hereafter QC). The minutes were printed and distributed in time for the yearly meeting in early June.

11. Larry E. Burgess, *Alfred, Albert, and Daniel Smiley: A Biography* (Redlands, Calif.: Beacon Printery, 1969), pp. 3-13; Biographical Catolog of the Matriculates of Haverford College: 1833-1922 (Philadelphia: Haverford Alumni Association, 1922). There were seven nongraduates in the class of 1849 of Haverford College.

12. Larry E. Burgess, *Mohonk: Its People and Spirit, A History of One Hundred Years of Growth and Service* (New Paltz, N.Y.: Smiley Brothers, 1980), pp. 15-20.

13. Burgess, *Albert, Alfred, and Daniel Smiley*, pp. 51, 74-75.

14. LMC, 1885, p. 1.

15. Roy W. Meyer, "Ezra A. Hayt (1877-1880)" in Robert M. Kvasnicka and Herman J. Viola, eds., *The Commissioners of Indian Affairs, 1824-1977* (Lincoln: University of Nebraska Press, 1979), pp. 161-62; Report of Committee of Inquiry, January 31, 1880, in Annual Report (hereafter AR), BIC, 1879, pp. 68-71. A. C. Barstow did not sign the report because he had not heard all the testimony in the investigation, but he considered the report's general statements to be fair and correct.

16. Investigation of Indian Bureau, April 1, 1880, AR, BIC, 1880, pp. 51-53. Smiley's chairmanship of both committees was mentioned in LMC, 1894, p. 38.

17. I am indebted to J. William Frost, director of the Friends Historical Library of Swarthmore College, for challenging and shaping my ideas about insularity, assimilation, and distinctiveness in Quaker history, as well as aiding my thoughts that appear later on Quakers and conferences.

18. Philip S. Benjamin, *The Philadelphia Quakers in the Industrial Age, 1865-1920* (Philadelphia: Temple University Press, 1976), pp. 100, 212-215.

19. Visit to Dakota—Report of Commissioners Smiley and Whittlesey, July 30, 1883, AR, BIC, 1883, pp. 33-38.

20. LMC, 1894, p. 38.

21. Visit to Dakota, AR, BIC, 1883, pp. 33-38; Albert K. Smiley's manuscript notebook of the Dakota trip, unpaginated, Mohonk Mountain House Archives, Lake Mohonk, N.Y.

22. LMC, 1889, pp. 98-100.

23. Ledger F, Mohonk Mountain House Archives; List of Members, LMC, 1890, pp. 151-56 and LMC, 1910, pp. 185-87; Larry E. Burgess, "The Lake Mohonk Conferences on the Indian, 1883-1916"

(Ph.D. diss., Claremont Graduate School, 1972), pp. 20-21.

24. Burgess, "The Lake Mohonk Conferences," pp. 19-20; Francis Paul Prucha, *American Indian Policy in Crisis: Christian Reformers and the Indian 1865-1900* (Norman: University of Oklahoma Press, 1976), pp. 145-46.

25. Prucha, *American Indian Policy in Crisis*, pp. 145-49.

26. LMC, 1885, p. 50; 1890, pp. 151-52; 1896, p. 114.

27. LMC, 1885, pp. 14-15; 1886, pp. 11, 43.

28. LMC, 1887, p. 63.

29. LMC, 1895, p. 49. For criticism of the Dawes Act by historians see Wilcomb E. Washburn, *The Indian in America* (New York: Harper & Row, 1975), pp. 243-44, and Arrell Morgan Gibson, *The American Indian: Prehistory to the Present* (Lexington, Mass.: D. C. Heath and Co., 1980), pp. 486-510.

30. LMC, 1898, p. 42.

31. Ibid., p. 93.

32. LMC, 1901, p. 46.

33. Visit to agencies in New Mexico, Arizona, and California—Report of Commissioners Smiley and Whittlesey, AR, BIC, 1884, pp. 15-17. In a letter to his younger half brother, Daniel, Albert Smiley said that the Pueblo Indians ". . . the people—their houses and habits resemble strongly the Syrians." (Albert K. Smiley to Daniel Smiley, February 26, 1884; A. K. Smiley Public Library Archives, Redlands, California.)

34. AR, BIC, 1887, pp. 17, 19-21; Walter C. Roe to Albert K. Smiley, June 11, 1907, and Smiley to Merrill E. Gates, June 12, 1907, Smiley Family Papers, QC.

35. Report of Albert K. Smiley, AR, BIC, 1889, appendix A; Report of Albert K. Smiley, AR, BIC, 1890, pp. 11-13; Report of Commissioner Albert K. Smiley of a visit to the Mission Indians made in the spring of 1894, AR, BIC, 1894, pp. 13-18; Diary of Albert K. Smiley for 1891 Mission Indian Commission, unpaginated, A. K. Smiley Public Library Archives, Redlands, California.

36. Prucha, *American Indian Policy in Crisis*, pp. 161-65.

37. Report of Albert K. Smiley, AR, BIC, 1895, pp. 12-14; LMC, 1895, pp. 18-20. The manuscript of Smiley's report to the Board of Indian Commissioners is in the Smiley Family Papers, QC.

38. LMC, 1897, p. 94.

39. LMC, 1903, pp. 80, 140.

40. Journal of the Fifteenth Annual Conference with Representatives of Missionary Boards, AR, BIC, p. 98.

41. Albert K. Smiley to W. A. Jones, August 5, 1913, Box 5-A, letterbook p. 270, Smiley Family Papers, QC; Burgess, "The Lake Mohonk Conferences," p. 198; List of Members, LMC, 1903, pp. 143-

45; 1904, pp. 167-69.

42. Charles Eastman's speeches are in LMC, 1890, p. 46; 1895, pp. 15-16, 66-68; 1907, pp. 176-77. Carlos Montezuma's words are in LMC, 1895, p. 68. Other proassimilationist Indians who spoke at Lake Mohonk include Chester Cornelius (Oneida), LMC, 1890, pp. 78-79; John Lolorias (Papago), LMC, 1901, pp. 75-77; Charles E. Dagnett (Peoria), LMC, 1907, p. 24; Simon Redbird, LMC, 1908, pp. 47-50; Henry Roe Cloud (Winnebago), LMC, 1910, pp. 14-16.

43. LMC, 1904, pp. 55-57. James M. Haworth's work among the Kiowas and Comanches is presented in Lawrie Tatum, *Our Red Brothers and the Peace Policy of President Ulysses S. Grant* (1899; reprint, Lincoln: University of Nebraska Press, 1970), pp. 166-202. Tatum served as the first Quaker agent to the Kiowas and Comanches. Haworth replaced him.

44. Benjamin, *The Philadelphia Quakers in the Industrial Age*, p. 113. Accounts of Quaker missions in the Indian Territory may be found in the closing chapters of Kelsey, *Friends and the Indians,* and Tatum, *Our Red Brothers.*

45. Minutes of the Associated Executive Committee of Friends on Indian Affairs were printed annually by the committee. The Quaker Collection at Haverford College has the minutes for 1886, 1889-1895, 1897-1898. The yearly meetings often heard from their delegates to the Associated Executive Committee. These reports appear in the minutes of the various Orthodox Yearly Meetings. In Smiley's case it is the minutes of New York Yearly Meeting which are also available at Haverford.

46. Stuart, *The Indian Office*, pp. 69-71.

47. Albert K. Smiley to Daniel Smiley, March 26, 1911, and Effie (Mrs. Daniel Smiley) to her husband, n.d. [approximately March 26, 1911], Box 32, item no. 209, Smiley Family Papers, QC. For a more positive assessment of the board's work, see Henry E. Fritz, "The Last Hurrah of Christian Humaniarian Indian Reform: The Board of Indian Commissioners, 1909-1918," *Western Historical Quarterly* 16 (April, 1985): 147-62.

48. NA, RG 75, Minutes of BIC.

49. Laurence M. Hauptman, Introduction, *Index of the First and Second Mohonk Conferences on the Negro Question* (New York: Clearwater Publishing, 1976); Laurence M. Hauptman, Introduction, *Index of the Proceedings of the Lake Mohonk Conferences on International Arbitration* (New York: Clearwater Publishing, 1976); *Riverside* (Calif.) *Daily Press*, April 27, 1908, clipping from Archives of A. K. Smiley Public Library, Redlands, California.

50. In the last years of the Indian conference Smiley seemed con-

cerned about "an undue preponderance of women" and added "very few feminine names" to the guest list because the meetings had taken on "a feminine touch and seemed to lack virility." Henry S. Haskins, secretary of the Lake Mohonk Conference of Friends of the Indian and other Dependent Peoples, to Charles S. Lusk, September 17, 1912, Bureau of Catholic Indian Missions, Correspondence, District of Columbia, 1912 (September), Marquette University Archives.

51. Edwin B. Bronner, "An Historical Summary" in Bronner, ed., *American Quakers Today* (Philadelphia: Friends World Committee, 1966), pp. 23-24; "James Wood" in William Bacon Evans, ed., "Dictionary of Quaker Biography," compiled typescript.

52. LMC, 1913-16, 1929; Lawrence C. Kelly, "Charles James Rhoads (1929-33)" in Kvasnicka and Viola, eds., *The Commissioners of Indian Affairs,* pp. 263-70. The quotation from the Hoover Commission report of 1948 is on p. 270. The Board of Indian Commissioners continued to hold its autumn meeting at Lake Mohonk from 1917 to 1928, although the "Friends of the Indian" conferences were no longer being held.

53. LMC, 1912, p. 268.

CHAPTER 6

1. For Whipple's reform career in its national context see Robert W. Mardock, *The Reformers and the American Indian* (Columbia: University of Missouri Press, 1971); Francis Paul Prucha, *American Indian Policy in Crisis: Christian Reformers and the Indian, 1865-1900* (Norman: University of Oklahoma Press, 1976); Henry E. Fritz, *The Movement for Indian Assimilation, 1860-1890* (Philadelphia: University of Pennsylvania Press, 1963); Helen M. Bannan, "The Idea of Civilization and American Indian Policy Reformers in the 1880s," *Journal of American Culture* 1 (Winter, 1978): 787-99. The institutional framework of Episcopal Indian missions is outlined in R. Pierce Beaver, *Church, State, and the American Indian: Two and a Half Centuries of Partnership in Missions Between Protestant Churches and Government* (Saint Louis: Concordia Publishing House, 1966).

2. Henry Benjamin Whipple, *Lights and Shadows of a Long Episcopate* (New York: Macmillan, 1899), pp. 1-10, 18-21; 26-27.

3. Ibid., pp. 30-31. See also Whipple, "Civilization and Christianization of the Ojibways in Minnesota," *Collections of the Minnesota Historical Society* 9 (1889-1900): 130.

4. Whipple to H. H. Montgomery, July 1, 1901, Henry Benjamin Whipple Papers, Minnesota Historical Society (hereafter HBW Papers).

5. Harold Hickerson, "The Chippewa of the Upper Great Lakes: A Study in Sociopolitical Change," in *North American Indians in Historical Perspective* Eleanor Burke Leacock and Nancy Oestreich Lurie, eds., (New York: Random House, 1972), pp. 182, 186-89.

6. Ebenezer Steele Peake to Whipple, February, 1862, HBW Papers.

7. Enmegahbowh to Mrs. [Cornelia] Whipple, January 13, 1862, HBW Papers; Enmegahbowh to Whipple, August 6, 1863, ibid.; Mane-do-wab to Whipple, March 21, 1863, ibid. These letters are representative of many pleas for and acknowledgments of material support. For the influence of such gifts on the status of a Christian Chippewa, see Shay-day-ess to Whipple, n.d., "written & translated by J. A. Gilfillan," ibid.

8. "Bp. Whipple's Visitation to Red Lake" [1862], ibid.

9. Whipple, *Lights and Shadows*, pp. 31-32, 82-83.

10. "Bp. Whipple's Visitation to Red Lake" [1862], HBW Papers.

11. Ibid.

12. Whipple, *Lights and Shadows*, pp. 142-45. See for example, Ma two Kon oon Nind and A se ne wub to Whipple, October 9, 1863, HBW Papers; George Bonga to Whipple, October 14, 1863, ibid. A letter to the Commissioner of Indian Affairs outlining the grievances of some of the Mille Lacs, Leech Lake, and Bad Boy's bands is typical. Whipple to William P. Dole, January 22, 1863, ibid.

13. Whipple, *Lights and Shadows*, pp. 145-47.

14. "The Story of Enmegahbowh's Life," excerpted from a letter to Whipple reprinted in ibid., pp. 497-98. See also John Johnson, Enmegahbowh, "Reminiscences," n.d., 45 pp., HBW Papers.

15. Whipple, *Lights and Shadows*, pp. 499-510.

16. "Bp. Whipple's Visitation to Red Lake" [1862], HBW Papers. This anecdote rests on Enmegahbowh's interpretation as reported by Whipple, and its self-serving nature should not be overlooked. At the same time it is instructive in establishing what both Whipple and his Ottawa protégé believed to be true concerning the Midéwiwin.

17. Enmegahbowh to James Lloyd Breck, January 23, 1862, HBW Papers.

18. Ruth Landes, *Ojibwa Religion and the Midéwiwin* (Madison: University of Wisconsin Press, 1968), p. 71.

19. Whipple, *Lights and Shadows*, p. 34.

20. Robert E. Ritzenthaler, "Southwestern Chippewa," in Bruce G. Trigger, ed., *Northeast*, vol. 15 in William C. Sturtevant, gen. ed., *Handbook of North American Indians* (Washington, D.C.: Smithsonian Institution, 1978), p. 754.

21. Whipple, *Lights and Shadows*, pp. 36-39.

22. See for example Friedrich Baraga, "Briefe an die Zentraldirektion der Leopoldinen-Stiftung und andere Adressaten," *Berichte der Leopoldinen-Stiftung* (1831-64): 5-25; J. B. Clicteur, "Lettre à M. Fenwick," Cincinnati, 3 juillet 1829, *Annales de la Propagation de la Foi* 4 (Lyon, 1830): 472-85; Auguste Dejean, "Lettres à M., à la Baie-Miamis, Rivière-aux-Hurons, l'Abre Croche," *Annales de la Propagation de la Foi* 4 (Lyon, 1828-31): 466-69; Frederick A. O'Meara, "Report of a Mission to the Ottahwahs and Ojibwas, on Lake Huron," *Missions to the Heathen* (London: Society for the Propagation of the Gospel, 1846), p. 6; Paul Radin, "Ottawa-Ojibwa" I-VII, manuscript 150 (Ott. 1-7), American Philosophical Society Library, Philadelphia [1926], as cited in Johanna E. and Christian F. Feest, "Ottawa," in Trigger, ed., *Northeast*, p. 783.

23. Robert F. Berkhofer, Jr., *Salvation and the Savage: An Analysis of Protestant Missions and American Indian Response, 1787-1862* (New York: Atheneum, 1972), pp. 123-24.

24. Whipple, *Lights and Shadows,* pp. 35-36, 161; Shadayence [Jr.] to Whipple, September 21, 1880, reprinted in ibid., pp. 161-62. Enmegahbowh to Whipple, July 20, 1863, HBW Papers, describes this man crying when he heard of his "praying boy." Another testimonial to the fervor of this convert is Joseph A. Gilfillan to Whipple, n.d., HBW Papers.

25. Shadayence to Whipple, n.d., "written & translated by J. S. Gilfillan," HBW Papers.

26. "Address of Bishop Whipple," *Proceedings of the Eleventh Annual Meeting of the Lake Mohonk Conferences of Friends of the Indian,* 1893, p. 34.

27. Whipple, *Lights and Shadows,* p. 263.

28. "Letter from Rev. J. J. Enmegahbowh," January 13, 1874, *Spirit of Missions* 39 (1874): 223-29.

29. Ibid., p. 226.

30. Whipple, *Lights and Shadows,* p. 263. For a similar version see Whipple, "Civilization and Christianization of the Ojibways in Minnesota," *Collections of the Minnesota Historical Society* 9 (1898-1900): 133-34.

31. "Letter from Rev. J. J. Enmegahbowh," January 13, 1874, *Spirit of Missions* 39 (1874): 228-29.

32. Whipple to H. Dyer, January 10, 1874, reprinted in *Spirit of Missions* 39 (1874): 222-23.

33. Whipple, *Lights and Shadows,* pp. 31, 264-65.

34. Wilcomb E. Washburn, *The Indian in America* (New York: Harper & Row, 1974), p. 116.

35. Whipple, *Lights and Shadows,* pp. 179-80, 183-86, 257-58,

317-18. For a list of Chippewa clergymen see Gilfillan to Whipple, July 10, 1884, HBW Papers.

36. Edmund Jefferson Danziger, Jr., *The Chippewas of Lake Superior* (Norman: University of Oklahoma Press, 1978), p. 86.

37. Enmegahbowh to James Lloyd Breck, January 23, 1862, HBW Papers.

38. Ebenezer Steele Peake, March 30, 1862, ibid.

39. William P. Dole to Whipple, August 1, 1863, ibid.; Whipple, J. L. Grace, Thomas S. Williamson to Dole, November 9, 1863, draft, ibid.

40. Whipple, Grace, Williamson to Dole, November 9, 1863, copy marked "Private," ibid.

41. Ezekiel Gilbert Gear to Whipple, October 3, 1860, ibid.

42. Whipple, *Lights and Shadows*, p. 178.

43. Enmegahbowh to Mrs. [Cornelia] Whipple, January 13, 1862, HBW Papers. For a brief discussion of the causes of Hole-in-the Day's discontent see Danziger, *Indians and Bureaucrats: Administering the Reservation Policy During the Civil War* (Urbana: University of Illinois Press, 1974), pp. 159-60. Mille Lacs band complaints are detailed in Gear to Whipple, September 9, 1862, HBW Papers.

44. On the alleged conspiracy, Hole-in-the-Day's activities, government strategy, and the destruction of Saint Columba, the letters of Peake are descriptive though replete with unsubstantiated rumors and speculation. See Peake to Whipple, September 5, 10, 11, 12, 14, 16, 19, 24, 1862, HBW Papers.

45. Whipple, *Lights and Shadows*, pp. 109-10, 529.

46. Peake to Whipple, September 10, 1862, HBW Papers; Enmegahbowh to Breck, September 6, 1862, ibid.; Peake to Whipple, September 19, 1862, ibid.

47. Ibid. For similar views, see Gear to Whipple, September 9, 1862, ibid.

48. Peake to Breck, September 30, 1862, ibid.; Peake to Whipple, October 13, 1862, ibid.

49. Peake to Whipple, September 10, 19, 24, 1862, ibid.; [Enmegahbowh] to [Whipple], September 29, 1862, ibid.

50. Peake to Whipple, October 13, 1862, ibid.; Enmegahbowh to [Whipple], November 10, 1862, ibid.; Gear to Whipple, November 2, April 1, 1863, ibid.; [Enmegahbowh] to Whipple, May 6, 1863, ibid.

51. Henry M. Rice to Whipple, March 18, November 21, 1863, ibid.; George Bonga to Whipple, November 10, 1863, April 14, 1864, ibid.

52. J. J. Johnson [Enmegahbowh] to Whipple, February 16, 1863,

ibid.

53. Enmegahbowh to Whipple, February 1, 28, March 13, May 18, July 20, 1863, January 11, 1864, ibid.

54. Whipple, *Lights and Shadows*, p. 252.

55. *Missionary Paper: Number Thirteen, By the Bishop Seabury Mission* (Faribault, Minn., February 1861), p. 3.

56. Gear to Whipple, April 7, May 1, November 17, 1863, HBW Papers; Enmegahbowh to Whipple, May 18, 1863, ibid.

57. Michael E. Stevens, "Catholic and Protestant Missionaries Among Wisconsin Indians: The Territorial Period," *Wisconsin Magazine of History* 58 (Winter, 1974-75): 144.

58. Gilfillan to [Whipple], n.d. [ca. 1885-90], HBW Papers; Wah boh nah god [Wahbonaquot] et al. to Whipple, n.d., ibid.; on the two clergymen see Whipple, *Lights and Shadows*, pp. 44-45, 176, 179-80.

59. Chief Twing (Meshakigijig) and Chief [Edward] Washburn (Mino-gijig) [Minogeshik] to Whipple, n.d., HBW Papers; [Enmegahbowh] to Whipple, May 6, 1863, ibid.; Gear to Whipple, March 11, 1863, ibid.

60. Whipple to Herbert Welsh, October 17, 1890, Indian Rights Association Papers (hereafter IRA Papers), Microfilming Corporation of America edition, reel 6.

61. [Enmegahbowh] to Whipple, May 6, 1863, HBW Papers, is typical of the Episcopal anti-Catholic genre.

62. Gilfillan to Whipple, n.d., ibid.

63. Whipple to Welsh, October 17, 1890, IRA Papers, reel 6.

64. "Bp. Whipple's Visitation to Red Lake," [1862], HBW Papers.

65. Whipple to William Welsh, November 17, 1873, IRA Papers, reel 1. For amplification of this theme see William T. Hagan, "Private Property: The Indian's Door to Civilization," *Ethnohistory* 3 (Spring, 1956): 126-37.

66. Whipple to W. Welsh, July 24, November 29, 1871, IRA Papers, reel 1; Whipple to Wayne McVeagh, January 5, 1884,: ibid.

67. "Fruits of Christian Work Among the Chippewas: A Letter from the Rev. Mr. Gilfillan," *Spirit of Missions* 39 (1874): 25-26.

68. Berkhofer, *Salvation and the Savage*, p. 114.

69. Gilfillan, *Spirit of Missions* 39 (1874): 27-29, 30-32.

70. Ritzenthaler, "Southwestern Chippewa," pp. 755-56.

71. Gilfillan to Whipple, n.d., [ca. 1889-92], HBW Papers. This letter cryptically mentions an Episcopal clergyman encouraging the ghost dance, a possible reference to Enmegahbowh or to one of the other Indians with whom Gilfillan sometimes bickered.

72. Ibid. Whipple, *Lights and Shadows*, p. 47.

74. See the excellent essay on Indian responses in James P. Ronda and James Axtell, *Indian Missions: A Critical Bibliography* (Bloomington: Indiana University Press, 1978), pp. 41–47.

75. For development of the theme of persistence of native spirituality see Henry Warner Bowden, *American Indians and Christian Missions: Studies in Cultural Conflict* (Chicago: University of Chicago Press, 1981), p. 197.

Bibliographic Note

Historical studies are often expansions on and debates with earlier works. In this volume two books have played a catalytic role. They are Robert F. Berkhofer, Jr., *Salvation and the Savage: An Analysis of Protestant Missions and American Indian Response, 1787-1862* (Lexington: University of Kentucky Press, 1965); and Henry Warner Bowden's *American Indians and Christian Missions: Studies in Cultural Conflict* (Chicago: University of Chicago Press, 1981). Indeed, both Berkhofer and Bowden served as commentators at the research conference at which early drafts of the chapters in this book were presented. Their books have scopes, styles of organization, and chronologies different from each other and from those of this volume. Nonetheless, readers may wish to turn to them to ascertain how some of our studies test aspects of their analyses. Most especially, our studies challenge some of the dynamics of factionalization presented by Berkhofer and some of the precedents of the colonial era stressed by Bowden.

A great number of books, articles, and dissertations have been written about specific denominations, particular missions, or distinct individuals and their work among the Indians. Studies of the Indians themselves and their religions are even more numerous. Fortunately, several impressive bibliographies exist that can guide readers to the appropriate works. All the volumes in the Newberry Library Center for the History of the American Indian Bibliographical Series, published by Indiana University Press, are very useful. Readers may wish especially to examine the volume in this series entitled *Indian Missions: A Critical Bibliography.* Following the for-

247

mat of the entire series, the authors, James P. Ronda and James Axtell, have selected 211 items ranging from Timothy Alder's *An Account of Sundry Missions performed among the Senecas and Munsees; in a Series of Letters* (New York: J. Seymour, 1827) to Sister M. Serena Zen's "The Educational Work of the Catholic Church Among the Indians of South Dakota from the Beginning to 1935," *South Dakota Historical Collections* 20 (1940): 299-356. Francis Paul Prucha lists 677 entries under "Missions and Missionaries" in *A Bibliographical Guide to the History of Indian-White Relations in the United States* (Chicago: University of Chicago Press, 1977). He has added 135 titles to this heading in the subsequent volume, *Indian-White Relations in the United States: A Bibliography of Works Published, 1975-1980* (Lincoln: University of Nebraska Press, 1982). An introduction to manuscript collections and archives is supplied by Gary Clayton Anderson in "The American Missionary in the Trans-Mississippi West: Sources for Future Research in Indian History," *Government Publications Review* 7A (1980): 117-27. In terms of one specific case study William G. McLoughlin has produced two outstanding books: *Cherokees and Missionaries, 1789-1839* (New Haven, Conn.: Yale University Press, 1984); and *The Cherokee Ghost Dance: Essays on the Southeastern Indians, 1789-1861* (Macon, Ga.: Mercer University Press, 1984).

The best guide to anthropological work on specific tribes and culture areas remains George P. Murdock and Timothy J. O'Leary, *Ethnographic Bibliography of North America*, 4th ed., 5 vols. (New Haven, Conn.: Human Relations Area Files Press, 1975). For individual Indian lives that often include a religious element see H. David Brumble III, *An Annotated Bibliography of American Indian and Eskimo Autobiographies* (Lincoln: University of Nebraska Press, 1981). The best overview of religious denominations is Sydney E. Ahlstrom's monumental study *A Religious History of the American People* (New Haven, Conn.: Yale University Press, 1972). Unfortunately, it has little to say about Indians or Indian missions.

General studies of the interaction between white Christian Americans and Indians are rare. The two significant exceptions that do exist are the books by Berkhofer and Bowden mentioned above. In studies of federal policy toward the Indians many works have examined the role of religious activists. Three important examples are R. Pierce Beaver, *Church, State, and the American Indian: Two and a Half Centuries of Partnership in Missions Between Protestant*

Churches and Government (Saint Louis, Mo.: Concordia Publishing House, 1966); Francis Paul Prucha, *American Indian Policy in Crisis: Christian Reformers and the Indian, 1865-1900* (Norman: University of Oklahoma Press, 1976); and Robert H. Keller, Jr., *American Protestantism and United States Indian Policy, 1869-82* (Lincoln: University of Nebraska Press, 1983).

The Contributors

W. David Baird is professor of history in Oklahoma State University. He has written or edited ten books including six volumes in the Indian Tribal Series. His most recent book, *The Quapaw Indians: A History of the Downstream People,* was published by the University of Oklahoma Press in 1980. He has been an active leader in both the Western History Association and Phi Alpha Theta, the national honorary society for historians.

Robert C. Carriker is professor of history in Gonzaga University. His book *Fort Supply, Indian Territory* (Norman: University of Oklahoma Press, 1970) is well known among western historians. He is also the author of *The Kalispel People* for the Indian Tribal Series and has published four archival guides listing more than 43,000 documents related to Jesuit missionary activity in the Pacific Northwest. In addition to his many articles and scholarly papers, he is an active board member of the Washington State Historical Society and the Lewis and Clark Trail Heritage Foundation.

Bruce David Forbes chairs the department of religious studies in Morningside College, Sioux City, Iowa, where he is associate professor. He has a special interest in the history of American Christianity. He also has taught courses in American Indian history and the history of the American West. His Ph.D. dissertation at Princeton Theological Seminary (1977) was on the topic "Evangelization and Acculturation Among the Santee Dakota Indians, 1834-1864." At present he is editing a book of documents to be titled *Christianity and American Indians: Voices in Exchange.*

Clyde A. Milner II is associate editor of the *Western Historical Quarterly* and associate professor of history in Utah State University. He has a scholarly interest in American Indian history and in the history of religion in America. In 1975-76 he was a research fellow at the Center for the History of the American Indian at the Newberry Library, Chicago, Illinois. His book *With Good Intentions: Quaker Work Among the Pawnees, Otos, and Omahas in the 1870s* was published by the University of Nebraska Press in 1982.

Floyd A. O'Neil is codirector of the American West Center and is assistant dean of humanities in the University of Utah. He has helped with the editing and publication of several tribal histories, including those on the Zuñis, Utes, and Southern Utes. He is the author or coauthor of numerous articles and is an expert on oral history and on the development of courses in American Indian history. He is serving as a scholarly consultant to both the Utes and the Zuñis in important land-claim cases. At the University of Utah he teaches courses on the history of Utah and on American Indian history.

Martin Zanger is professor of history and department chair in the University of Wisconsin-La Crosse where he has helped direct archival and historical projects for the Winnebago Indians. He is also writing a major history of this tribe. From 1974 to 1976, he held a postdoctoral fellowship and served as associate director of the Center for the History of the American Indian at the Newberry Library. At the Newberry he coedited the first six volumes of the Center's American Indian Bibliography Series. Several of his published articles have considered American Indian historiography.

Index

Abbott, Lyman: 159-60
Adams County, Ill.: 82
Africa: 30, 67
Ak-ik-hun-nah: 10
Alaska: 129-30, 133
Albert Horse Memorial: 66
Alcohol: 179, 181, 186, 205-206
Algonkian Indians: 193
American Bible Society: 23
American Board of Commissioners
  for Foreign Missions: 5-8, 10-11,
  16, 18ff., 23, 25ff., 28ff., 31,
  34, 40, 67, 208
American Fur Company: 110
American Missionary Association:
  157
American Revolution: 147
Americats: 86-89
Amherst College: 159
Anadarko agency: 46, 48, 49, 51,
  53ff., 61, 65, 66, 68; church,
  54; Kiowa church, 66
Anadarko School: 55; see also
  Methvin Institute
Anderledy, Anton: 129
Anderson, Rufus: 67
Andover Theological Seminary:
  6ff., 10
Andrews Hall (Faribault, Minn.):
  194

Aoute (Kiowa): 62
Apache Indians: 46, 69, 164
Arizona: 102, 106, 164
Arkansas: 21, 35
Ash Creek: 93
Assimilation: 6, 49, 73, 105, 107,
  118, 123, 125, 136, 138, 154-57,
  163, 168-70, 173-75, 182,
  211, 213
Auburn Institute (Auburn, Ga.): 41
Avant, Mrs. M. B.: 52

Babcock, Sidney: 45
Babinap (Peter Parker,
  Chippewa): 210
Bad Boy (Chippewa leader): 203
Baltimore, Md.: 110
Baptists: 10, 45, 49, 145
Barnum's Museum (New York): 197
Barstow, A. C.: 145-46, 153
Battey, Thomas C.: 48
Beall, Emma Louise (Mrs. John
  Jasper Methvin): 42, 56, 65
Bean, George Washington: 77, 82-
  86, 90-96, 98-99, 102-104, 106
Beckx, Peter, S. J.: 111
Beecher, Henry Ward: 159
Belpre, Ohio: 35
Benjamin, Henry: 206
Benjamin, Philip S.: 155

253